ANALYZING AMBASZ

ANALYZI

JERRILYNN D. DODDS
PETER HALL
CATHERINE INGRAHAM
DEAN MacCANNELL
FELICITY D. SCOTT
LAUREN SEDOFSKY
MICHAEL SORKIN EDITOR
ANTHONY VIDLER
JAMES WINES
LEBBEUS WOODS

AMBASZ

THE MONACELLI PRESS

First published in the United States of America in 2004 by
The Monacelli Press, Inc.
902 Broadway
New York, New York 10010

Library of Congress Cataloging-in-Publication Data

Analyzing Ambasz / edited by Michael Sorkin ... [et al.].
    p. cm.
Includes bibliographical references.
    ISBN 1-58093-135-9
1. Ambasz, Emilio—Criticism and interpretation. 2. Architectural
practice, International—New York (State)—New York. 3. Architecture,
Modern—20th century. I. Ambasz, Emilio. II. Sorkin, Michael, 1948 –
    NA839.A66A89 2004
    720'.92—DC22

                            2003019719

Design: Distant Station Ltd.
Printed and bound in Canada

PHOTO CREDITS
Aldo Ballo: 159
Santi Caleca: 25 (right)
Cartello Torri & Notte Pesce: 161
Louis Checkman: 23 (lower right), 24, 25 (left), 33, 43, 50,
    51 (both), 54 (both), 64, 78, 181 (right), 187 (top left
    and right)
Poltrona Frau: 167 (left)
Felipe Palomino Gonzalez: 187 (bottom)
Janos Grapow (courtesy of Ilva Pali Dalmine) 172
Hallmark (courtesy of) : 23 (lower left)
Mike Hirst: 29
Industrial Foto: 165, 167 (center and right)
Ryuzo Masunaga: 168, 171, 175, 179 (left)
Museum of Modern Art (courtesy of): 121, 125 (all), 126
    (all), 127 (both), 128
Nichii: 23 (top right)
Frank Poole: 169
Richard Scanlan: 15, 61
Superstudio: 108
Christiano Toraldo Di Francia: 117, 118
Hiromi Watanabe: 66

ILLUSTRATION CREDITS
Emilio Ambasz & Associates: 33
Mark Mack: 80
Studio PM: 23 (top left)
Suns Hung: 56, 57 (both), 62, 75

LUNCH WITH EMILIO
Michael Sorkin

This book is the result of lunch. Every few years Emilio Ambasz circles like a comet into my life and we sit down together. I look forward to these encounters: Emilio is a genial companion and an old friend, his work is always interesting, and he is a master of dish and tall stories, the most joyful teller of tales that I know. No sooner do we sit down than it begins. Titanic architectural accomplishments. Amazing encounters with the rich and powerful. Prodigies of financial legerdemain. Cruel and delicious denunciations of the competition. Tales of hush-hush activities on behalf of the oppressed of Latin America. The more incendiary items are related in the strictest confidence, including scandals that could ruin any number of careers, not to mention tales of personal derring-do of Brobdingnagian proportions.

The experience of Emilio's simultaneous charm, self-effacement, and grandiosity produces a singular effect, rendering me nearly speechless. Can life truly be this fabulous? While the tales Emilio tells in such dazzling sequence run from the verifiable to the certifiable, each is fascinating and beautifully wrought, and the more he recites, the richer the fabric he weaves. Although it might seem churlish to question stories of such evident charm, the author of "Design Tales for Skeptic Children" demands it irresistibly, reality and fantasy conflating with disarming verve as the line is insistently blurred by his fearless poetic latitude. For the sympathetic listener (grown more so in this case by a good bottle of wine), the impulse to keep the delirious Scheherazading going is powerful. After all, much of this can be confirmed. Ambasz is rich, famous, cultured, and accomplished. His digs in New York, Bologna, and Venice are luxurious, he is greeted effusively by the maître d's at Aureole and the Four Seasons, the excellent Vertebra chair is visible in every airport and auditorium on the planet, the charismatic architectural images leap from the pages of the journals. Could all the rest be true as well?

At the end of our most recent lunch, Emilio revealed—casually, disarmingly—that it was his sixtieth birthday, and told a moving story about never celebrating the occasion during his childhood lest he remind his parents of their own age and mortality. I was honored and flattered to be included on such a sentimental occasion, but a sliver of doubt nevertheless pierced my brain. Returning to the office a little later, I immediately checked the part of the story that I could. And he was born on June 13, 1943. Caught again in the Ambaszian *gotcha*, that fabulous netherworld of uncertainty and promise. My skepticism rebuked, the embarrassment is palpable. Admiration reauthorized, a project is formed to try to account for this fascinating case, and I relinquish myself to enjoyment and suitable penance. Colleagues are recruited to help unravel this seductive and singular enigma, and this volume is the result.

The insistent fabulation is a value at Ambasz's creative core. Emilio's wily self-invention jibes precisely with his architectural project, which likewise smoothly elides the fictive and the world, producing a not quite terrestrial place dedicated to the beautiful idealized. Emilio's Platonic optimism—the principle, the "wager" that gives the work its social valence—is simply that what has been represented *exists*. Mediated by the gnomic fables that form his main written self-account, this imaginative space was born, largely intact, early in his meteoric career and has been pursued with teleological zest ever since. Upholstered in that famous Technicolor blue and green, it seems, at first glance, to be a heaven-on-earth for upmarket angels, the state of nature with plumbing. But this is to miss both the reach and the joy of the message: wishing his mark on everything from the pencil to the city, Ambasz excels at the design of all and, by extension, for all.

Whatever the private enigma, the cultural point of entry is precise. Leaving Argentina as a teenager, Ambasz attended Princeton in the sixties and departed, after an accelerated stay, to work at the Museum of Modern Art, where he conducted a curatorship of refinement and gusto. Which is not to say he entirely missed the mellow, funky side of the times, rather that he has always related to the counterculture at the source, at a distance. The hippie idyll *began*, after all, in the eighteenth century, and Ambasz shares the long lineage of believers in the possibility of paradise, life lived for pleasure. And, like his more recent predecessors (including, among others, Archigram, Ant Farm, Drop City, Kiesler, Soleri, Superstudio, et al.), he speaks with eloquence through the machine/garden dialectic that founds one of the key dialects of modernity. Ambasz is possibly the last great architect of the eighteenth century.

Emilio Ambasz's project spans the culture of design—exemplary, relational. As an architect, he has been a pioneer of the ideology, if not the technicality, of the light lie of building on the land, an avatar of greenness, a sylvan philosopher. He has advanced the ongoing project of inventing nature via the modernist medium of landscape design—that confidently totalizing successor to mere gardening—blending architecture into the expanded field pioneered by the earth art that was at its conceptual apogee during his student days. As a product designer, Ambasz has defended and extended the space of the modern object of mass consumption by his careful attention to use and his graceful tinkerer's sense of mechanism, pre-electronic and decidedly nonvirtual.

Ambasz describes his work grandly "as if it were built by the last man of the present culture for the first man of a culture which has not yet arrived." Is Emilio the last man? Finding the archaeological tools needed to excavate this yet-to-be-realized future obliges a return to its author, who is, perhaps, a little too eager to be helpful. Wishing us to know that he is both dreamy poet and canny pragmatist, he frequently dilates on the two sides of his personality, which he calls "Emilio" and "Ambasz." Glossed along with his fabulous tales, we are forced by the tenacity of this shtick into maddening, impossible speculations: are we dealing with St. Francis, Leonardo, or Michael Milken? One day, Ambasz seems Gatsby rendered by Borges, a melancholy misfit. The next, the most salivary and canny entrepreneur. The next, Adam before the Fall. The next, after.

Emilio's forebears, the Romantics—modernity's founding poets—replaced God with nature and religion with the sublime. In their addictive pastoralism, they virtually invented lifestyle as both politics and self-expression. While it may be hard to imagine Ambasz, the rootless cosmopolitan, happy for long in the countryside, this only allows him to adore it more (and more abstractly), like a ghetto shut-in longing for the unseen Jerusalem, lovable only to the degree that it is imagined afresh as the last, best dream of a righteous life. The Edenic spaces he designs—where difference is a wisp—surely domicile our better, more generous selves. At night we repair beneath the sheltering earth, take up nobody's space, entombed in quietude. Who knows if our trashy, mundane desires can exist in a place where nightmares never happen.

But the project is not simply misty hope. Ambasz has participated forcefully in the transformation—the reformation—of contemporary architectural speech, and not just via his poeticizing style. As design curator at MoMA, he energized the discourse with prodigies of concise taste, filially celebrating figures and forms that were sources of his own aesthetic. This clear vision ranged from the revelation of Barragán's moving, rich simplicity, to the diversity of postwar Italian design and its investigations of the politics of the object, to the cultural and technical intricacies of the manufacture of taxicabs. He helped flesh out the image of late modernism for which the MoMA Italian show represents a defining moment, a design-world 1848 with its high hopes of apotheosis. And he cleaves to the ethic of functionalism, still the best available account of architecture's cooperation with human needs.

Ever the brilliant curator, Ambasz has a demanding eye for the object and believes sincerely that the idea must inhere in the thing. This produces, however, a flip-side disdain for the theoretical, and Ambasz speaks of being "intermittently embarrassed and irritated by the woolly-mindedness" of contemporary theory. In this studious rejection, he diverges from his first posse—the group that coalesced around Peter Eisenman and the Institute for Architecture and Urban Studies, for which Ambasz was an early board member and author of bylaws. He looks balefully at colleagues who produce those fat apologies, filled with memos and plane receipts, sketches and construction photos, friendly essays by fellow travelers, obscure, self-referential graphics, and mock Talmudic interior voices. Ambasz sees their impossibility: attempting to infuse the object of architecture with the capacity to absorb meaning like a sponge, such volumes have the effect of rarefaction, divorcing architecture from the social, robbing building of the power of—and responsibility to—its effects.

Theorizing seeks to infuse architecture with metaphysical importance, a sense of its connectedness to larger desires and explanations. Scientistic modernity—still a dominant model—put virtually all of its explanatory eggs in the basket of objectivity, in the fundamental rationality of the architectural act. Ambasz seeks something more spiritual than science to undergird his project ("the architecture I create is steeped in mysticism"), and he works overtime to get that *The Earth, the Temple, and the Gods* vibe cooking. Like the Doric, the Ambaszian order is at once spare and highly iconic, replete with polyvalent symbols of spirit, columns taken back to their origins as tree trunks, an almost automatic architecture. In Emilio's garden, architecture is like Topsy, it jes' grew.

Still, Ambasz carefully provides an authorizing discourse that can stand in the position of the theoretical and has long provided, via his "fables," an end run around the conventional uncertainties of architectural argument and the evidentiary burdens of theory. "I opted to be a fabulist rather than an ideologist because fables retain the ring of immutability long after ideologies have withered," he has written. His well-known fables are tightly delineated ideograms, analogous to sketches, foundational, "innocent" moments. They are carefully composed, the work of single authorship, fables in guise, but really celebrations of the absent presence of offstage erudition and knowledge. And by pretending to accumulation and consent, they stand in for a consensual longing that makes them candidates to be read politically. They are addressed to a "skeptic," highly precocious child, suggesting the integrity of both motive and explanation. Who would lie to a child?

Ambasz, with his world-record frequent flyer account, delights in being a force acting at a distance which, as a statical matter, can be either a multiplier or a reducer. This question of presence establishes a fault line between the industrial design, where the deliberation (not to mention the original and ingenious mode of production) seems more intense, and the architecture, where it is more spare—between the intimate tactility of the object and the untouchability of the (to be) inhabited space. There's a precision in the objects, answerable to detail, that is (carefully) less clear in the architecture, which at larger scale sometimes feels generic. Although Ambasz has suggested that, to guarantee freedom of action, the designer should organize and specify less as scale increases, the argument is not clear-cut, albeit very seductive.

Design, as a political project, occurs at various sites, and both architecture and the mass-produced object can spread the word—this was the MoMA Design Department's foundational credo. Here we are in the realms of both organization and propaganda, and the vim behind Ambasz's political postures is surely more astringent than the limousine liberalism of those like Frank Gehry, whose politics seem to have no important effect on his artistic project, beyond a certain sanction to formal freedom. Such politics "on the ground" are obviously fraught territory for someone as nimble as Ambasz in circulating between the halls of power and a living conscience. Emblematically, Ambasz recalls that during the divisive and angry staff strike that occurred during his tenure at MoMA, he was so torn between loyalties on both sides that he developed ulcers, enabling him to stay home in bed, rather than confront the picket line.

The fabulous aura that surrounds his work can, however, distract attention from deeper political meaning, and Ambasz has his own dark side. He seems, for a green architect, to have a peculiar affinity for the petrochemical industry, one he may have acquired early in life. He often quips about Peter Eisenman's insistence that his wealth could only have come from oil money, to which he replies, yes, his father owned a gas station! Never mind the delectable image of the teen Emilio pumping gas, his client list does include a substantial number of firms that are not exactly embodiments of the environmentalist agenda: Schlumberger, Cummins Diesel, Mercedes-Benz, and ENI, the Italian oil cartel—the very axis of internal combustion. It is surely legitimate to ask whether shrouding the ENI headquarters with rows of trees is camouflage or a gentle reminder to those toiling within to seek another way. To Emilio's credit, it's a tough question to answer.

The vanguardist political affect, the idea of being ahead of—indeed, of transcending—the curve, also reflects Ambasz's deep desire for his work to be seen as *sui generis*. His own well-cultivated mysteriousness is paralleled by the sense of solitude imparted by a striking repertoire of images in which no one is ever in the frame, a communism of invisibility. Ambasz's politics are hard to gloss from his projects but clearly mix both red and green tints and are embodied in his call for "a new philosophic definition of Nature, encompassing architecture as one of its inseparable component elements." In the incumbent culture, the environment has become a general surrogate for the political sphere, and Ambasz's work argues for an architecture of responsibility by this reverent tithing of the authority of "Nature," universal signifier of the good.

Given the durability of the motif in Ambasz's work, these green projects do argue for another view of architectural form. In the repetitive, minimalist character of his architectural object-making—the prosody of greenhouses, berms, reflecting pools, plumes of steam, barges, and excavations—Ambasz overleaps the empty innovation and arcane formalism of the more theoretically certified work of his peers and gets right down to business. The work is simply beautiful and offers a firm riposte to the tedious but persistent critique of green architecture as irredeemably homely. Most important, Ambasz identifies architecture with the earth and its gravities, with a terrestrial future. Although his renderings sometimes seem utopian to the point of antigravity, true visionaries and poets do not require literal loam, a substance which, transformed by Ambasz's geometric abstraction, acquires a more metaphysical status, phlogiston of life.

It is precisely in the simultaneous earthiness and mystery of his vision that Ambasz so brilliantly—and usefully—situates, validates, and gives shape to his project of amelioration. In paradise, innocence always trumps theory as an ethical stance. We look for lineage, not an ideology, relying on a prior authority, the wisdom of the ancients. Filled totemic referents, both the architectural project and the fabulation, assume a consistent—and reassuring—relationship to a set of fabulous sources: sacred mountains, holy rivers, Kubla Kahnian ruins, magic mists, overgrown ruins. But Ambasz artfully works both sides of the street, twinning the unapproachable pith of the mock myth with a deadpan account of the proper application of gunnite. He sports with the high-minded styles of legitimation practiced by his peers via radical simplification, creating a history of minimalism, from Imhotep to Ambasz. Insisting that all must be read into these sparse armatures, Ambasz at once conceals and reveals the meanings of his projects. The message is that there's more than meets the eye, more concealed than dreamed of in all our philosophy. The fables surround the architecture with a nimbus of sagacity and alterity.

Anxiety over an uncontrollable future, over "growing up," is resolved by this mythic past of saturated color, blue skies, dappling sun, and the purity of an endless horizon. Standing in heavenly (postapocalyptic?) isolation, uncontaminated by neighbors or inhabitants, almost heartbreaking in its aspiration to goodness, this architecture, it would seem, conveys tremendous disappointment. The sadness is paternal, godly even—dismay, perhaps, with the venality of human desires, a wish to be part of a race better than ours, secure in its uncomplicated wisdom, never-never land before Peter met Wendy. This architecture of tumuli and purification bears the weight of tragedy and the burdens of hope, Rousseau made shapely and concrete.

The greatest contemporary master of the rhetoric of innocence (and immanence) in architecture was John Hejduk. For Hejduk, the attitude of simplicity suffused the life, a complete performative package. From his shamanistic self-presentation, to the mellifluous lyric of his poetical invention, to the outpouring of his wonderful hand, Hejduk was the model of the architect as wild man and priest, obsessed with the inner meanings of forms. Truly larger than life, Hejduk was both a poet and a paranoid, a man who saw monsters all around him. The transparency of form and feeling was his gift to us, the idea that authentic magic could reside in architecture, his foundational church. He was a man who genuinely believed in angels.

The ideal subjects of Ambasz's arcadia are also innocent creatures but far more palpable than Hejduk's cherubim and suicides: the nameless trees and plants that cover and order his work. Ambasz generally refrains from the precise stipulation of social life in his projects, preferring an architecture of setting rather than orchestration. Flora, though, submit uncomplainingly to strict discipline and precisely adorn the facades of his buildings, like the Elgin Marbles. This architecture of gardens and conservatories, of grape arbors and Babylonian hang, is a paradise of the undifferentiated, weirdly uniform—the antithesis of the jungle. The science behind his relentless botany springs from the understanding that we rely on the field of flora to purify our exhalations, our exhaust assimilated and transformed into the substance of our survival, the life-giving air. Building acts as a filter and a pump, a giant respirator for a planet that has been polluted by too much building. Ambasz reports with glee on the success of a project in Japan for a tree suspended by a truss over a hole in the roof of a parking garage: "The tree's roots drew savory nourishment from the carbon dioxide the cars exhausted."

Ambasz seeks to reverse architecture's banishment from Eden, and we love him for it. But the apple has been bitten and the nakedness appears. Ambasz sympathetically drapes it in foliage, concrete and steel obscured behind a chlorophyll veil. Or one of earth. The occluding berms both identify architecture with planetary harmony and save building from the detail that Ambasz identifies with fashion and ornament. Purging it through minimalism, camouflage, interment, he seeks to create an architecture of fundamentals—a jointless, seamless construction that speaks little of the humdrum of its own stability and connectedness. The aspiration is to go off the grid, not the Cartesian one exactly but certainly the social and the electrical. Powered by sun and wind, insulated by a blanket of earth, these buildings eschew the rigidities of society and the dependencies of interconnection and infrastructure, burying themselves where they can more safely assume the informality of the curvilinear, forms less seemly aboveground where decorum and convention rule, the datum of geometry. Disorderly pleasures are best conducted underground.

This architecture suggests a hyper-irony, a self-conscious paring away to get closer to the edge, invention via distillation. The method unites minimalism and surrealism, combining the grand poverty of Heizer or Serra with the strangeness of De Chirico or Delvaux. Corralled within those depopulated expanses of geometric earth, we constantly stumble upon the unexpected *thing*, the errant Mercedes, the Barbie doll, the classical *tempietto*, the winged aviator, the log column, the miniature facade. These punctuating quirks activate the interior life of the projects, a wink from the creator, letting us know that his is a wry and "skeptic" innocence. The surrealism is *critical*, the working method of modern life, the casual weirdness of the unexpected juxtapositions that culture constantly throws at us. Ambasz cherry-picks the strangeness as an antidote to the dour bigness of the minimalists and colossalizing earth movers of the art world.

Julio Cortázar has written, in response to the reception of his work in the U.S., "American critics are upset by an Argentinian or Mexican who has a universal, European spirit rather than writing about shacks, capuli, tequila or melancholy gauchos. An Argentinian has no right to be cosmopolitan. But what would Hemingway, Scott Fitzgerald, Gertrude Stein and so many Americans have produced without their great experience in Europe? That doesn't even occur to them when they accuse us of being 'playboys of Frenchified literature.'"

Ambasz shares these exiles' resentments, the compensations, excesses, expatriations, strivings, complexes, anxieties, and complications. The tremendous desire for vindication on the loftiest field of play leads him to take, as his project, nothing less than the project of paradise. As Paris was a utopia for previous generations of expatriates, Ambasz has produced his own recombinant millennial field of action, including New York, Bologna, Tokyo, and the stratospheric space of flows through which he soars. This creative geography is also an assemblage, his beloved bricolage. But, despite his claims, this is not the working method of his own creativity, which is decidedly not about cobbling together found objects and practices but lies in the certainties of single vision. For Ambasz, architecture is a confident gift to the species, a vision of a democracy at the top: a world where everyone flies first-class.

Let us call this magical modernism, a yoking that is nothing if not optimistic. I sometimes wonder why there are so many successful Argentine architects in New York. Fascinated with modernity and strongly inclined to power, many see New York as a crucible of self-invention, the place where magical realism can become material, a portal between the imaginative and the concrete, where the commercial possibilities of imageable weirdness are second nature. I have also been told that there are more people undergoing Lacanian psychoanalysis in Buenos Aires than anyplace on the planet, and I can certainly understand the appeal to the analyst and analysand both. The linguistic model of mind is most Borgesian, the precise but inscrutable science of irrationality. Ambasz, as neurotic as the rest of us, is too worried about the world to want to know his own secrets and so he speaks and makes another, perhaps better, truth.

And this is the elevating contribution of the work of Emilio Ambasz. At a time when architecture is obsessed with chasing the tail of formalism and power, Ambasz's work reminds us that the highest calling available to builders and dreamers both is the happiness, comfort, and dignity of others. He roots us at architecture's conceptual core with his unwavering faith in the possibility of a reconciliation of the arts of building with the future of our planetary home.

IDEOLOGICAL CASTLES
Dean MacCannell

[On the Burmese frontier, Kuki] houses were not so much built as knotted together, plaited, woven, embroidered and given a patina by long use. Those who lived in them were not overwhelmed by great blocks of unyielding stone; these were houses that reacted immediately and with great flexibility to their presence, their every movement. The house was, in fact, subject to the house-holder, whereas with us the opposite is the case. The village served the villagers as a coat of light elastic armor; they wore it as a European woman wears her hats. It was an object of personal adornment on a mammoth scale, and those who built it had been clever enough to preserve something of the spontaneity of natural growth. Leafage and the springing branch were combined, in short, with the exactions of a carefully planned layout. The inhabitants seemed pro-tected in their nakedness by the fronded velvet of the partition walls and the curtain-fall of the palms. And when they went forth from their houses it was as if they had just stepped out of an enormous dressing-gown of ostrich-feathers. Their houses were caskets lined with down … and their bodies the jewels within them.

—Claude Lévi-Strauss, *Tristes Tropiques*

Daphne [is] transformed into a tree under the pressure of a pain from which she cannot flee. Isn't it true that the living being who has no possibility of escape suggests in its very form the presence of what one might call petrified pain? Doesn't what we do in the realm of stone suggest this? To the extent that we don't let it roll, but erect it, and make of it something fixed, isn't there in architecture itself a kind of actualized pain?

— Jacques Lacan, *Seminar VII: The Ethics of Psychoanalysis*

Emilio Ambasz could easily have had Lacan's and Lévi-Strauss's words in mind when he wrote,

> [T]he ideal gesture would be to arrive at a plot of land which is so immensely fertile and welcoming that, slowly, the land would assume a shape—providing us with an abode. And within this abode—being such a magic space—it would never rain, nor would there ever be inclemencies. . . . In a perfect nature, we would not need houses.[1]

Ambasz's "ideal gesture" apparently does not originate in architecture. It originates in myth and in the unconscious. This much is already well established in the critical embrace of Ambasz's creative works.[2]

Myth is the most frequently recurring trope in the writings about Emilio Ambasz and his work. For one who is steeped in the anthropological and critical study of myth, it is somewhat unexpected and touching to find this architecture submitting itself to an anthropological framing. Unexpected, because it does not appear to submit itself to any other framing. It eludes conventional architectural discourse; it is architecture-beyond-architecture. In a sympathetic essay, Ettore Sottsass remarks that Ambasz's buildings are "not architecture." They are more like "wagers."[3] The evocation of myth is touching, because technically Ambasz's work has no real need to be propped up with supernumerary theoretical discussion of its supposed mythic qualities. If anything, our understanding of myth will benefit more from its connection to Ambasz than vice versa. Anthropology should be honored that this exceptional architecture has reached out to it. In this essay, I will attempt to return the tribute.

It is Ambasz himself who authorizes mythic interpretation: "It has always been my deep belief that architecture and design are both myth-making acts."[4] And from his "Credo": "There is in all of us a deep need for ritual, for ceremony, procession, magical garments, and gestures."[5] Professional colleagues and critics have eagerly seized Ambasz's suggestion that his masterworks be understood in terms of their mythic significance. Peter Buchanan praises the architecture for renewing myth and "reenchanting" and "reintegrating" our "desiccated" and "fragmented" world.[6] Michael Sorkin names *Arcadia* as the mythic landscape of Ambasz's projects and thinking.[7]

After Saussure, Propp, Lévi-Strauss, and Barthes, our understanding of the operations of mythic thought is quite a bit advanced. We know that language is composed of phonic and grammatical oppositions and that myth derives its power from modeling itself on language. Myth is a viral copy of an original code. The building blocks of myth are bits of language that are detached from their historical coordinates and reassembled in persuasive ideological forms. The ideological function of myth is to allow its believers to live with social and cultural contradictions as if they do not exist, or if they do exist, to live with them as if they are neutral or meaningless.

MYTH-LITE

When "myth" is summoned in writings by and about Ambasz it is not in terms that immediately resonate with anthropological or critical understanding. In the discussions surrounding Ambasz's projects, "myth" mainly references past epochs when humans were thought to have lived in closer harmony with nature, and were on more intimate terms with primordial mysteries. This critical strategy suggests that we should approach Ambasz's appeal to the "mythic" in design as a kind of "myth-lite." The Ambasz commentary only wants to go far enough to invoke the mystical, spiritual feel of "myth"; or the mythical surface of myth; or a sense of a mythic past; or a mythic oneness with nature. The commentary does not engage the structure of myth in any technical sense. An anthropological or critical consideration of myth would appear not to have a place in the discussion surrounding Ambasz's projects.

This tendency is evident in Peter Buchanan's essay, which pushes Ambasz's work quite hard in the direction of a New Age interpretation. According to Buchanan, Ambasz's projects "evoke certain urgent universals."[8] He praises Ambasz for reintroducing the mythic into architecture and design, claiming that it enables us to see beyond cause and effect and the bottom line, getting us back in touch with our primordial emotions.[9] He aligns Ambasz with the "two patron saints for the nineties, Carl Jung and Joseph Campbell," as well as the "Gaia hypothesis," "feminine archetypes," the "Mother Goddess," and other

theoretical elements that "encourage more nurturing, non-exploitative relationships between people, and between people and the planet."[10]

Without wishing to detract from the evident goodwill of Buchanan's and
similar views, I am going to recommend against this version of "myth" as a
way of understanding Ambasz's (and anyone else's) contribution. Elsewhere I
have argued that this appeal to "primitive innocence" is not itself innocent.[11]
We are supposed to identify with "old or perhaps wiser societies" because we
too are good. But we have been expelled from Arcadia. In the "New Age" we
understand ourselves as condemned to live in a too-complex world, overwhelmed by thousands of meaningless, impersonal relationships, disconnected
from family, from ethnic roots, and from an authentic sense of place. The New
Age image we have created of so-called primitive peoples makes them the
opposite of all this. They are simpler, more unified in their beliefs, more in
touch with themselves and with nature, more spontaneous, intimate, altogether more magical, wonderful, and so on.

Thus, by a nasty theoretical sleight of hand, we see *ourselves,* not colonized native peoples, as the primary victims of our social and technological
complexity. In this context, and against the expressed desires of those who
advocate it, New Age mythology functions effectively as the enabling fantasy
for the petty viciousness and actual violence that are the other marked
features of the modern world. The suburban community undertakes to make
itself a better place to live by mocking up a version of primitive homogeneity
and uniformity of beliefs, by ridding itself of people who are "different,"
and by surrounding each household unit with a patch of symbolic nature.
This is an ideological perversion of the myth of the primitive. A gated suburb
is a highly self-interested, motivated simulacrum of a "primitive isolate,"
a fantasy of a fantasy. When it is examined in the light of a more rigorous
understanding of myth, the embrace of putatively "primitive" beliefs and
practices by hippies, New Agers, suburbanites, and other modern peoples is
no less septic than forcing nonsustainable western technologies and extractive
economies upon recent ex-primitives and peasants. The two sets of practices,
which may want to see themselves opposed, are but the obverse and reverse
of the hegemonic coin.

It seems unlikely, on the face of it, that this is the direction Ambasz's work
is taking us, that his work is advancing some New Age hegemonic fantasy.
Should we simply drop the mythic interpretation? I don't think so. Let me

recommend that in place of a New Age mythology we reexamine Ambasz's projects in the light of more rigorous theories of myth.

LÉVI-STRAUSS'S "SCIENCE OF THE CONCRETE"

Lévi-Strauss's monumental lifework is a series of volumes that treats the meaning and function of one thousand American Indian myths culled from tribes covering the territory from the Bering Strait to Tierra del Fuego. What is remarkable about these myths, and Lévi-Strauss's handling of them, is that while they were independently collected from hundreds of quite distinct cultural groups, they can be seen as being composed from a restricted set of basic cultural oppositions, using a singular underlying transformational logic.

This method of understanding myth is not the same as that of Jung. It makes no appeal to "universal archetypes." In fact, Lévi-Strauss goes in an opposite direction. Where there appears to be a common mythic theme shared by different peoples, Lévi-Strauss shows how each culture bends and twists it, turns it inside out, transforms it into its opposite, and otherwise reshapes it so it works in the immediate cultural context—not as something borrowed, but as a crucial stitch in the local cultural fabric.

The anteater appears to be an "archetype" in South American myth, but in one group he is found resolving the tensions produced by an incest prohibition, while in another he shows the people the way to a more habitable territory. There may be figures that appear to be "universal," or nearly so. But no figure is universal in its meaning and function—that is, there are no mythic archetypes. There are only more or less effective strategies for trying to understand the world and our place in it. According to Lévi-Strauss, myth is protoscience. Does this make it less heartfelt or emotionally satisfying? No. It serves to mark and to honor intense creativity, our most human attribute.

Lévi-Strauss discerns in the myths he studied a speculative thinking of the sort our ancestors must have needed to create the great inventions of the Neolithic revolution: writing, kinship, universalistic religions, plant and animal breeding, ceramics, calendars, and, relevant to the topic at hand, architecture. Native American myths provide an integrated framework for our most durable form of theoretical thought: the systematic effort to fit everything in the world together in a way that "makes sense." So-called primitive societies must contain and somehow resolve primary and secondary structural oppositions: for example, nature versus culture, or the raw versus the cooked. Myth inserts itself between these oppositions and builds structural sets out of the "debris of events,"[12] or, "ideological castles" from the remains of discourse.[13] Even though myth restricts itself to existing symbolic constructs, restless "mythical reflection can reach brilliant unforeseen results on the intellectual plane."[14] Myth orders events in a search for meaning. Science orders ideas (meaning) in order to produce events.[15]

Myth, according to Lévi-Strauss, permits people to live with the structural contradictions peculiar to their cultural arrangements, as if they were not contradictions. It operates at the collective level and also at the psychic level. Or, as Lacan put it, "Myth is always a signifying system or scheme, if you like, which is articulated so as to support the antinomies of certain psychic relations."[16]

AMBASZ'S "SCIENCE OF THE CONCRETE"

Ambasz has not tried to discourage an interpretation of his work in terms of "myth-lite" à la Jung, Campbell, Buchanan, and New Age clichés. Indeed, there can be little question that he has actively sought to make his work accessible in these terms. But there is another side to Ambasz's self-analysis, at once darker and more reflective, like an obsidian mirror, that suggests a harder stance on myth and politics. This alternate line of thought about myth and mythmaking is summarized in his essay "Coda—A Pre-Design Condition."[17] "Coda" begins with some (insider?) observations of the Events of May, Paris, 1968. On the first page, Ambasz expresses disappointment that the revolution succumbed to its own myth of immediacy. He sadly observes that nothing remains except the "paper barricades." The rest of the essay is his effort to recoup from the failed revolution his youthful enthusiasm for social change. By the second page of this fascinating text, Ambasz is engaging in speculation about "structure" that is either heavily indebted to Lévi-Strauss or a dramatic case of "parallel invention."

> Man creates structures that are the meeting grounds between two incommensurable realms. . . . A structure . . . is designed to reconcile the discordant interface. . . . [P]articular instabilities are likely to follow its attempted resolution of the conflicts between the two realms.
> A structure may act as a pattern breaker; it may dissolve established correspondences between thought and matter and introduce new ones; it may induce a physical rearrangement in the infrastructure and an epistemological renewal.[18]

Lévi-Strauss sought to explain how mythic thinking, constrained to work with a bricolage of existing cultural elements, could lead to the intellectual creativity that produced the inventions of the Neolithic revolution. How did our primitive ancestors, in possession of nothing more than mythic thought, no Galilean insight, no Cartesian method, no experimental research design, and no mathematics, reach "brilliant unforeseen results on the intellectual plane"? Nowhere does Lévi-Strauss describe the likely process any more succinctly than Ambasz does here.

Ambasz consciously locates his architecture (indeed, all architecture) in the space of myth, not "myth-lite," but the mythic operations that are located "between two discordant realms." In the following sections I offer a listing of the fundamental oppositions, the "discordant realms" underlying Ambasz's architectural practice.

PRIMITIVE/MODERN

Of the series of oppositions that Ambasz interrogates through his work, the most obvious for an anthropological reading is "primitive/modern." It is also the most reflexively self-conscious opposition in his architectural idiom. It is what miscued some of his admirers into thinking his work can be contained by a New Age reading.

Adroit critical handling of the primitive/modern opposition requires us to scrape it clean of its encrustation of sophistry about crystals, feathers, magic mushrooms, and the mother goddess. Ambasz's projects embody the essence of the Primitive. Yet, in their presence we do not get a whiff of someone "going native" or "playing Indian." In fact, if there was ever a contemporary artist whose work is free of literal references to the "primitive" and "primitivism" it would be Emilio Ambasz. He returns us to a primitive state without returning us to a primitive state. The question for the critic is, How does Ambasz work this peculiar magic?

Alessandro Mendini tells us that Ambasz's work "is born from an obsessive search for primary principles."[19] It does not, however, reproduce the primitive state and hold it up as an example. It restages the fundamental problematics that we, as humans, have had to deal with from the beginning. Ambasz's creative response is on the same footing as that of our primitive ancestors', but time has passed and he must address the cultural crudation that has grown up around the original solutions, in addition to proposing new solutions. This is why Ettore Sottsass can say of his work with such evident

truth that it looks like "a thousand hours after the cataclysm" when humankind
has found a way to "restructure some form of mental and physical survival,"
to "build a stairway leading to who knows where."[20]

Michael Sorkin astutely retraces a trajectory that was first calculated by
Claude Lévi-Strauss, transforming "primitive/modern" into "minimal/elabo-
rated." Sorkin remarks with a Rousseauistic twist that Ambasz's work embodies a "pared down integrity of innocence" without "irony or suspicion."[21]
And, "it is not about being simple. It is about being concise."[22] We might add
that it is a minimalism without a trace of Puritanism. Ambasz does not elevate
the primitive over the modern, but he treats the two as a technical opposition
that provides an opening for rigorous interrogation of what is basic and true
about human emotions, relationships, and creativity.

NATURE/CULTURE

We have before us skyscrapers of trees, mountains of glass, buildings
that are floating islands, and a train station that is a desert oasis.
Ambasz comments:

> I seek rhetorically to eliminate architecture as a culturally conditioned
> process and return to the primeval notion of dwelling. I seek to
> develop an architectural vocabulary outside the canonical tradition
> of architecture. It is an architecture that is both here and not here.[23]

Ryuichi Sakamoto suggests the oeuvre taken as a whole is a metaphoric
scale model of planet earth. It reminds him of "a gigantic space station
endowed with desert and savanna areas where ten million people dwell."[24]
In this new architecture, "nature/culture" carries no weight as an *opposition*,
but it carries ultimate weight as a *pair*. Sorkin elaborates in landscape terms:
"About the work is an abiding sense of the ecological, nature's own system of
decorum. The sort of reticence about grade that the work persistently displays
is part of this, a deference to mother nature."[25] And with regard to the other
member of the nature/culture pair, Sakamoto tells us the work is not about just
one building after another, but it "always bears in mind an entire culture."[26]
Sakamoto goes on to state that the work promises to "reestablish a pact of reconciliation with nature."

Tadao Ando says Ambasz uses "nature on a massive scale," presenting
"the entire environment as a constellation from which architecture draws its

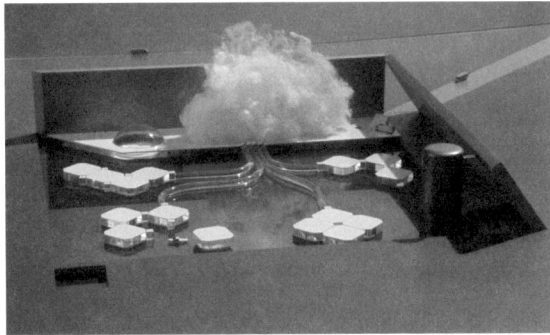

essential being." And, "there is . . . no prior example of nature governing architectural creation with such power and haunting seduction."[27] To this we could add that there is no prior example of architecture governing nature with such power and seduction. In the Houston Plaza, the cubic geometricism of the trees below and the dance of vapors above constitutes a new form of the nature/culture opposition. Ambasz takes pains to create places that are neither "God given" nor "man-made," but precisely suspended between the two realms.

There is a critical consensus that Ambasz's architecture "defers" to Mother Nature. It embodies an "ethic of growth" that is "decorous," "reticent," "innocent," given to "gentle gradients," "nurturing," "nonviolent," and "nonaggressive." Can't we just call it "green architecture"? Yes, but it is a unique kind of "green architecture," one that does not permit itself to succumb to crude do-it-yourself aesthetics. Ambasz's heroic efforts to hold himself accountable to principles of ecology *and* cultural history has the mythic potential for tragedy. There is always something sorrowful here, because the work already stands for the loss that accompanied the millions of pieces built by others in the progressive desolation of earth.

Houston Center Pla
Houston, Texas, 198

FACING PAGE, LEFT:
Casa de Retiro Espi
Cordoba, Spain, 197

FACING PAGE, RIGHT
Banques Bruxelles L
Lausanne, Switzerla

FRONT/BACK, SURFACE/DEPTH

It has been said of postmodern architecture that it is all surface and no depth. Fredric Jameson and others have taken this to be the organizing metaphor for postmodern culture in general: there is no depth of understanding, feeling, or historical sensitivity. Most of the writings about Ambasz comment that his work does not contribute to the postmodern aesthetic. To distinguish it from postmodern exercises, Buchanan states that Ambasz's work has "little in the way of facades."[28] Buchanan must mean "facade" in the sense of false fronts, or overly decorated fronts, not in the original, structural sense of the "face or front of a building." All architecture has some kind of facade to divide inside from outside and front from back. It would be better to say that the facades of Ambasz's buildings work a mythic inversion of front and back and renew our involvement in the passage from inside to outside and out to in. In his interiors he favors walls made of light. And at the Casa de Retiro Espiritual, there are walls without an inside. No one has theorized this better than Ambasz himself:

> You always have a sense that behind the walls of these projects are absent presences or present absences. The notion of that which is in front of you and what happens behind the wall has always appealed to me. There is a

certain anima or spirit behind the wall. The berms act as symbolic fortresses through which you pass to discover a terribly benign giant. . . . I have no wish to provoke anguish.[29]

In execution it gets even more interesting. In a characteristic gesture at the Banque Bruxelles Lambert, he installs the building's facade inside, in the lobby. He speaks directly to the complexities of psychic desire for intimacy. The designs promise us access to a mysterious interior and at the same time allow us a way out. Like an understanding illicit lover, they are not cloying; they never trap us in an unwanted intimacy.

Ambasz's handling of inside/outside disrupts the taken-for-granted alignments of architecture's conventional antinomies. Tadao Ando complains that, in modern times, "nature came to be treated as a mere visual accent, a mere aspect of landscape, a subject of adornment, and too often it [is] relegated to the margin of the site."[30] Not with Ambasz.

	Inside	Outside
Culture	MODERNIST AESTHETICS	AMBASZ
Nature	AMBASZ	MODERNIST AESTHETICS

Modernist aesthetics took pains to elevate culture over nature, and postmodernism elevated surface over depth. Ambasz strives to hold the two poles of both oppositions in a relation of perfect equality. And he allows the balanced oppositions to oscillate around each other, functioning as mythic operators, producing "brilliant unforeseen results."

SACRED/PROFANE

A few of Ambasz's projects have called on him to produce sacred sites or to deal directly with spiritual themes. These include the Casa de Retiro Espiritual in Spain, the convent in Singapore, and the small underground chapel for the agricultural workers' collective in California. While the numbers of specifically sacred buildings are small, the commentary on Ambasz's work as a whole very often invokes its alignment with sacred values. Buchanan generically calls the work "sacramental." Here again, Ambasz lends his own authority to this critical turn, commenting, "We should allow designers to act openly as once the shamans of 'old' societies, perhaps wiser societies, acted."[31]

It is commonplace to the point of being taken for granted that contemporary life is no longer infused with a strong sense of the sacred. Buchanan says that our lives are "drained of the radiantly sacred . . . dried up and fallen apart."[32] This belief that we have lost our ability to Believe lends a certain urgency to comments about the "sacred" quality of Ambasz's architecture. The claim is that he is helping us find our lost spirituality and making us whole again. I propose that there is something important going on here, but this is not it. If a spiritual sense of the sacred really "drained" out of modern life, the opposition "sacred/profane" would merely coincide with "traditional/modern," and a renewed sense of the sacred would be a simple reprise of traditional forms, a kind of retro spirituality à la the Family Values Movement. This does not feel like Ambasz on the face of it. Something more complex is happening.

Technically, a sense of the sacred, the awe that the sacred inspires, requires a special kind of "writing" on objects and events that simultaneously marks them as embodying ultimate values and separates them from secular, profane objects. Durkheim said that the sacred is the original "value added."[33] Sacred "writing" comes from the social group, but the group must always convince itself that it comes from without. Among the oldest forms of this kind of writing that designates parts of the world, the law, and experience as *sacred* are the hallowed *names* that are given to places and individuals and protected by ritual.

The notion that the sacred has departed modern life is simply untrue. This is another of those myths of modernity that are necessary to secure the position of ruling interests in our modern societies. (See "Myth Today" below.) If we the people are convinced that we have become separated from our own deep spirituality, then corporations, politicians, and other phony casuists can profit by selling their diluted versions of morality and spirituality back to us. This is how it became possible for abortion, which has no political significance whatsoever, to become a major "political issue." ("At last, an issue you can believe in.")

While any body would serve, the easiest proof of the continued deep resonance of sacred values in contemporary societies is the "ideal" feminine body nicely shrink-wrapped as it is in moral lustrations. Our sacred bodies can be tainted by even the slightest odors. Our garments—indeed our very being—are defined by the smallest stain. Our teeth must be at least three shades whiter or we shouldn't dare to open our mouths. The world that we live in continues to be much more religiously defined than we admit. As Goffman once famously commented, "Many gods have been done away with, but the individual . . . stubbornly remains as a deity of considerable importance."[34] Only now the commandments are brought down from the mountain by Proctor and Gamble and the Republican National Committee. Every modern person, especially the pitchmen, seducers, connivers, and big liars among us, is surrounded by a wall of morality that protects the sacredness and dignity of the image they want to claim for themselves. None of this would be possible if our world was devoid of sacred meaning.

I disagree with the comments to the effect that Ambasz is reintroducing a sense of the sacred back into architecture and contemporary life. The sacred has been subject to theft and manipulation, but it has not departed the modern social world. Power continues to depend on controlling sacred values as it always has. The strategy for taking the sacred away from the people is fully formulated. It requires two steps: (1) convince the people that their ordinary, everyday lives are drained of all spirituality, devoid of heightened meanings, and (2) offer the people compensation for their lost spirituality in the form of commercialized entertainments packaged as "spectacle," blockbuster movies, show trials, celebrity weddings, beauty pageants, and so on. The pretense that nothing significantly meaningful or of spiritual value can occur in the ordinary, everyday life of an average person runs precisely counter to the insights of the human sciences. According to Marx, Freud, and Goffman, everyday human relationships are the basis for our most intense psychic dramas. Conflicts, the formation of identity and character, and the everyday relation to production form the engine of history.

By decrying the "loss of the sacred," the most passionate critics of contemporary social arrangements hand victory to their enemies on a silver platter before any discussion or debate even begins. It is only to the extent that we actually believe our everyday lives are drained of the sacred and the consequential that we can have our humanity stolen from us and a crappy version of it sold back to us. It is only when we think our lives are meaningless that we turn to corporate authority to tell us what recreational vehicle is needed to commune with nature, who is the current god of popular culture, who has a *perfect* body?

In this context, all serious architecture can be seen as a form of sacred writing. It is not possible to rearrange a pile of stones without invoking the sacred. The issue here, for Ambasz in particular and architecture in general, has to do with the *placement and definition of the line between* the sacred and the profane, and the ownership of the means of production of the sacred. Does architecture express the dignity and meaning of the everyday, or does it seek to impress us with the putative insignificance of our ordinary lives? Ambasz does not bring back a sense of the sacred. Rather, he moves the battle lines between the sacred and the profane as they have been defined in the recent culture wars, or, more properly, in the current corporate war against culture. This is clearly enunciated in his "Credo":

> In my architecture I am interested in the rituals and ceremonies of the twenty-four-hour day. I am not interested in the rituals for the long voyage. . . . [W]hat a tragedy to discover that for the sake of those long-term dreams, we have sacrificed our daily lives. No, I am interested in daily rituals: like the ritual of sitting in a courtyard slightly protected from both the view of your neighbors and the wind—looking up at the stars. Dealing architecturally with that type of situation attracts me.[35]

Ambasz's architecture informs us that the raw materials for constructing an opposition between the sacred and profane are more or less evenly

distributed between peoples, localities, and historical moments. He takes the humblest materials, a quiet moment in a courtyard, a depression in the earth, a small tree that appears to have volunteered to grow on a stairway, and transforms them into sacred objects and events. Sottsass poetically remarks:

> I see [Emilio Ambasz] as an imaginative and illuminated young man, resembling some old Chinese priest who, first for months, and then for years, uses ancient techniques to polish the surface of a great disk of green jade which will allow him, perhaps, to penetrate beyond the daily, or better still, which will allow him, even for just an instant, to place daily existence in some exalted architectural domain.[36]

What is Ambasz up against? Corporate dream merchants adept at convincing the people that they are not competent to comprehend and shape materials to satisfy their spiritual needs. Ambasz's shamanistic practice is to make examples, to establish grounds for collaboration, to assist the people to trust their own insight when it comes to moral and aesthetic judgment. This is the way Ambasz understands it:

> We should allow designers to act openly as once the shamans of 'old' societies, or perhaps wiser societies, acted when they were more attuned to the human imperatives of dealing with passions, emotions, wonder.[37]

There is still a great deal of work to be done before everyone can see that we are capable of creating our own meaningful moments, that the women in the street are more beautiful than the women in the beauty pageant, that the important building doesn't have to be a phallic monstrosity.

SOLID/LIQUID/GAS

Since Aristotle, these categories have appeared on every list of concepts that permits us to think about essential differences in the form of substance, and of substantiality itself. Along with time, space, class, and number, they are among our most precious instruments of thought. Architecture, by convention and by code, is inscribed mainly within the category of *the solid*. Insofar as concepts require representation, buildings, along with their favored material, stone, are among the most privileged *signs* of solidity.

Emilio Ambasz's buildings do not sit proudly on the surface and appear to be gloating about their solidity. Instead, they hang in the air, or they are rhizomatically connected to everything that is underground. They are an affront to the kind of architecture that asserts its substantiality by mimicking the cube. Ambasz has created a distinctive architectural vocabulary that delights in its alignment with fluidity and insubstantiality. This has been pointed out by Ettore Sottsass, who remarks, "Such a quest for a constant state of fluidity, such a perception of existence as an ever-changing process pervades everything that Emilio has ever designed."[38] The play of forms that are more proper to a liquid than to a solid animates even the most prosaic details of his construction. Ambasz explains that before he buries a mobile home, he calls in a swimming-pool contractor to blow gunite around the outside of the structure that will be under the earth: "I can take a normal house, a Levitt house, or even two trailers perpendicular to each other and cover them partially with earth. . . . For projects of this sort, I employ people who build swimming pools. . . . Waterproofing is the last step before extra earth is brought in and mounded against the walls."[39] What is this thing except a pool turned inside out and made into an underground dwelling?

Here, for reasons that should be evident enough in a moment, I feel a strong need to go back to Lévi-Strauss's study of myth. Few of the myths Lévi-Strauss analyzes articulate the origins of house-building or architecture. The following Mataco myth may be the only one. It was collected by Métraux in the 1930s in northern Argentina about 750 miles from where Ambasz was born. The Mataco people were nomadic hunters and gatherers ranging in the Gran Chaco region of Argentina, near disputed borders with Paraguay and Bolivia. According to Mataco mythology, in the beginning there were no houses and no knowledge of methods needed to build them. We can pick up the story the way Lévi-Strauss re-tells it:

> [A]n Indian one day heard a noise at the bottom of a lagoon. He dived in and saw people building a large house under the direction of a master carpenter. This carpenter was none other than the skate [sting ray], who taught the Indian the art of house building. . . . [T]he skate was the first carpenter.[40]

I do not know if Ambasz has heard this story. I would like to know. No other story slips so easily into dialogue with Ambasz's imaginary. The theme of the submerged house, of drawing inspiration from nature, and from unlikely sources in nature: everything in the Mataco myth has found its expression in Ambasz's work.

If there are underlying principles to Ambasz's architectural practice, one of them would certainly be that in the solid/fluid opposition, architecture should align itself more with the fluid and less with the solid. The Schlumberger Research Laboratory calls for a prairie with some "natural" features: hills, valleys, a stream, and a lake. The earth of the prairie is strategically cut to accommodate offices and laboratories, half-underground. The individual offices of the scientists are to be parked here and there under the landscape. Each office unit is self-contained and mobile, allowing the scientists to select their neighbors according to their preferences and collaborations of the moment, and to select their views according to their inspirational needs. The flexibility of this arrangement would seem to respond directly to Lacan's dictum (in *Seminar IV*) that the most basic human desire is to be somewhere else. It also answers Lévi-Strauss's invidious comparison of Western architecture to the Kuki houses he describes in the passage at the beginning of this essay: "Those who lived in them were not overwhelmed by great blocks of unyielding stone; these were houses that reacted immediately and with great flexibility to their presence, their every movement. The house was, in fact, subject to the householder, whereas with us the opposite is the case."[41]

The same principle is found in the proposal for the Seville Exposition. The pavilions are floated on artificial lagoons. The entire design acknowledges the impermanence of international expositions. It is made to be recycled into a university campus. And when each of the pavilions becomes a university department, these can be flexibly arranged and rearranged into colleges in response to changing patterns of interdisciplinary collaboration. Of course, not everyone would be comfortable with so much flexibility. Resistance to this plan would nicely reveal irresponsibility in the face of choice, and hypocrisy in the embrace of freedom.

This inversion of the solid/fluid opposition is found in the program of many works, and it is also evident in the aesthetic elements of virtually every design. Exterior surfaces woven from living trees recall the Yuki houses described by Lévi-Strauss. The original design for the Fukuoka Prefectural International Hall called for a folded and inclined lake, as if not even the fluid is flexible enough for Ambasz. In summary, I will again paraphrase Sottsass: "Emilio's buildings are not objects. They are not architecture. They invoke the presence of architecture. They are more like wagers."[42]

Ambasz's architectural practice contains the outlines of an alternative modern mythology—not myth-lite. Fumihiko Maki comments that Ambasz has created something new through "violent oppositions."[43] This remark appears to stand in direct contradiction to Sorkin's and others' assessment that the works are "reticent," "innocent," "gentle," "nonaggressive," and "nonviolent." Can both claims (for violence and for nonviolence) be correct? I think so, at the level of mythic transformation. What Ambasz creates is non-violent. But it is necessary for him to do violence to conventional oppositions and hierarchies to arrive at his distinctively nonviolent architectural result. Thus his work stands not just as architecture but as strong critique and comment on the state of the world we live in, set up as it is to underwrite all forms of violence. The particular revisions Ambasz is making to the antinomies that underlay everyday life is the reason his work is inclusive. It is compelling not just to architects and artists but to anyone who might stumble across it. This is not because it invokes "universal mythic archetypes." It is because it enters and works the gaps in human consciousness that have been created by myth.

MYTH TODAY

Roland Barthes extended the study of myth to cultural arrangements under late capitalism. According to Barthes, modern myth is not necessarily found in formulaic narratives or in other material that announces itself as myth. For example, his essay on "Ornamental Cookery" focuses on the presentation of food in the French magazine *Elle*.

> Glazing, in *Elle*, serves as a background for unbridled beautification: chiseled mushrooms, punctuation of cherries, motifs of carved lemon, shavings of truffle, silver pastilles, arabesques of glacé fruit. . . . [I]t is because *Elle* is addressed to a genuinely working class public that it is very careful not to take for granted that cooking must be economical. . . . [O]rnamental cookery is indeed supported by a wholly mythical economics. This is an openly dream-like cookery, as proved in fact by the photographs in *Elle*, which never show the dishes except from a high angle, as objects at once near and inaccessible, whose consumption can perfectly well be accomplished simply by looking.[44]

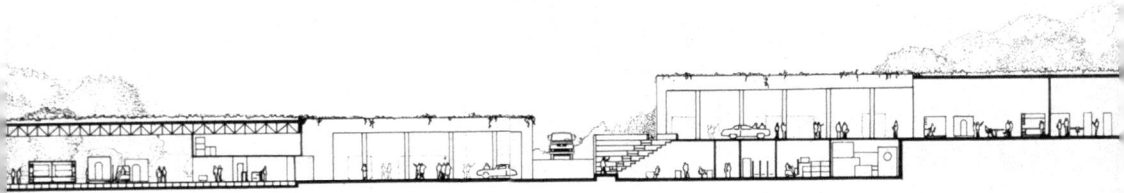

According to Barthes, myth today is not so much "built from" the "debris of discourse" as it is embedded in it. We do not relate our myths so much as we bear them on our persons and in our belongings, in figures of speech, clothing styles, automobile design, advertising formulas, representational strategies, motion picture clichés, retro and nostalgic architectural styles, decoration, toys, and gadgets.

While Lévi-Strauss's and Barthes's theories of myth were given to us in very different forms (Barthes's was in several short essays, not several heavy books), they are markedly similar in their essentials. Modern myths, no less than "primitive" myths, are ideological castles built from scraps of discourse, exactly as Lévi-Strauss suggested. But Barthes's words about myth work are much stronger than Lévi-Strauss's. Barthes says that myth is "parasitic," that it "appropriates" and "nourishes itself" on history, and "distorts" language for its own ends.

What kind of work does myth do in late capitalist society? Again, it is precisely the same as that posited by Lévi-Strauss for American Indians. Our myths permit us to live our social contradictions as if they are not contradictions. The difference between primitive and modern myths are the actual historical contradictions that the myth-work covers up and supports. How do we reconcile the democratic principle of human equality with the racism that is still rampant in democracies, or with the enormous difference in life's possibilities for the wealthy and those for the impoverished? Modern myth glosses over these differences that have specific historical origins by pretending they are not historical but a part of the "natural" order of things. Thus, we have a thousand variations on the myth that free enterprise is human nature; or the myth that blacks are naturally inferior to whites, but are suited to certain types of work, good at sports, and capable of loyalty. Myth appropriates language to suppress history. It transforms conservative values into "facts." It enables a kind of right politics that appears to operate beyond merely political considerations by wrapping an elevated class perspective in pretentiously "a-political," "universalistic" rhetoric. Conservative mytho-politics hides its specific agendas

33

behind vapid generalities: "All people have the right to be free from government regulation of their authentic human potential."

While the fundamentals of the theory of myth remain remarkably stable and constant across the primitive/modern divide, the moral and ethical implications are entirely different. Why? Because the histories are incommensurate. No primitive society ever had to deal with the kind of human inequality that we moderns face on a daily basis. When Montaigne sent his servant to interview a chief who had been brought to Europe from the recently discovered Americas, he inquired first of all about inequality, or the material consequences of status difference. Did chiefs dress any differently, or eat better food, or live in larger or more comfortable houses? No. Were there *any* differences then? Yes. The chief proudly proclaimed two differences. When the group was on the move through the forest, his subjects would pull back the foliage to make it easier for him to pass. And the second difference? When his people went into battle against a mortal enemy, it was the chief who was privileged to lead the charge.

Evidently we're not in Arcadia anymore.

How do we reconcile this critique of myth under capitalism with an architecture that simultaneously espouses democratic values and wants to think of itself as myth-work?

Barthes does not directly suggest, though he strongly implies, that the gap between rich and poor under extreme capitalism is great and unbridgeable. The middle class might be pivotal, but there is simply too much ideological terrain to bulldoze, and our collective understanding of history is too weak. Accordingly, the "middle class" spends its considerable wealth and energy on compensatory myth with which it is endlessly preoccupied. Whatever revolutionary potential the middle class might possess has been completely neutralized by its distinctive consciousness built from the droppings of mythic discourse: gleaming domestic surfaces indicate social standing; the appearance of compassion is equal to the reality of justice; the natural destiny of woman is to be a wife and mother; the wealthy work harder for their money than the poor; social and other kinds of friction can be made to disappear from our lives; if someone fails it is their own fault; brilliant economic success is the result of a good business plan; shopping is patriotic; it is possible to insulate oneself from socially undesirable elements by living in a gated community; with sufficient social and other prophylaxes sex is completely sanitary; and so on. According to Barthes, the bourgeoisie is historically nothing except what has been pasted together from these and similar mythic beliefs. He calls the bourgeoisie a "joint stock company" and remarks, "Ideologically, all that is not bourgeois is obliged to *borrow* from the bourgeoisie."[45]

Where does Ambasz stand on the matter of modern mythology having been fully co-opted in the service of reinforcing existing social hierarchies? For example, myth today as nothing more than the ideological support for the singular opposition in late capitalist societies: that between wealth and poverty, between surplus and lack. This is more difficult for Ambasz, and for us, than his alignment with Lévi-Strauss's theory of myth. He is clearly ambivalent on the matter of the politics of his mythic experimentation. Sometimes he denies that his works have any political significance: "I want to be a fabulist, not an ideologist."[46] At other times, he deals directly, and often bravely, with political questions and theory. He prefaces these moments with a quick move to dissociate his work from "traditional" class-based critiques.

> [T]he traditional agent of change, the class subject, is spottily assumed by a lucid and sensitive few who place themselves on the periphery of the system. They may attempt to establish alliances with those who are dispossessed or deprived of their rights, but these are now outside channels of production and wield no power; and the alienated ones who do take part in production can no longer recognize themselves as a social class.[47]

I read this as fully acknowledging the effective political neutralization of all class perspectives except, of course, the highest one. In other words, according to Ambasz, myth won, not Barthes's exposé of its inner workings. This would be a bitter pill for both the old and new Left to swallow. But the Far Right should not begin their final victory dance. None of the problems that gave us Left and Right have gone away. If anything, they have intensified. Ambasz does not stop with his critique of leftist rhetoric, he immediately tries to shift the struggle for the soul of humanity onto a different ground.

> Formal organizations . . . legitimize social relations, the ownership of resources, etc. . . . . [T]he structures that man designs, the myths he creates, are temporary crystallizations in the perennial state of dialectical transaction between the fears and desires underlying the

individual's aspirations and the assembled forces of the natural and socio-cultural worlds.[48]

In short, the historical framing of human aspiration in terms of social class position has only driven revolutionary sentiments deeper underground. The class positions that have been proffered are not attractive choices: to be an oppressor, or to desire to be an oppressor. Ambasz wants to start with a clean sheet on these matters, which makes his architecture historically interesting indeed.

[E]ven though the old [class] distinctions have been blurred, conflicts, albeit of a different nature, still exist between infrastructure and super-structure. The strategy that is called for is the design of structures which, mediating between the two levels, attempt to resolve their new kinds of conflict, and to cause in both changes that are wanted. What these struc-tures can and ought to be cannot be known in advance of their existence. However, as we have seen, in an advanced industrial society the conditions *do not exist* which permit the emergence of structures that may bring about significant change. We are, so to speak, in a pre-design situation.[49]

Are we, so to speak, in a perpetually prerevolutionary situation? I can think of no more frustrating place for humanity to end up. But this is also the exact point of theoretical and critical impasse. Where do we go from here? Toward the prospect of a revolutionary bourgeoisie? Or straight to cyber-nuclear-fascism?

This is not just a problem for the Left. The Right has its work cut out for it as well. At this moment, the Right has positioned humanity between traumatic responses to staged events and nonresponses to actual cataclysms. If anything, this is a tougher space to work one's way out of than the impasses on the Left. There is no middle way out of this dilemma. Or there may be, but the so-called middle way is always further to the right than the conservative way. Recall that Hitler and the Nazis extolled the virtues of German National Socialism as the sensible "middle ground" between the "excesses" of American capitalism and Soviet communism. And they knew excess.

It is important to continue to examine the role of myth in society today. Clearly, Barthes's version of myth is not the same as Ambasz's. Barthes was incensed by myth's capacity to neutralize the historic role of the working class and to deny its contribution to our general well-being. He was equally incensed by myth's capacity to disguise the cruel, self-interested manipulation of all of our lives by the controlling class. In short, Barthes was infuriated by myth's capacity to drain all historical meaning out of the structural opposition that sustains capital. Ambasz's strategy is to step around social class and interrogate the superstructure that supports it. Ambasz does not place one member of an oppositional pair over the other, or try to drain all the meaning out of both. Rather, he seeks to create a new balance and to infuse both sides with sumptuousness. Even the member that had been privileged by previous cultural movements is enriched in his hands. It is a matter of aesthetics, but it is also political.

Ambasz has selected the most consequential terms possible to frame his own work. He has thrust himself and his critics into the historical game with the highest stakes. ("His architecture is more like a wager.") If it is just a stronger kind of glue to hold an ultimately unsustainable class structure together, it will only serve to make the eventual explosion that much more destructive. If, on the other hand, it is a brilliant engine for generating alternative human arrangements and new models of governance, there are grounds for hope.

1   Emilio Ambasz, "Fragments from My Credo," in *Emilio Ambasz Inventions: The Reality of the Ideal* (New York: Rizzoli, 1992), 55.

2   Michael Sorkin, "Et in Arcadia Emilio," in *Emilio Ambasz: The Poetics of the Pragmatic* (New York: Rizzoli, 1988).

3   Ettore Sottsass, translation of catalog essay in *Architettura naturale: Emilio Ambasz progetti e oggetti* (Venice: Electa, 1995), xxii.

4   Emilio Ambasz, "I Ask Myself," in *Emilio Ambasz: The Poetics of the Pragmatic*, 24.

5   Emilio Ambasz, "Fragments from My Credo," 53.

6   Peter Buchanan, "Emilio Ambasz: The Relevance of Resonant Ritual," in *Emilio Ambasz Inventions*, 27–29.

7   Sorkin, "Et in Arcadia Emilio," 19.

8   Buchanan, "Emilio Ambasz: The Relevance of Resonant Ritual," 15.

9   Ibid., 29.

10   Ibid.

11   Dean MacCannell, *Empty Meeting Grounds: The Tourist Papers* (London: Routledge, 1992), 292ff.

12   Claude Lévi-Strauss, *The Savage Mind* (Chicago: University of Chicago Press, 1966), 22.

13   Ibid., 21.

14 Ibid., 17.

15 Ibid., 22.

16 Jacques Lacan, *Seminar VII: The Ethics of Psychoanalysis* (New York and London: W. W. Norton & Company, 1992), 143.

17 Ambasz, "Coda—A Pre-Design Condition," in *Emilio Ambasz: The Poetics of the Pragmatic,* 49ff.

18 Ibid., 50.

19 Alessandro Mendini, catalog essay in *Emilio Ambasz: The Poetics of the Pragmatic,* 16.

20 Sottsass, catalog essay in *Emilio Ambasz: The Poetics of the Pragmatic,* 10.

21 Sorkin, "Et in Arcadia Emilio," 17, 21.

22 Ibid., 21.

23 Ambasz, "I Ask Myself," 28.

24 Ryuichi Sakamoto, "Return of the Entire Humankind to Earth," in *Emilio Ambasz Inventions,* 11.

25 Sorkin, "Et in Arcadia Emilio," 22.

26 Sakamoto, "Return of the Entire Humankind to Earth," 9.

27 Tadao Ando, "Amplitude's Promise Fulfilled," in *Emilio Ambasz Inventions,* 43.

28 Buchanan, "Emilio Ambasz: The Relevance of the Resonant Ritual," 17.

29 Ambasz, "I Ask Myself," 27–28.

30 Ando, "Amplitude's Promise Fulfilled," 41.

31 Ambasz, "Architettura Radicale," in *Emilio Ambasz Inventions,* 76.

32 Buchanan, "Emilio Ambasz: The Relevance of Resonant Ritual," 29.

33 E. Durkheim, *The Elementary Forms of the Religious Life* (New York: The Free Press, 1965), 363.

34 E. Goffman, *Interaction Ritual: Essay on Face-to-Face Behavior* (New York: Anchor Doubleday, 1967), 95.

35 Ambasz, "Fragments from My Credo," 53.

36 Ettore Sottsass, translation of catalog essay in *Architettura naturale,* xxiii.

37 Ambasz, "Architettura Radicale," 76.

38 Sottsass, translation of catalog essay in *Architettura naturale,* xxii.

39 Ambasz, "I Ask Myself," 27.

40 Claude Lévi-Strauss, *The Naked Man: Introduction to a Science of Mythology,* vol. 4 (New York: Harper & Row, 1981), 549.

41 Lévi-Strauss, *Tristes Tropiques* (New York: Atheneum, 1968), 198–99.

42 Sottsass, translation of catalog essay in *Architettura naturale,* xxii.

43 F. Maki, "Primary Architecture," in *Emilio Ambasz Inventions,* 45.

44 Roland Barthes, *Mythologies* (New York: Hill and Wang, 1972), 78–79.

45 Roland Barthes, *Mythologies,* 139 [Barthes's emphasis].

46 Ambasz, "I Ask Myself," 27.

47 Ambasz, "Coda—A Pre-Design Condition," 50.

48 Ibid., 51 [emphasis added].

49 Ambasz, "Coda—A Pre-Design Condition," 51 [my emphasis].

PERIPHERAL VISION
Lauren Sedofsky

Given the sheer quantity of attention that has been directed over the past two decades toward the limits, the margins, the peripheries of artistic and intellectual practices—their repressions, suppressions, and proscriptions—it would seem only logical that Emilio Ambasz's work should have been picked up and picked over long ago as a unique effort to carry architecture across one of its most forbidding lines of demarcation into landscape. Yet, to date, even the seemingly inevitable observation that Ambasz has engaged in a conspicuous inversion of the respective weights conventionally assigned to the architectonic and the natural terrain has never been made, much less examined, with the clarity that it fully requires. The question is why, at a particular historical moment, this line of demarcation would have elicited Ambasz's disruptive investigations, while at the same time obscuring their implications for the potential power of landscape to intrude upon the autonomy and legitimacy of a bona fide architectural object. To state the issue baldly: Ambasz has brought the house down to the ground. And if familiar critical boundaries are fortified against such a move, it may be time to explore the unfamiliar.

As far back as 1980 Manfredo Tafuri was to count Ambasz among architecture's young ironists.[1] By irony he meant an "interrupted criticism,"[2] the intermittent allusiveness of a poetic image. If the illustrations in *The Sphere and the Labyrinth* are any indication, Tafuri was thinking of Ambasz's proposal for the Grand Rapids Art Museum, involving the insertion of a monumental inclined stepped-plane cascade between the Beaux-Arts wings of an unused federal building. Right on target, Tafuri identified this massive intrusion of reflected sky into the building's academic vocabulary as an effort, typical of the Argentinian contingent in New York, to achieve a "masked architecture," which he equated with a "dissimulated language."[3] But what Tafuri ignored in Ambasz's "too-simple instruments" was their illicit foreignness. What he misjudged, out of a commitment to the totalizing power of architectural language, was the extent to which the masking gesture might constitute a historically determined statement. For, in the intervening years, Ambasz has developed just this gesture into a full-fledged, relentless principle, one that today, in its deliberately ex-centric way, would satisfy Tafuri's criterion for a genuinely critical architecture: "the systematicity of the heresy."[4]

The twist in architectural logic that has become Ambasz's *modus operandi* is hardly removed from the pivotal debates of the moment. The furious oscillation between classical and modernist canons that seemed so much the issue in the late 1970s was to evolve rapidly into anxious investigations of a conceivable noncanonical architecture. Polemics between "Whites" and "Grays" yielded to a far more direct and devastating confrontation with the rout of modernism—not through the proliferation of its sterile or bastardized versions, or even the revolution in our reading of the avant-garde movements—but from within its indelible richness. For it might be argued that with Wright's Guggenheim Museum and Le Corbusier's Ronchamp the architectural object had already turned resolutely and definitively *sui generis*. Nonetheless, some of the most provocative speculative projects over the last fifteen years have consisted precisely in demonstrations of this new deregulated condition. Daniel Libeskind's collages, Bernard Tschumi's dismantling, Coop-Himmelblau's instabilities and contradictions, OMA's darkly witty allegories, and Peter Eisenman's flatbed superimpositions all create the impression of an architecture that wants out and is in despair of finding a viable exit. All of them seem to be raising the elemental question of what an edifice could possibly *be* now, what kinds of concerns or extrinsic concepts might conceivably legitimate the generation of form.

We make a distinction between architecture and landscape, a distinction that would appear inescapable. This condition of adjacency promotes to this day unqualified assertions that they each participate in irreconcilable orders. To be sure, the architectural treatises have traditionally provided for neighborly negotiations, modulations of the edifice in view of a disparate environment: the perennially recast recognition of site-specificity. But no amount of consecrated green space—not SITE's Forest House, not Le Corbusier's Plan Voisin or Ville Radieuse, not Wright's Fallingwater or Broadacre City, not the Garden City or Olmsted's parks, not Kew, Versailles, the Palladian villa, or the Renaissance and Baroque gardens, not even Buontalenti's most elaborate version at Pratolino—has ever been given license to invade the tectonic integrity of the edifice. A troglodyte mentality figures as essentially alien to a tradition that posits strict perimeters for its vehicles of high signficance. But, between Western metaphysics' considerable investment in positive aboveground building—which finds its most distilled expression in Hegel's *Aesthetics*—and a tradition of architectural treatises that has invariably grounded the validation of the orders in natural laws, there exists a paradoxical neglect of the *materia prima* that serves as the seat and the resources for all construction. The displacement of the naturalistic paradigm to the human body, like the prestige of the archetype accorded to the primitive hut, reposes on the same quid pro quo, in that each promotes a psychic screening of architecture's fundamental ablation of the earth.

Read Ambasz and note, in his lexicon of predilection, an avowed conception of architecture as a "poetics," constitutive of mythmaking and quotidian rituals, ceremonies, and processions, dedicated to what architects like to call the "myth of Arcadia." Taken at face value in a period of fierce demythologizing and demystifcation, these reference points verge on an anachronic preciosity. They have no doubt dampened the interest of more than one historian or critic and led several of Ambasz's more literal-minded commentators to advance the notion that he might be, at once, Wordsworth and Magritte, Ledoux and Jeff Koons, a family-oriented Nietzsche and a New Age Joseph Campbell. Now look at the photographed models, whose carefully composed graphic significance is manifestly at odds with any ultimate realization. The projects are posed in radical isolation, overwhelmed by a preponderance of sky and earth. Only Ettore Sottsass has had the perspicacity to remark that Ambasz's earth is not at all the picturesque botanical compendium of the pastoral.[5] There is nothing Romantic about this green desert, this turf or tegument stretching to infinity. No historical inflection impinges on the ambient pregnancy released uniquely by the incidence of architectural intervention. Earth, sky—now bring in, as Ambasz's statements tend to do, the personalized rites that inform daily routine, the local deities that reign over place, and consider to what extent these coordinates correspond to those that orient the Greek temple[6] or the bridge[7] in Heidegger's elaboration of "authentic dwelling."

A chasm separates the strict Heideggerian doctrine of the ongoing historical production of meaning from the "existential" reception that architecture theorists have reserved for it.[8] And the errant path of Heidegger's resonant phraseology passes through the latter's humanistic screen directly into Emilio's Folly, where the philosopher's better-known philosophemes find their most literal construction. Within the speculative genre of the folly, Ambasz presents a design that unambiguously and unconditionally "brings forth the earth," not merely by burying the canonical Mediterranean villa and thereby elevating the surrounding grounds, but, with demonstrative emphasis, by inserting into the villa's courtyard pool an incongruous micromountain, visibly excised from the nearby terrain. To this enigmatic terra incognita he appends a narration or, as

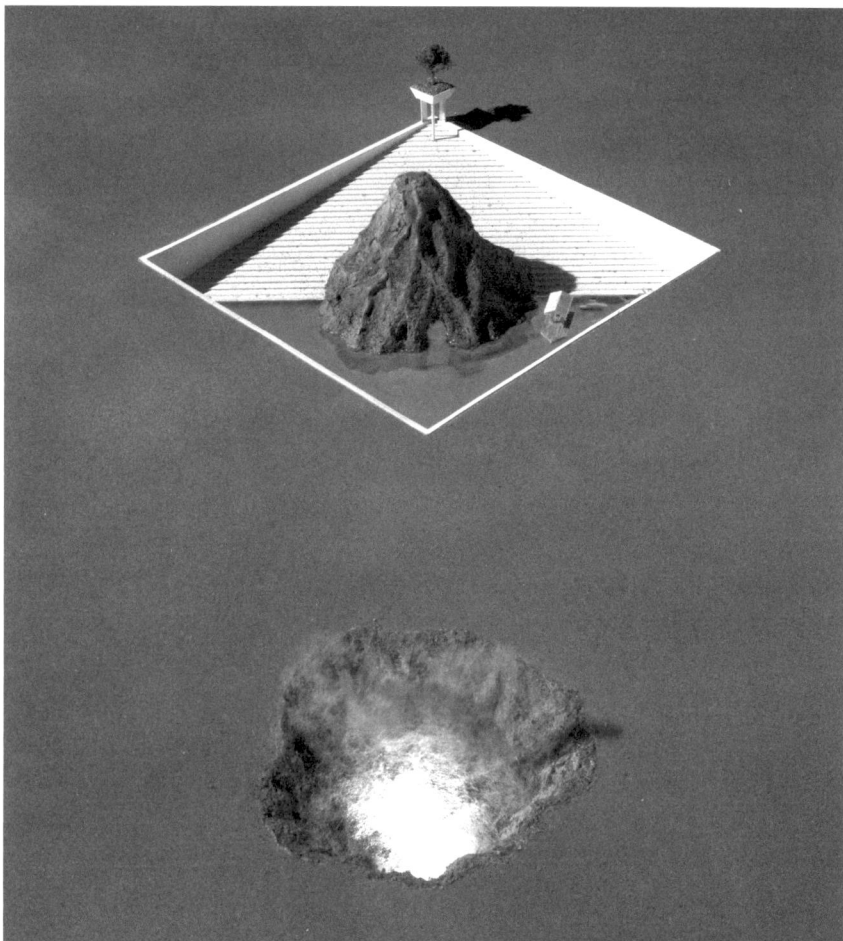

he would have it, a "fable,"⁹ which foregrounds architecture's specifically discursive feature as it relates, in a first-person voice, a "thrownness" into this preexisting geo-tectural situation and the consequent progressive personal mapping and appropriation of "what is at hand." No socius legitimates the emergence of significance here, as it must for Heidegger, nor does the architectural object relay attention to the social and historical rootedness of the site. Nonetheless, the signal act of "disclosure," animated by "care" for the successively revealed facets and usages of this location, as well as by a self-reflexive recognition of its temporal dimension, incontestably "opens a world." And that "openness," figured both topographically and phenomenologically, would appear to infuse Ambasz's "poetics" with the more compelling semantic force of *poiesis:* the distinctly human agency involved in the construction of meaningful presence. In the folly's highly synoptic and playful version, how-

43

ever, the "combat" that Heidegger posits between the "world" and the "earth," that is, between the infinite range of possible human meanings and the inherent constraints of the natural environment (which includes all preexisting worlds)— both largely concealed, each dependent on the other for its historical revelation—becomes the model for an architecture that will take *à la lettre* the terms *world* and *earth* and afford to their relative "concealment" and "unconcealment" the enhanced relief of a rhetorical figure.

The emergence of the earth *over and against* architecture produces a singularly unfamiliar topography in Ambasz's work, one that scuttles the customary conjunction of solids and voids, and topples the generally recognized hierarchy of primacy and secondariness. Such a deployment of architecture and landscape has been difficult to characterize, because it has been difficult or seemingly impossible to historicize. Only ancient astronomical observatories, Japanese gardens, labyrinths, processionals, and oases offer similarly unclassifiable, hybrid configurations. Far from a territorialization of the site—whether construed as a friendly regionalism or an ominous Heideggerian descent into native soil and the destiny of a people—Ambasz's supra-architectural conception evokes instead the transtemporal, transcultural enigma of a paleolithic vestige: dislocated, anonymous, without particularities. Like the ruin dating from a time *before* architecture, which incorporates or recapitulates the natural features of a tract of ground, his structures engage the dynamics of the hidden and the revealed with a categorical shift that overwhelmingly privileges earth surface. On this point Ambasz has been clear. As early as the the Casa de Retiro Espiritual in Cordoba, the explicit issue was "to eliminate architecture."[10]

It is important to take the measure of this assault on the seemingly ineradicable gestalt associated with the architectural object, especially in view of the tortuous recent history of the notion of the "frame" and its implications for the kind of unified and finalized object that architecture implies. If Heidegger had allowed that a constellation of meanings could be harnessed by a certain stability or en-framing, say, in the work of art (at least until the paradigms of modern techno-science had rigidified the dynamics of meaning to the point of reification), Derrida later detected the cheating, principally in the overarching designs of philosophical systems, that had been going on all along. What he designated the *parergon* and was to become the springboard for Peter Eisenman's Carnegie-Mellon Center (1987–88) represents an accretive frame that results from the remedial plugging of conceptual holes. Such as Derrida describes it in *The Truth in Painting*,[11] the apparently extrinsic *parergon* is a threatening, critical "additive," a stop-gap, a "prosthesis," "half-oeuvre, half-hors d'oeuvre," neither simply outside nor simply inside, detachable but difficult to detach, riveted as it is to what is missing. Countering this ideational assemblage, the text decrees a "general law": make the frame crack. And, indeed, it is in adherence to this law or, more precisely, its *image*, that Eisenman tackles the problem of designing an edifice that exhibits its own disruptions, disjunctions, and instabilities. To generate the form of the *Center,* he conceives of the frame as a linear cube, projects it in n-dimensions, cuts it axially, and rotates the segments, seeking the cube's complex, virtual relations.[12] But Eisenman's choice of the cube as a point of departure tells the whole story and returns us to square one. The end product of this process, for all of its formal breaks and lattice extensions, constitutes a necessarily static, constructable unit, which may illustrate its generative principle, but amounts *in toto* to nothing more than a reframing. And reframing, together with the dream of no frame at all, are the two contradictory gestures that Derrida has labored so hard to deconstruct.

The receptacle for habitation shows a remarkable resistance to contemporary theories of process and dynamics. No obsolete metaphysical imperative, the sheer material necessity for closure and immobility has been problematized in our time far beyond anything Bruno Zevi might have dreamed of in extolling the traditionally neat, invaginate relations between the shell and core of a solitary edifice. To the dilemma of introducing a kinematics into architecture's statics, Ambasz responds with an unequivocal negation of tectonic symbolization, in its place consigning the edifice to literal interment and leaving "process" to the surrounding soil. A thorny question arises, then, as to just what kind of frame landscape might provide, and nothing is more ambiguous. In Ambasz's projects, a strict heteromorphism exists between the habitation and its landscape boundaries; their respective contours remain distinct and arbitrary. The clearing that landscape affords the site predominates, surrounding the habitation, submerging and sometimes invading it with the material substance of an improper territory. As a frame, the terrain is bivalent: while it surely serves to harness the site, at the same time, it opens it up, allowing it to expand and dissolve into the wider surroundings. When the philosophical text overflows and cracks apart, Derrida was to remark, it is condemned to find only other texts.[13] When the architectural object overflows and cracks apart—the accumulated history of architectural models notwithstanding—ultimately it joins the natural continuum, of which it is merely one type of articulation.

Ambasz's grafting of landscape onto architecture retains an outlandish aspect only so long as architecture maintains its status, according to the habitually parochial view, as an autonomous enterprise cut off from simultaneous permutations in the visual arts. In New York in the late 1960s and into the '70s, where and when Ambasz's ideas were taking shape, boundaries were becoming exceptionally permeable. Painting had already come off the wall in a full recognition of its three-dimensionality, and sculpture was taking a decidedly unclassifiable turn. As Rosalind Krauss was to sum it all up at the end of the decade, the hitherto freestanding object had surprisingly invaded formerly unoccupied regions delimited by the normally extrinsic architecture and landscape, positively or negatively defined: *landscape* and *architecture, not-landscape* and *not-architecture, landscape* and *not-landscape,* and *architecture* and *not-architecture.*[14] Crossbreeding produced hybrids: site-constructions; earth mounds and excavations; marked sites, inserting man-made natural structures into the natural environment; and axiomatic structures, seeking to simulate aspects of architectural experience. In the mapping of this logical expansion, Krauss recognized the "lifting of an ideological prohibition to think the complex," which represented an unequivocal "historical rupture." What is astonishing, in retrospect, is not only that she should have bolted her argument to evidence that "other cultures had been able to think the *complex,*" specifically identifying examples of *both landscape and architecture* (mazes and labyrinths, Japanese gardens and ancient processionals), but that the reciprocal implications of this "historical rupture" for architecture itself was to remain obscure. Seen today in the context of Ambasz's work, Michael Heizer's *Two-Stage Liner Buried in Earth and Snow* (1967) and *Compression Line* (1968) or Robert Smithson's *Partially Buried Wood Shed* (1970) look like rough preliminary drafts for an integral architectural program. For the underlying urge, as Smithson emphasized in his writings, was to arrive at something "sprawling and embedded in landscape, rather than putting an object on the landscape."[15]

Minimalist art has occasionally been evoked to characterize Ambasz's use of simple geometric forms. But the minimalist mind-set, pushing ineluctably toward the earthwork mutation, had a much more far-reaching and subversive objective: a total rejection of the work's inner logic. The black boxes, L beams, cages, and floor tiles established an art object that was nonrelational, opaque, and external. All that mattered was the materiality of the object, its mass, bulk, density, and volume. The meaningful core, the composition, the interior had been leveled to an inexpressive, enigmatic surface that, in its tension between self-evidence and impenetrability, converts the viewer's experience of a shared space into an inhabitual confrontation with what Krauss so rightly designated, with regard to Lewitt and his peers, as *aporia*.[16] Consequently, the kind of inscrutable *found object* that the minimalists were trying to achieve finds its correlative in Ambasz's projects, in point of fact, not at all in his use of simple geometric shapes, but rather in his appropriation of landscape. Once you have buried the box (as Lewitt did, quite literally) or consigned the receptacle for habitation to some arbitrary location, lurking in the bowels of the earth in an indeterminate way, the issue of the architectural object's inner logic is dead. The work turns centrifugal: its familiar natural surface, defamiliarized by an indecipherable architectural organization, becomes a marked point of fascinating estrangement. As architecture, landscape, in its striking inevidence, stares back at the observer with dumbfounding undecidability.

Ambasz's purism, a purism that often reflects a Scarpa-like refinement in the articulation of detail, studs a much larger design. When visible, the strictly architectural fragments—an undulating wall, the intersection of two planes, a beveled sphere, receding tiers, a curvilinear stairway, a trellis or lattice—obey a principle of extreme reduction, even as they establish a rudimentary signaletics of the site. What is being carried out is something on the order of a demonstration of the least number of units required to *mean* architecture, not unlike those employed by the Mexican architect Luis Barragán, whose work Ambasz was to unearth and exhibit when he was curator of design at the Museum of Modern Art in New York. Master of the isolated architectural element—the gate, the reflecting pool, most notably, the self-supporting wall—Barragán proposed a form of architecture that verges on both sculpture and scenic design. His use of brilliant color and the backdrop of a raw and antithetical Mexican landscape in which his elements acquire enhanced relief, however, serve only to augment the assertive force of his structures as autonomous modernist "works of art." Barragán's work, in its way, is all purism, whereas Ambasz's version takes on its specific resonance as a counterpoint to landscape's predominating effect of *contamination*. If an "impure-purity," as Smithson maintained, was to become the hallmark of visual art in the late 1960s and early '70s, clearly in the wake of a renewed Duchampian invitation to spoliate a presumably pristine modernism, in architecture this tendency was to take the form of recourse to vernaculars and revivals. Smithson wrote of his generation's enchantment with "the mood of bad architecture"[17] and the transtemporal richness of 1930s Ultramoderne eclecticism[18] some time before Robert Venturi, Charles Jencks, or

Paolo Portoghesi turned their attention to those wellsprings. And it would be left primarily to the visual artists of this generation to extrapolate the implications of earth-surface and seize upon the *promenade architecturale* as their own veritable medium.

A house conspicuous by its absence troubles the imagination. In Ambasz's most prototypal residential designs, the House for Leo Castelli, Manoir d'Angoussart, and Casa de Retiro Espiritual, something habitual in the habitation has been wrested from the site, and what is left belongs to a rhetorical *topos* hotly debated in France during the period of their inception: the *rest*. The rest is a throwaway in underground works like the Philip Johnson Gallery or Norman Foster's bunker house. Yet the rest was traditionally a regulator in the definition of the suburban or country villa—a regulator later perceived as a source of suspicious deflection. As Wölfflin remarks laconically in *Renaissance and Baroque*, the crossing of art and countryside seems to take the art out of art.[19] And, in much the same vein of urban reticence, Tafuri continues: "In the landscape context, from an absolute object architecture becomes a relative value."[20] But, indeed, it is just this relativity, implicit in the conception of the suburban dwelling from Martial and Terence to Alberti, that contributes to a principle of intervention into landscape requiring development, not in height, but at ground level and out into a larger *promenade architecturale*. The intriguing issue that Ambasz raises, then, pertains to the purview of that principle, that is, the extent to which the architectural work might be conceived in its entirety as a promenade, in and around and even over the house. Bird's-eye views of his designs—a vantage for which he appears to have particular affection—suggest precisely this kind of unified, all-over surface, guided by sculpted roads and extruding markers. "The landscape," much the way Smithson imagines it in his proposal for an "Aerial Art," "begins to look more like a three-dimensional map than a rustic garden."[21]

Ambasz's early professional association in Buenos Aires with Amancio Williams alone would have sufficed to acquaint him with an acute Wright-inspired concern with landscape. Williams's Casa del Puente (1943–46), for example, engulfed by an overgrowth of lush Mar del Plata vegetation, assumes the posture of an enclosed bridge that straddles the river, bolstered by a frank curvilinear support. But, quite apart from his reputed accessory obsession with horizon lines, Williams was to oversee the construction of a design that contains *in nuce* an assortment of architectural impulses recognizable in Ambasz's disparate but often repeated gestures: Le Corbusier's sole work in South America, La Casa Curutchet (1949) in La Plata. At street level, this suburban villa distinguishes itself notably by a detached, prismatic portal. The four stories of the structure, accessible via interior ramps, however, closely encase a foreign body: a fully mature tree, rooted at ground level and sprouting upward past openings in the facade and beyond the roof, like a mammoth, domestic potted plant. That is to say, this arborescent hostage occupies an open core around which the *promenade architecturale* leads with its unraveling logic up to a baldachin-covered approach to a terrace-garden, overlooking a green panorama. Within the continuity of tree, garden, and panorama, the axis of the villa's alternative facade shifts the garden door into the position of a second principal entrance, allowing the promenade to function both top down and bottom up. Here, on high, it becomes entirely possible to imagine the application of a strict rule of architectural non-necessity, much as Ambasz has done, which would lift the terrain to the terrace level and sink the villa out of sight.

If the impulse, then, is to achieve extension without interruption, orientation within the architectural work will depend upon a set of signals that consist of architectural fragments. Like a latter-day Piranesi detailing sections wrenched from the ruins of modernism expressly for an excavationlike installation, Ambasz elaborates a series of detached, isolated, incomplete forms that *point* indexically to the physical presence of an unapparent buried structure. At the same time, the resonance of each extrusion and each void fans out, effacing any notion of a perimeter or end to the work, thereby foregrounding the underlying natural continuum. Gordon Matta-Clark's excisions and micro-demolitions in existing architectural structures, which encourage reciprocal relations between inside and outside, between spatially and temporally disparate cultural fabrics, were typical of a postminimalist concern with the capacity of the work to absorb and to be absorbed by a preexisting physical environment. Ambasz's interpretation of this concern for architecture can best be seen in the constructed Private Estate in Montana, gobbled up as it is by the real brute terrain, a steep slope from a dense pine forest down to a lake. Pierced with oversized windows, the facade stands alone in its elegant, antithetical concavity, more void than solid, an annunciatory or exclamatory marker in the wilderness. Excavation miraculously deromanticizes Arcadia. Eruptions from below, those chthonic forces thought to rise and haunt, were devaluated and evacuated by positivistic scrutiny. In the earth's elevations and depressions, Darwin and De Beaumont found a different sort of "legend" by

which to gauge the hidden, sinking strata from above.[22] We read the earth through its geomorphic plan, the way we read the body through its skin.

Ambasz's hidden corpus reawakens what might otherwise be taken as the stale analogy or homology between the edifice and the human form. Philosophically charged, yet curiously unsubstantiated in its Greco-Roman and Renaissance versions, the model and even the later Modular seem to have withered away. Now architectural truncations of all descriptions suggest contemporary resurgences, with the Lacanian morselated body as a facile guarantee. What lives and breathes in landscape is the green tegument, the expanse of dermis, the long-neglected, underestimated, undervalued organ called the "skin." The modernist glass sheath seems a thin and brittle metaphor in comparison with this geological metaphor for the cutaneous, unpeeled and elastic, neither

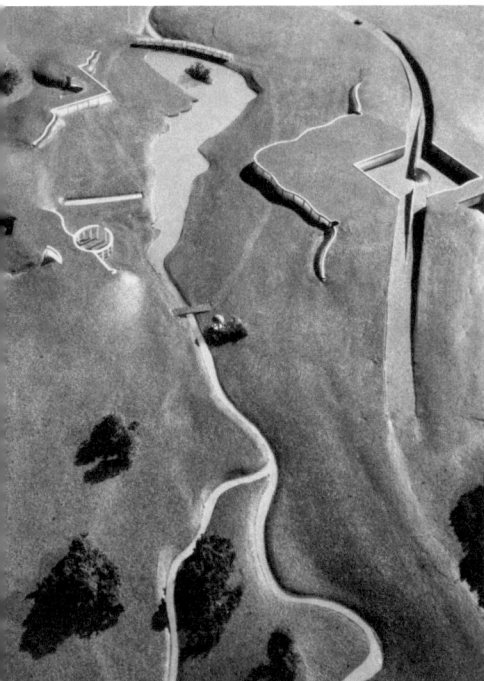

merely outside nor merely inside, ectomorphically one with the brain, nerves, and sensory organs—quite literally, as Ambasz employs it, an immunological layer, a thermo, hydro-regulator, its orifices communicants with the interior milieu. Look at the villas, the Schlumberger Research Laboratories, or the Lucille Halsell Conservatory and remember Walter Benjamin's detection of a shift in the artist's identity—picked up by Tafuri as so pertinent to architecture—from magician to surgeon.[23] However much Ambasz has been associated with the abracadabra of his mists and vapors, clouds and odoriferous shrubs, it is hard not to see in these schemata operations of the the scalpel's deft effect, the clean incision. Engraved here is no anthropomorphism, but rather passages traced for bodily experience, which transits with phenomenological drive through a preeminently material world.

Neat carvings in the earth, linear inscriptions, divulge the composition of Ambasz's berms. What is a berm if not the edge, the ledge, the limit of some larger surface, taken as primary? From this primary solid, the habitation becomes negative void. Berms and grottoes, caves and bunkers, subterranean temples, catacombs, mines and basement playrooms, vaults of the modern urban infrastructure (to which Ambasz would write an early encomium), not to speak of the effervescent artistic and political hollows of "underground" activity, attest to an atavistic sense of this space's cultural availability. But the issue of "The Burrow," in Kafka's penetrating analysis,[24] swings gravely between a second skin for the peaceful fantasies of intrauterine repose and a labor-intensive crypt fit only for apprehensiveness and terminal anxiety. Being below ground level invites this uneasy acknowledgment of womb and burial. Cut any of Ambasz's structures axonometrically and find the paradigm: the burial mound, the tumulus. Slice a tumulus in a similar fashion, however, and find a not-uninviting abode, quiet and impregnable. This bivalence, of course, informs all architecture. Any hole in the wall, as Bachelard observed, can become an insular sanctuary, just as architectural aspiration, to believe Boullée and Adolf Loos, finds its apotheosis in the funerary monument. The quintessential cenotaph, as formulated in Boullée's *architecture ensevelie*, reduces architecture to its bare essentials, its "skeleton," a naked wall without a plinth.

Far from the hermetically sealed enclosure, however, Ambasz's berms surprise by their openness. Every edge and every ledge reiterates the geological phenomenon of an open-air depression in the earth. At bottom, the plan for the houses reinstates the model of the Mediterranean villa, whose rows of rooms open onto an inner court. Sources of ingress and egress, light and ventilation, repeatedly pierce the buried structures with unexpected stairs and skylights, or the gaping glass embrasure of a doubly exposed entrance-reception room. Claustrophobia and the fear of asphyxiation cede in the villas—which force the outside in and inside out, establishing a delicate balance between protection and exposure—to a much more complex phenomenological experience of the architectural opening toward the agora, wide-open space, green prospects sometimes within and always just beyond the roof. But the berm's outward thrust involves as well a deviation from the habitation's ordinary rootedness. Given the disjunction between the habitation's form and the landscape configuration, the superficially buried cubicula could multiply under the earth in any direction, its segments in no way regulated by the hierarchy implicit in the central trunk of a conventional edifice. With no beginning and no end, anchored in the earth by a minimal foundation, so like a foundation in itself, this root canal inevitably sprouts upward—a detached facade, a mirador, a solar energy unit, a ventilation duct, a rooftop rim—like an orchid, an iris, a dahlia. Deleuze and Guattari's figure of the rhizome, the loosely planted, horizontal, nomadic root effects a shift in logic from the Western forest to the Oriental steppe or garden, desert or oasis, in which the cultivation of the tuber fosters the development of more tenuous and unpredictable relations. "In the last analysis," they were to say, "it is always the grass that has the final word."²⁵

What is commonly referred to as the "fusion" between architecture and landscape in the garden provides a necessary but insufficient *topos* for Ambasz's procedure. Ultimately, the question is not the extent to which architecture has been given free rein to design a highly wrought, quasi-autonomous, artificial natural environment, but the extent to which this natural environment can be deployed as the gestalt itself of the primary architectural object. For this, there are no clear antecedents other than the idiosyncratic cases of Taut's speculative Alpine Architecture or César Manrique's constructions in the Canary Islands. The baroque imitation of the organic in stone suggests a similar impulse; yet, in its very mimetic principle, it turns antithetical. Only Buontalenti's adventure at Pratolino fully embodies the effort, not merely to implant tectonic elements in the landscape or to organize the landscape in a tectonic manner, but to create an artificial universe of forms, sounds, and visual effects, purposefully variegated and irregular in its overall design, out of brute matter. Where the rationalism of the Medici court that carried the desire for urban evasion toward an extensive investigation of available botanical, hydraulic, and mechanical techniques for expanding the definition of landscape brings the enterprise to its full achievement—and abrupt halt—is just beyond the southern entrance to the villa. Situated in a lower-level terrace, the multi-chambered grotto, which merited a detailed description of its movable decors, automata, and cascade music in Montaigne's *Journal de Voyage,* in no way impacts on the especially austere villa that stolidly contains it. Buontalenti's Pratolino was nonetheless to remain an object lesson in the garden's formal potential, just as the legacy of the Renaissance and Baroque gardens persists in a summary vocabulary, each term of which figures conspicuously in Ambasz's work:

Axes. Ambasz's incisions, his edges and ledges, follow a remarkably consistent pattern: almost invariably straight lines that meet at right angles, counterpointed by an undulating curvilinear stroke. At most, the undulation expands into a hemisphere or circle. This highly reduced, abstract script, as in the plan for the Schlumberger Research Laboratories—a site plan exceptionally loose in organization, potentially extensible or modulable, as are the detachable, movable individual units buried below—effects a singular topographical inversion: pedestrian paths on the expanse of grass-covered terrain are left unmarked, whereas the tectonic elements instead assume the forms typical of the garden

LEFT: Mercedes-Ben
Showroom. New Jer

RIGHT: Manoir d'Ang
Charleroi, Belgium, 1

axes. All of the villas show a similar configuration of pedestrian freedom and axes solidified into architectural components. Emblematic of this pattern, the Mercedes-Benz Showroom, most appositely, consists in nothing more than the most basic consolidation of a crossroad or axial intersection.

Pergolas. In a similar reduction seen in Ambasz's project for the Cooperative of Mexican-American Grapegrowers, the pergola, together with its attendant fruits, makes a claim to architectural self-sufficiency. As a more conventionally integrated structure in the plan for Frankfurt's Eschenheimer Tower, the arbor provides an open-work enclosure for urban connections in a way that recalls Hector Horeau's projects for covered avenues in Paris. The point is not obscure: the trellis/lattice/grid plays on a homology between armature and vine and, at the same time, maps a space, shuttling it back and forth between the determinate and its implicit infinite extension. In this way, Manoir d'Angoussart's ghostly trellis facade announces entry into a *locus solus* that elicits the sense of a phantom habitation floating over its material double, one that has slipped out of view into invisible subterranean reaches. An uncomplicated combinatorial process makes of the trellis and the garden axes the constitutive elements of the Nishiyachiyo New Town Center, emphasizing their sufficiency even in the radically isolated, monumental proportions of a town center in an as yet undeveloped region. The grid, by turns angular and curvilinear, void on one side, solid on the other, plots an implicity open perimeter, studded serially with the garden's proverbial potted flowering tree. Railway axes orient the design toward two thirty-five-story office buildings in the guise of a traditional Oriental Torii Gate.

Pools: The sunken central courts of the Casa de Retiro Espiritual, the House for Leo Castelli, or the Phoenix Museum of History in no way establish a bottom. A reflecting pool, often amorphously shaped, deflects from the strict delineation of the dwelling proper, directs the promenade, and intimates unspecified further depths, both downward and upward, in its reflection of sky and contingent resurgences of the surrounding landscape. Thus, the swimming-pool technology that assures the berm's feasibility also assures a rhetorical function. At Casa Canales a triangular rooftop pool camouflages the house below and and emphasizes both contiguity and continuity with its containment of a patch of mirrored firmament. At the Schlumberger Research Center, the body of water meanders, yet not without further Italianate accessories: the bridge and *isolotto*. The sinking remnant of land mass, in its imaginative, artificial version, constitutes a key chapter in Ambasz's "scientific autobiography." His inaugural high-tech workstation barges at the Center for Applied Computer Research, perhaps with a slight bow to Le Corbusier's floating Asile, have been relaunched on several occasions and for less self-exegetical purposes than the allegorical mound in Emilio's Folly: the floating galleries for the New Orleans Museum of Art, the enlargement of preexisting bodies of water at Paseo del Lago or the Shikoku Marine Resort Community provide an elemental, liquid trope available for repetition in an accessory horizontal rhizomelike motif within the wider context of site-specificity and land development. The progressive elaboration of this liquidity brings the isolated cascade at the Grand Rapids Art Museum, as well as the seemingly gratuitous cascade and pool at Houston Center Plaza, into relief as historically grounded garden motifs.

Grottoes. The significance of an axonometric cut in an edifice buried under a layer of topsoil was not unknown to Enlightenment architects. What you have, at rock bottom, is a grotto. No amount of civilization can dislodge this void as a mythic *locus* of habitation. Nor can the most ponderous work of architecture avoid the interior void it must, of necessity, define. Ambasz's excavations represent mock grottoes that stress an empty core within a first principle of terrestrial or subterranean substantiality. In this way, the burrowing of the berm offers an escape route from architecture's historical veneer of solidity. When called upon to intervene inside a preexisting empty core, however, Ambasz once again inverts the formula. His proposal for the reuse of Union Station presents a scene that at first glance might be taken for a cataclysmal eruption of landscape from out of the structure's bowels into its poised gaping

Great Hall. In its assertion of a contaminating force, this invasion summons
up the image of Brongniart's Project for a Mountain in Saint André Cathedral.
The breach of decorum sought by French Revolutionary secularization finds
something of an aesthetic equivalent in this geological insurrection against
architectural language *tout court*—a stand reinforced at Union Station by a
design that appears to urge the adjacent Liberty Park to rush down a steep
drop, like a cataract, and flood these academic precincts, seeping deep into the
building's lower levels, nearly rejoining the earth below. As solutions to outdoor urban reconversion, Houston Center Plaza and Plaza Mayor both insert
public space within a subterranean cavity that converges with Ambasz's villa
prototype. At Plaza Mayor, however, the requisite ground-level green carpet
has been tufted by a tree-lined parterre.

Terraces & Stairs. Ground level is relative, easily displaced. Ambasz's descents
might appear timid when compared with Le Vau's exceptionally elastic conception of the light and air available in great depth: a 330-tiered orangerie, for
example, set beneath the terrace of a seventeenth-century chateau. From the
moment the garden terrace dismissed the lay of the land and, with agronomical
authority, reproduced its layers in ascending or descending tiers, the plan in
extension was turned on its side. The garden became a vertical enterprise: terraces, tiers, the *place à gradin* (theater, amphitheater, circus), the step, the
stair—the *ziggurat*. With Ambasz's emergence from below stairs into freestanding structures, the plateaux have simply multiplied and mounted. What is the
Fukuoka Prefectural International Hall if not fifteen one-story receding terraces,
that is to say, a monumental stairway? It would be reasonable to see the cascade

flowing down to a theater below as a playful wink at the Villa Aldobrandini and accept the extension of the preexisting park, up and over the building out to the sea and sky, as merely one more example of Ambasz's obsession with landscape continuity. But the dramatic accentuation of an essentially heavy, truncated, stepped-back form forces an association with the turning point in the deployment of the garden-stair: Bramante's Belvedere at the Vatican. Like Bramante, Ambasz employs terraces and stairs—theater below, belvedere above—to articulate the gap between two preexisting architectural blocks. His version, however, is detached, literal, repetitive, in a way that conforms to a contemporary minimalist or rhizomatic logic: segmentation, stratification, one thing after another. "A plateau," as Deleuze and Guattari insisted, "is always in the middle, neither beginning nor end. A rhizome is made of plateaux."[26]

Under the foliage, a plateau: Deleuze and Guattari's "Rhizome" was conceived as a position paper for an alternative philosophical discourse, no longer systematic or unified, but infinitely extensible by way of tangents: *mille plateaux*. Derrida surely figures as the signal reference point. His repeated, fragmented, differential reentries into the seminal texts of Western metaphysics is revealingly summed up in a single phrase from *The Truth in Painting:* "I do not know what is essential or what is accessory."[27] The point is graphically reinforced by illustrations of Fantuzzi's ornate, self-proliferative frames that become the work itself around an empty center. Taking an impulse discernable in Lequeu's Sépulture near Voorhout to an extreme point of integration, the site plan for Ambasz's Worldbridge Trade and Investment Center shows an expansive indeterminacy that dilates any accepted architectural notion of a "shell," spreads it out in amorphous lateral and centrifugal botany-encrusted layers from a hollow core to the virtually undifferentiable landscape. Only the free-form surrounding clearing detaches the structure. With its echoes of Boullée's cenotaphic *enceinte,* the truncated conical core refutes its centrality as the hold of habitation, which has been shifted to a peripheral interior. What emerges at Worldbridge is not merely multiplied earth surfaces. Their irregular outer contours, which could be taken for the terraces of the tilled field, coalesce into an unmistakable protozoan form. With this instance of zoomorphism, not to speak of the gigantic entrance tear at Fukuoka, as if the building were made of natural tissue, a landscape premise predicated on the literal infusion of organic matter into architecture has been reformulated to admit symbolic reiteration.

Greenhouses. Organicism is both the *bête noire* and the holy ghost of late-twentieth-century thinking. The naturalistic metaphor of the rhizome surprises. Yet the same Smithson who had denounced Wright's Guggenheim Museum as an "inverted intestine," a "concrete stomach,"[28] filled with a suspicious and obsolete anthropomorphism would later stare into his own earthwork, *The Spiral Jetty,* and observe: "Following the spiral steps we return to our origins, back to some pulpy protoplasm. . . . I was slipping out of myself again, dissolving into a unicellular beginning, trying to locate the nucleus at the end of the spiral."[29] The shift in focus in the visual arts from organicism to physical science goes awry, attesting in the end only to unsettled scores with natural phenomena. For the earth is a powerful vehicle: a tough membrane, most easily likened to a single, living cell. Ambasz was to receive his first green light for construction with the Lucille Halsell Conservatory. In San Antonio, the earth's insulating capacity made climatic sense, and Ambasz's high-tech peaks of glass and steel not only rise as sleek variant indices of sublevel structure but concretize his unequivocal relation to an auxiliary architectural tradition: the greenhouse. All of the unsettling ramifications of Ambasz's extrapolations of organic matter were to have found initial acceptance, ironically enough, within the context of vegetation in captivity.

The greenhouse microclimate takes on a particularly enigmatic dimension at the Nichii Obihiro Department Store: a two-and-a-half-acre building draped in greenery and encased in a confoundingly irregular, multifaceted bell jar. This green promontory or mountain-mall on the Siberia-like Hokkaido Island flirts with mimesis, even though its organicism and inorganicism reference no known geological formation—that is, apart from the entry to the cyberspace Free Zone in William Gibson's *Neuromancer*[30]: the interior walkway through a deep canyon; the subtle angles of the boutiques and enclosures that dissimulate its walls; the light from above that filters through masses of green vegetation cascading down from numberless terraces and balconies. Ambasz's state-of-the-art transplant, however, reverses this anomalous green valley core in the overarching exterior configuration of an equally anomalous green mountain peak, which exasperates (to use Tafuri's term) the greenhouse genre by forcing a Taut-like Alpine flashing of glass in the crystalline environs to contain a visible chunk of disparate and thoroughly artificial geography. Smithson warned of the mind-bending and unnatural associations produced by "quality gardens."[31] With this extravagant example of hothouse domestication, Ambasz's interpretation of Louis Kahn's wrappings veers toward the purely rhetorical statement, even as the structure's hermetic closure instills a disturbing sense of our estrangement from the material substance kept in confinement inside.

"Nature" has not yet been evoked, not once, and for good reason. Here it emerges, harnessed by quotation marks, a citation of an antiquated common place. Facile references to this historically eminent *topos,* a frequent, mindless reflex, have gone far to obscure the thrust and timeliness of Ambasz's work. Is landscape "Nature"? An abyss opens, in this spot, between sheer physical matter and the universal history of human concepts and techniques. Were landscape in its symbolizing power still an adequate vehicle for some natural totality, it would be nonetheless legitimate to ask: what "Nature"? To confine the question only to the West: Pre-Socratic first principles? The Greek *physis*? The Roman *natura*? The alternatively secularizing, moralizing, or redemptive Renaissance "Book of Nature"? The object of Copernican or Newtonian speculation? A Leibnizian monad? Kant's sublime unknowable? Enlightenment natural laws? Hegel's suicide victim? Romantic poetry's visionary resource? Positivism's captive? Bergson's *élan vital*? All of this and more haunt the generic noun, filling it with an unsuspected heterogeneous surfeit of meaning to the point of utter opacity. But the opacity, the illegitimacy, the pure emptiness of landscape, as a statement in itself, is exactly what defines Ambasz's architecture as so pointedly contemporary. At a time when architectural demonstrations of depletion of meaning, rebuttals, and refusals of signficance prevail, landscape shows itself to possess a unique capacity to store its unparalleled illustrious connotations, flirt with them, subvert them, and to persist, even in its stark semantic nakedness, with untarnished autonomy.

To take Ambasz's architecture as resolutely nonurban—a throwback to Wright's disgust with the metropolis and his search for agrarian alternatives—

would be to ignore a dramatic alteration in cultural options and sources of value. Surely the parallels are real: the "fusion" of architecture with landscape, the influence of the artifical Italian garden, the reliance on technology to make the earth a viable habitat, and even the penchant for what Mumford would call "solo performances." Still, in Ambasz's case, the urban/nonurban distinction seems null and void. His production involves a prototype developed, not in the country, but in total isolation, a pure laboratory product. What it rejects is an evolution of architecture within a typically urban setting, myopic vis-à-vis architecture itself. To this extent, Ambasz's reading of Arcadia, a varied literary genre of urban evasion, sometimes halcyon, often elegiac, turned "myth" only for architecture, would seem much closer to what Smithson was to label "land reclamation." For if the artistic recycling of a spoliated or dilapidated landscape might best be achieved by earthworks, within the context of architecture's habitual ablation of the preexisting site, construction might well be conceived as a preservation or a resurgence or, at the very least, a reemphasis of natural terrain. What has often been construed as a flagrantly ahistorical architecture, oblivious to the site's temporal strata or the architectural language of contiguous elements, responds, in reality, to another equally forceful historical imperative: to move outside just those perennial coordinates.

La Venta is Ambasz's most synoptic project. With an extreme freedom of design that admits the amorphous, the truncated, and the aleatory, the seven buildings instate the same carefully cut, raised-earth-surface, terraced principle. Only ramps to the roof have been added for motorized access and attenuation of any sense of scale. Engulfed in a dense, dead pine forest, these tiers planted with saplings set in motion an odd dialectics of dead and alive. Our capacity to discriminate between the preternatural and the natural, the cultivated and the brute, wavers. Smithson experienced a similar perceptual upheaval when faced with the interpenetration of the dead salt lake with his *Spiral Jetty*: "My dialectics of site and nonsite whirled into an indeterminate state, where solid and liquid lost themselves in each other. It was as if the mainland oscillated with waves and pulsations, and the lake remained stock still." At La Venta the animation of the inanimate, however, is no effect of the optical imagination. The dead pine forest, itself man-made, had been asphyxiated by its density. To redress that human miscalculation, Ambasz converts architecture into the cultivated grounds for its regeneration. In consequence, La Venta might be read as "Nature's" cenotaph. The "mythmaking" that he has always seen as architecture's vocation arises, then, in the mythic moment of a historical threshold: the

death of "Nature" and the emergence of its complex materiality. Or, perhaps, the death of "Nature" and the advent of the hybrid form: an architecture of the graft, a mutant in the age of genetic interventions, in which human calculation exerts an unimpeded projective power, and the parterre is everywhere.

An earlier version of this essay was published in 1994.

1   Manfredo Tafuri, *La sfera e il labirinto: Avanguardie e architettura da Piranesi agli anni '70* (Turin: Einaudi, 1980), 365.

2   Manfredo Tafuri, *Théories et histoire de l'architecture,* trans. SADG (Paris: SADG, 1976), 155. An English translation appeared under the title *Theories and History of Architecture,* trans. Giorgio Verrecchia (New York: Harper & Row, 1980).

3   Tafuri, *La sfera e il labirinto,* 365.

4   Tafuri, *Théories et histoire de l'architecture,* 160.

5   Ettore Sottsass, "Ettore Sottsass, Milan, Italy," in *Emilio Ambasz: The Poetics of the Pragmatic* (New York: Rizzoli, 1988), 10.

6   Martin Heidegger, "L'Origine de l'oeuvre d'art," in *Chemins qui mènent nulle part,* trans. W. Brokmeier (Paris: Gallimard, 1962), 32–35.

7   Martin Heidegger, "Bâtir Habiter Penser," in *Essais et conférences,* trans. André Préau (Paris: Tel Gallimard, 1980), 180–85.

8   The reference is of course to Christian Norbert-Schulz, Alberto Perez-Gomez, and, most important, Kenneth Frampton. See Kenneth Frampton, "On Reading Heidegger," in *Theorizing a New Agenda for Architecture: An Anthology of Architecture Theory, 1965–1995* (New York: Princeton Architectural Press, 1996), 440–46; originally printed in 1974.

9   Emilio Ambasz, "Emilio's Folly: Man Is an Island," in *Emilio Ambasz: The Poetics of the Pragmatic,* 162.

10 Emilio Ambasz, "I Ask Myself," in *Emilio Ambasz: The Poetics of the Pragmatic,* 28.

11 Jacques Derrida, "Parergon," in *La Vérité en peinture* (Paris: Champs/Flammarion, 1978), 19–168.

12 A parallel might be drawn between Eisenman's examination of the cube and Sol Lewitt's cubic structures of the 1960s. In point of fact, however, the German artist Manfred Mohr had by the mid-1980s established a body of work, initiated in the early 1970s, based specifically on computer projections of the n-dimensional cube in rotation. See my "Linebreeder," in *Algorithmische Arbeiten* (Bottrop: Josef Albers Museum, 1998).

13 Jacques Derrida, "Tympan," in *Marges de la philosophie* (Paris: Minuit, 1972), xx.

14 Rosalind Krauss, "Sculpture in the Expanded Field," in *The Anti-Aesthetic,* ed. Hal Foster (Port Townsend, Wash.: Bay Press, 1983), 31–42; originally printed in *October* 8 (spring 1979).

15 Robert Smithson, "A Sedimentation of the Mind: Earth Projects," in *The Writings of Robert Smithson,* ed. Nancy Holt (New York: New York University Press, 1979), 89.

16 Rosalind Krauss, "Lewitt in Progress," *October* 6 (fall 1978): 60.

17 Robert Smithson, "Entropy and the New Monuments," in *The Writings of Robert Smithson,* 11.

18 Robert Smithson, "Ultramoderne," in *The Writings of Robert Smithson,* 41.

19 Heinrich Wölfflin, *Renaissance et Baroque,* trans. Guy Ballangé (Paris: Livre de Poche, 1967), 305.

20 Tafuri, *Théories et histoire de l'architecture,* 114.

21 Robert Smithson, "Aerial Art," in *The Writings of Robert Smithson,* 92.

22 Francois Dagognet, *Une Epistémologie de l'espace concret: Néo-géographie* (Paris: Vrin, 1977). See especially Chapter 2: "Reliefs et paysages, pour une épistemologie de la géomorphologie."

23 Walter Benjamin, "L'oeuvre d'art à l'ère de son réproductabilité téchnique," in *Poésie et Révolution* (Paris: Denoël, 1971), 196.

24 Franz Kafka, "The Burrow," in *Franz Kafka: The Complete Stories,* trans. Willa and Edwin Muir (New York: Schocken, 1971), 325–59.

25 Gilles Deleuze and Felix Guattari, "Rhizomes," in *Mille Plateaux* (Paris: Minuit, 1980), 28.

26 Ibid., 35.

27 Jacques Derrida, "Parergon," 73.

28 Robert Smithson, "Quasi-Infinities and the Waning of Space," in *The Writings of Robert Smithson,* 33.

29 Robert Smithson, "The Spiral Jetty," in *The Writings of Robert Smithson,* 113.

30 William Gibson, *Neuromancer* (New York: Putnam, 1984), part 3, p. 10.

31 Smithson, "The Spiral Jetty," 91.

CORPOREALITY
Lebbeus Woods

Ecologically sustainable architecture is an idea that has threatened for some forty years to become a major movement, but has somehow never managed to do so. There has never been any doubt that the formulation of an ecological architecture, which has shared a kind of stalled pregnancy with kindred concepts like renewable energy and the recycling of waste, is one of the most worthy of endevors and that its presumed fruits would be among the sweetest and most nourishing imaginable. Everyone knows that the planet is in the early but irrefutably detectable stages of serious trouble and that the exploding human presence is the cause. Everyone knows that something must be done to reduce the negative human impact on forests, lakes and rivers, farmland, countless species of flora and fauna, the atmosphere, and the weather. Huge chunks of Antarctica are breaking off regularly and floating up-ocean, and if that isn't enough of a warning, a hole in the ozone layer, caused by fossil fuel emissions, decaying batteries, leaky cooling systems, and millions of spray cans emptied every day to paint people's lawn furniture and hold their hair in place, is expanding at a rate that actively threatens future generations with terminal sunburn. Everyone knows, but so little happens.

That a full-blown ecological architecture has failed to emerge is no doubt due to the same dreary set of reasons that the global environment continues to deteriorate, regardless of the warnings, the evidence, and—remarkably—the presence of viable antidotes that are simply ignored. At the head of the list is economics. The global economy is too dependent on its wasteful, toxic ways to change significantly anytime soon. So we'll cut down—later—we promise. Next on the list is denial. Sure, it's happening, but is it really that important? Next is politics: I don't want to be the president/prime minister/monarch/ruler/dictator who will be remembered for bringing his/her people to economic ruin, especially not for some elusive, long-term goal. Nestling among these and other rationalizations are the architect's: my clients all want it, but won't pay for it. I'll do my best. And one more: ecological architecture looks so boring. And so it does.

For some considerable number of years, Emilio Ambasz has worked to redress this last objection by formulating an eye-friendly architecture, and in an age that values image as highly as the present one, his approach is not misguided. It is unlikely that the vegetation-laden architecture he has designed for sites ranging from the pastoral to the densely urban could actually affect the steady decline of the earth's ecosphere, but that is certainly not his goal. His hyper-designed landscapes join architecture's geometric abstractions with nature's organic complexities, inviting us to see that ecological architecture can, well, look good.

One of the first things that strikes you when looking at the books cataloging Ambasz's works is their supreme self-confidence. The models and drawings of the projects betray no doubts, no second thoughts, no *pentimenti*, no questions lurking around rough edges—in fact, no rough edges. One might expect or hope for such self-assurance in a finished building, but it is unexpected and unnerving in unbuilt works. It is as though they were born, like Athena from the head of Zeus, fully grown and mature. They are like children without a childhood, perfectly poised and eerily lacking the awkwardness of learning's confrontation with the not yet fully understood. This is an aspect of the work I shall return to later and explore more deeply, because it helps illustrate its stance relative to ecology. The model photos and drawings bring to mind the impeccable presentation drawings from the Ecole des Beaux-Arts in the nineteenth century, extremely skillful renderings that inspire awe for their completeness, their particular kind of perfection. Yet, for anyone with even a trace of existential doubt, they remain at an emotional distance. They are, in a sense, closed subjects, inviting neither discussion nor critique.

Ambasz has built a number of estimable buildings, some of which, like the Fukuoka Prefectural International Hall in Japan, have been justly celebrated. Yet his books place substantial weight on his unbuilt works. This strongly suggests that he considers himself a man of ideas. For a man of ideas, though, it is strange that his books reveal so little of his thought processes. There are no sketches, no tentative first, or second, or third steps, no ruminations, no studies. There is only the finality of a vision in which, as I look across the table at opened copies of his books, in the admittedly compromising light of my workspace, it is difficult to tell the difference between images of the built and the unbuilt projects.

Yet, looking closer, differences do appear, and some explication of Ambasz's thinking process might help us understand them. In the design presentation model of the Fukuoka project, the guiding concept is quite clear. A large glassy curtain-wall building faces rather densely built streets on two sides, a canal on the third side, and a large public park sprinkled with trees and facilities buildings on the fourth. The side of the thirteen-story building facing the park is stepped-back in even increments to form a gradually ascending phalanx of terraces, which are laden with greenery and other naturalistic amenities, an extension of the park and then some. This vertical and highly unnatural displacement of greenery is a continuing theme in many other projects as well, and is an Ambasz innovation.[1] In the Chiba New Town Center,

65

also in Japan (and unbuilt), trees fill standing, undulating Cartesian frames wrapping both building and public open space, in a regimented, one-tree-per-module manner. In the Museum of Modern Art and Cinema for Buenos Aires, where the existing building shell and outdoor screens wrap a rectilinear block of green stuff, the same. For the ENI Headquarters high-rise in Rome, the same. And so on. Nature—represented, one might almost say, symbolized, by greenery—submits, or is made to submit, to human design. The Romans understood this approach well, as did the Japanese. The French, in their gardens, mastered it completely, leaving it to the English, in theirs, to turn it upside-down. No matter. In the domain of principle, Ambasz is in very respectable historical company. In the Fukuoka design model, he arrays his greens with convincing effect.

What is masterful, in the Fukuoka design, is not the regimentation but the rather rough, organic, perhaps somewhat English way the greenery climbs the terraced building hillside, as though plant life had been liberated to the point of challenging or even threatening human presumptions of its immobility. And then there are the amenities: a great waterfall occupying the upper floors and spilling down the terraces to a cave reaching the park level, from which emerges a swooping white rectilinear mass. This sequence of water and movement and geometry is quite mysterious, and appealing. We are not only being given the refreshing sound and play of splashing water, but also an allegory of the natural and the designed that seems, at least, to promise an unconventional understanding of what they mean together.

How disappointing, then, that the built building omits these very features. The waterfall is gone, replaced by a glazed mass piercing the upper terraces. The cave is gone altogether, and the swooping white mass has been replaced by a sedate block with a triangular opening, having no more cave from which to mysteriously emerge. And the greenery, well, it no longer wildly climbs the hillside, but sits, politely perched, on the stepped terraces. What are we to make of these differences between the designed and built? Were they compromises forced on the design by practical or economic considerations? If so, then the book merely details the usual, sad story of a failure of ideas in their confrontation with reality, and casts a pall over the entire body of work consisting of projects waiting to be realized. Or are these differences at least in part the result of the architect's rethinking? Even if his rethinking has been forced by other than primary considerations, how did it evolve into the built form?

Some elaboration of thought process, design methodology, or simply some history of the journey to construction would help to rescue us from despair.

The answers to these questions may lie in the understanding that, for Ambasz, an idea is something to be objectified: a product. All traces of process, and thus all potential for inference, are necessarily erased or concealed. The product of Ambasz's design is an object, or an *ensemble* of objects aesthetically arranged and conceptually consistent, even to an uncanny degree. The object, the ensemble, which includes natural elements—trees, shrubs, lawns, ponds, creeks, lakes, skies, whole expanses of clouds and startlingly blue firmament—must carry the whole weight of the architect's intentions and their foreseeable consequences. So he presumes.

Architecture is predominantly a visual art. When we see a building, the seeing itself must give us a clear sense of what it actually is. Critics and commentators only provide shortcuts to judgment, for those without the desire or ability to see for themselves. But with unbuilt projects the case is not the same. The built building is a fact, like it or not. We can debate its successes and failures, but we must live with it. The unbuilt projects, on the other hand, are not facts, but arguments. Most often the argument is to build the project. Sometimes, though rarely, and certainly not in the examples Ambasz offers, the unbuilt can be an argument for ideas. Either way, it necessarily requires a different form of understanding than the built building. Because it is primarily a means of persuasion, to be effective it must include insight into the thought process that underlies the argument for a building's necessity. Considering the mounting ecological disaster confronting us, it cannot be assumed that new buildings are needed at all. Entropy may rule the universe, but empathy may yet rule the world. Can't we recycle the buildings we already have, upon which so much of human energy and natural resources have already been spent? Can't we formulate a new ethic, that we will build no new buildings, unless we really demonstrably need them? This is the radical ecological view, no doubt. But isn't there some merit to it? If there is, then the unbuilt, and especially the ecologically inspired, must convince us of its need to exist.

The view that has increasingly gained acceptance since the early 1960s is that nature is a complex, ever-evolving system, of which the human is but a part. In this view, which is aligned with others broadly labeled as postmodern, the human is interdependent with other life-forms, to such an extent that, if you follow theories of chaotic phenomenology, a butterfly flexing its wings in Haiti can cause a drought in China. Today, causal chains are considered something far more complex and interrelated than in the old days of intellectual hubris when Aristotle's law of identity ($A = A$) seemed to give each element in a chain total independence and autonomy, when it was still possible to believe that one thing naturally leads to another. Today, one thing leads to many things at the same time, the hierarchy of which may only be known later, the effects of which may never be entirely known at all. Any thing—including the objects of human production—has multiple, often contradictory, or even conflicting identities, because there is no fixed or ultimately privileged point from which anything can be viewed, judged, understood, or hierarchically arranged. A tree in the rain forest "sees" us differently than we see ourselves. Today, it seems quite useful to consider the standpoint, if not exactly the viewpoint, of that tree, much more particularly and strategically than we have in the past.

It is noteworthy that the trees in Ambasz's projects are shown as green and full. It is late spring, maybe high summer. Always. They are perfect trees, at the height of their powers. Of course, in the models they are only representations, but what do they represent? We might say that they represent a happy, healthy nature, living in friendly agreement with the buildings designed by Ambasz. As symbols, we might also say that they represent nature's reconciliation with the human, but a reconciliation that amounts to a kind of taming of nature, its subordination to human design. Nature doesn't mind being moved around and placed by human beings wherever they want to put it. A quite convenient view of nature, one that comes from the self-assurance, the supreme self-confidence, that nature exists to serve the human, that it does not have its own agenda, possibly quite indifferent to human goals.

Clearly, Ambasz is no postmodernist. He is not interested in multiple viewpoints and readings. He is not interested in the possible ambiguity of the objects of design production. He is not concerned with the vicissitudes of interpretation, and the messiness of ambivalent meanings. This does not mean, however, that he is a hard-boiled rationalist, or even a strict determinist. He is an idealist, and his works single-mindedly aim to realize a quite specific ideal, one that places nature unequivocally under human control.

From our present perspective, this sounds rather sinister, if not downright threatening. Human control of the human, for a change, would be more welcome than more of the millennia-old view of nature as an adversary that must be conquered.[2] Conquering nature has been a very expensive enterprise, particularly as the size and the impact of the human presence on the planet has dramatically increased. It has certainly been proven, in the last 150 years, that nature can be controlled, if not by fair means, then by foul. Dams can be built, rivers rerouted, forests cut down, the very contour of nature's dominion pushed back or erased. All by conscious and maybe even responsible design. But where design fails, at the limits of human control, then indifference and neglect take over. Air, water, and soil pollution are not intended consequences of human production, but they are tolerated as though they were. They are weapons in the human war against nature that have succeeded to a degree far surpassing all attempts to reshape it by design. Nature is simply being killed,[3] on a routine, daily basis, and to an extent that now begins to threaten the human presence. Humans may win this war, may make this conquest, but will do so at the expense of their own well-being, if not their survival. Hence, the welcome emergence of the postmodern view, the systems-theory view, the complexity view, any view that makes the human part of nature, that reverses the hierarchy and the priorities, giving nature, if not the upper hand, then at least an even break.

Some tough questions emerge from any study of Ambasz's work. Are large buildings, such as the Fukuoka project, covered with shrubs and trees, really ecological? This is a case that must be proven, or at least argued convincingly. It cannot be assumed unless we want to be in league with those in the corporate boardrooms where decisions of planetary consequence are made, in feudal fashion, as the privilege of an economically empowered few. It could be said of Ambasz's institutionally commissioned buildings that they are wolves in sheep's clothing, disguised monsters that consume resources at the same reckless rate as their more nakedly rapacious brethren, only with edges softened by greenery. Does this greenery return an ecological benefit in any proportional way to the ecological deficits of the buildings' construction and maintenance? Of course it does not, and in today's world no one would reasonably expect that it should. But, then, perhaps in the conceptual sense, as images of a harmonious interweaving of the human and the natural? That is a fine reading, if we take greenery as representing nature and concrete or steel and glass as representing the human. But why cannot steel and concrete and glass also be seen as representing nature? Is it conceivable to imagine an ecologically sensitive architecture that does not rely on the presence of greenery to convince us of its "naturalness," or its friendliness to nature? While I admire the aspiration of the designs to reconcile the human and the natural on both aesthetical and practical levels, I am disturbed by the conventionality of the identities thus assigned to the human and the natural. If we judge from the ecological crisis mounting everywhere around us, these conventional views have not served either well.

The Lucille Halsell Conservatory stands as something of an antidote to the nature-as-greenery stance of many of Ambasz's other projects, both built and not. This one happens to have been built, in Texas, some years ago. (The architect annoyingly omits from his books the dates of his projects, another example of his desire to erase marks of process, including evidence of chronology, confirming that his *veritas* is eternal.) In this project—a botanical center—the game is reversed: greenery is encased in a series of abstract, geometrical prisms that stand without apology or compromise in an open Texas landscape. Here one has the sense that architecture becomes, or is becoming at last, a form of nature, that it emerges, with all its human baggage, to assume a place in a larger hierarchy than human design has yet devised. The glass structures stand over underground rooms in which plants are protected, cultivated, and, we might say, acculturated. There is no pretense that a park is naturally extended, no assumption that trees and grasses and pools and waterfalls are accomplices to design. There is only the frank concession that when design intervenes in nature, it alters natural balance and placement. Encased in the prisms, trees and plants are captives of human curiosity, its categories and purposes. An ultimately modernist view. What goes beyond this view, happily, is the organic disposition of the prisms and other site elements, which follow an intuitive schema, more related to perceptions of the site than to dogmatic or ideological formulas.

Clearly, Ambasz's work leaves me with mixed feelings. I admire the skillful and sometimes poetic nature of the designs for buildings and the landscapes they inhabit. I am disturbed by the unhesitant character of the designs in the face of the complex questions they confront. Some humility before problems of recycling, energy sources, allocation of resources, ecological balance, and the host of intractables confronting design today would be more encouraging than brusque self-confidence that, in effect, brushes them aside. I admire the high degree of refinement of the formal elements of architecture and landscape. I deeply question the sacrifice of step-by-step experimentation in order to achieve and sustain this degree of refinement. Taking a few risks, in the name of learning something not known before, would more than justify a measure of formal roughness.

Whatever the virtue of these defenses and criticisms of the works of Emilio Ambasz, there is no doubt that they speak with a voice that is distinctly his. In this time when the new is pursued exhaustively by everyone hoping to get a little attention—or a lot—it is not so easy to create something uniquely one's own. This can only be done by sustaining an idea over the long period of time it takes to convince us that the idea is essential to consider against the backdrop of devilishly complicated contemporary problems. If it is not, then it is merely fashion, highly disposable and justly dismissable. It doesn't hurt if the driving force in one's work is entangled with some urgent problem or question of the day, in the way that Ambasz's work is. Regardless of whether it answers the burning questions in any universally acceptable way, the very fact that it places them in the foreground is a high recommendation of its seriousness of purpose and worthiness of consideration. But it is not, in itself, enough to claim an ethical position or establish a clear point of view. To achieve that, an architecture, built or not, must set out a way of thinking and, if possible, a way of acting in the world that holds the promise of eventual answers and solutions. More than that, it must allow for the presence of others who can not only follow but participate in constructing the means to the longed-for ends. It is here that Ambasz's instinct for the generic, for the typological, for the corporate, corporeal product may—just may—succeed. The stamp that he places upon all his work—the curious anonymity, the unemotional quality to the models and buildings, the utopian distance and institutional coolness—may indicate a way to ecological sanity that is the very opposite of the individual, the expressive, the small-is-beautiful approach advocated by those who believe, or hope, that a better future will come from the bottom up. The way things are going now, with the advent of globalization and of the market-state, with the decline of individual initiative and responsibility under the homogenizing pressures of mass culture, solutions to big problems like the destruction of the ozone layer and the rain forests are more likely to come, if they come at all, from the top down. If that is true, then the boardrooms and bureaucracies that are the obvious audience for his work can learn from it. But they can also learn from its critics, who insist on broadening and deepening its tenets.

[1]   Every innovation has its precedents. In this case, they range from the Hanging Gardens of Babylon to the Oakland Museum, designed by Kevin Roche in the early 1960s.

[2]   See Lebbeus Woods, *Earthquake: A Post-Biblical View* (New York: Princeton Architectural Press, 2002).

[3]   Something like three thousand species of plant and animal life are "terminated" every day as a result of human activity planetwide, a kind of holocaust that as yet avoids convincing moral condemnation.

ARCHITECTURE & ISLANDS
Catherine Ingraham

The little village was in the grip of fear. . . . One of the men started to build
a construction, circular in plan. . . . He used stone, wood, and mud. . . .
Then using a rod he had taken from the temple, he erected a large hut. . . .
When he died, his body was laid down inside the hut . . . and his son covered
the entrance with the large stone slabs. . . . Some people say this was how
architecture started.
—Emilio Ambasz, *Working Fables:*
A Collection of Design Tales for Skeptic Children

What are the children skeptical of in this "Collection of Design Tales for
Skeptic Children"? Perhaps the words themselves: *Some people say this was
how architecture started.* Is it the dead body plus the hut plus the covered
entrance that equals architecture? Perhaps they are skeptical of the unresolved
questions: did the architecture erase the fear or make it worse? Is this a true
story? Perhaps it isn't true.

Furniture designers historically thought of a chair as a relatively rigid spatial
object with which the fluid biological body had to negotiate. Gerrit Rietveld
made chairs of flexible material—tubular metal, wood, cane, leather, plush—
to put the chair in the same field as the mobile posture of a seated human
body.[1] Ambasz's famous Vertebra seating system takes this idea further by
attempting to make chairs automata, so the body can find its elusive comfort
almost without negotiation. The chair is fully at the service of the body. But
the ergonomics of this system are sly; they are not adequately summarized by
the word *service.* As Ambasz remarks:

> In the case of the Vertebra chair, which looks like such a highly mecha-
> nized artifact, I was deeply concerned with creating an anthropomorphic
> and anthropofunctional object that accompanies the movement of the
> body completely and unselfconsciously, just as a glove moves with the
> hand that wears it.[2]

We will return to the force of the "anthro" shortly.

But for now, let's take architecture: perhaps Le Corbusier. Even in those curvaceous houses riding on piloti legs, as at Villa Savoye, is that from which architecture has extricated itself, even if at the last possible moment. In contrast, Ambasz's famous earth architectures (House for Leo Castelli; Schlumberger Research Laboratories; Manoir d'Angoussart; Center for Applied Computer Research; Private Estate, Montana; Focchi Shopping Center; Realworld Theme Park; Phoenix Museum of History), all legless and partially embedded in the ground, seem to put buildings at the service of a "natural" nature. But the skeptical children ask again, Is this really what is happening?

Everywhere in Ambasz a simultaneously humble and omnipotent force of architecture and design offers itself to the natural world as a gift of (pragmatic) idealism about both sides of the nature/artifice divide: the "natural world" that his buildings sit within are also constructed, and the "artificial world" of architecture that Ambasz designs emerges from the ground as an "almost natural" form. The skeptical children might want to know if the world really works in this manner; if we can expect things to go out, and come back to us, in this way. The skeptical children run tests. They give powerful lectures to their stuffed animals in the darkness of their bedrooms, saying, "I will test your magical powers by asking you to do something for me. If you don't do it, you're not alive." And when the animals don't do it, the children become skeptical of the power of magic, their own will, idealism. They learn the questionable solace of scientific distance, rationality, and the power of binary oppositions such as life/death and nature/culture.

And so it is, in general, with architecture. The question is, Does Ambasz really persuade us otherwise, even for a second? I think he does, but it's not straightforward.

The problem has become—for those who have been studying it—that the skeptical children no longer can hear, innocently, most of the words that Ambasz's architecture speaks: nature, myth, environment, poetic form, pragmatism, ritual, mysticism, primacy.[3] These references are now fully glossed. We note, cynically, that the romance of the land is nowhere to be found in the acid green false turf of the models, and we pitilessly critique the brownness of the grass in the built work. The myriad nuances of everyday life refuse mystical summation. Form does not take form in the hopeful way that architecture once portended. Poetry, as a form of architectural speech, is particularly suspect.

bottle, 1986.

Architects, Ambasz among them, seem to believe that poetry is an appropriate form of language for architecture because of its presumed capacity for transcending the weightiness of language through pithy reduction. They do not see that poetry belongs to all the parts of language they hate most: excessiveness, diffusion, critical and pedantic tendencies. For these, and other, reasons it is now almost impossible to speak of Ambasz; it is certainly impossible to speak of him in his own terms—although his own terms are both complex and insightful.

It is therefore noteworthy that Ambasz's work continues to be interesting. Not only part of an interesting history, some of his work continues to exhibit the character of unresolved, congested, nonsmooth architectures. A few random examples of nonsmooth architectures might be Rem Koolhaas's Kunsthalle in Rotterdam, Le Corbusier's Carpenter Center in Cambridge, Lewerentz's St. Peter's church in Sweden, Scharoun's Berlin Philharmonic Hall, as well as certain biomorphic digital projects (paradoxically, since smoothness is everywhere desired in the digital). In a sense, the usual suspects. It may seem odd that the sleek designs of Ambasz—sleek in innumerable ways that are almost perfectly recapped in the functional beauty of his design for a Vittel water bottle (1986)[4]—should be connected to these nonsmooth architectures. And I should qualify my definition of "unresolved architecture." The failure of a building to resolve itself aesthetically or structurally is neither good or bad, but a sign of how something, perhaps some idea on the part of the architect or some fortuitous event, exceeded or overran the architectural desire and ability to close things up. The architectural idea was never abandoned in such buildings and projects, in spite of its excess, even in the final stages of the building project. The architectural idea continues to pressure the project, keeping it open, awkward.

I want to further investigate this nonsmooth aspect of Ambasz's work by taking some of his claims at face value; for example, the idea that while there is a primal connection between architecture and nature, to be a human in Ambasz's architectural terms is, in effect, to be an island. "Emilio's Folly: Man Is an Island" is one fabulistic project that suggested explicitly how "man is an island" might be as an architectural proposition, but the theme crops up in many places. Ambasz famously remarks on the two "Emilios"—one, a "solitary, cheerful man, anguished . . . because he hopes through his architecture to be welcomed by angels," the other, a "sociably sad man, anxious because he wants his products to be well received by men." He continues, "I am cheerfully

sad and sociably solitary."[5] Human consciousness has always noted its evolutionary isolation from other species and its psychological isolation from other humans—sometimes cheerful, sometimes not. The loneliness and islandlike condition of Ambasz's architecture should be evaluated in light of this isolated consciousness.

Recently I have been writing about the relation of architecture to the history of the idea of human life, a notion that gained the status of an idea only in the last two hundred years.[6] The "human" is a recent invention, as Michel Foucault reminded us twenty years ago. Before this invention, humans were simply living beings among other living beings. Morphologically, one of the defining characteristics of humanness—when that idea coalesced in the eighteenth century into various disciplines, among them paleontology—was the demonstration of an upright posture. Uprightness was understood by scientists to be a moment of absolute differentiation between two possible evolutionary paths. According to one relatively contemporary theorist, once the path of uprightness was embarked on, everything else apparently followed: the hand was freed, the face shortened, and a larger brain developed.[7] From the bipolar coordinations of brain/hand and brain/mouth comes both technical ability (pragmatics) and language (poetics). The philosopher Georges Bataille remarked famously, "Man would seem to represent merely an intermediary stage within the morphological development between monkey and building."

It is an oversimplification, but still a useful one, to say that humans combined their techno-linguistic powers to produce architecture as an extruded upright body that can carry symbolic meanings. Like other technologies, architecture enters onto its own evolutionary path but maintains a technical and morphological relation to the upright body from which it was put forth. And like other technologies, architecture, over time, is increasingly removed from the slow evolution of the biological body.

Architecture has pursued the path of uprightness—where else could it go?—not only in its built form, but, at least since the Renaissance, also in its moral posture. Some would refer the contemporary formal verticality of architecture to serendipitous technological developments such as the elevator, but at least part of the history of upright structure is a form of homage to, and simultaneously a refutation of, the biological burden of the human form that architecture defers to, and outstrips. The evolution of technology outruns the evolution of the body very early on in human development, and yet of course the body remains as some kind of custodian of these technological advances—the elevator operator, so to speak.

Some of Ambasz's architectural cosmology—the configuration of architecture, nature, and island—rests inside these propositions. "I seek, rhetorically," he writes, "to eliminate architecture . . . and return to the primeval notion of dwelling . . . within the abode . . . [where there would never be] inclemency of any sort."[8] Dwelling, for Ambasz, is made "primeval" partly by its burrowing aspect, its pre-vertical (pre-ideological, pre-curtain-wall) state. This is a return to an earlier era—an era of a pre-human, although not animal. But it is interesting that the moral and morphological fate of humans is intimately tied to the moral and morphological fate of their dwellings.

The island site that houses Ambasz's ideal architect/occupant is frequently a vast green terrace or horizontal landscape, frequently not a natural landscape but often an artificial landscape rendered as natural. Occupants are perched in small outlooks at the top of a long, steep white staircase or deep inside a hill, or both. (Examples include Casa de Retiro Espiritual, Mycal Cultural and Athletic Center at Shin-Sanda, and Worldbridge Trade and Investment Center.) This is not a Darwinian island, not part of the Galapagos Islands, for example, where isolated bird species demonstrated, in their difference, a common ancestry. These isolated locales in Ambasz's work are places where humans are almost indistinguishably affiliated with architecture—an affiliation of two structures with moments of uprightness (skeletal and technical privilege) but dominantly horizontal perspectives because of trabeation, horizon lines, landscape, and the human eye.

Buildings—completed structures—are among the slowest moving of technological artifacts, partly because they act both sympathetically and regressively toward the slow evolutionary needs of the biological body. Although architecture intersects with speedier material and digital technologies, it frequently counterbalances these high-tech moments with slow-tech moments. Architecture tries to exalt the body that it houses—in scale, attitude, material difference—but it also stoops to this body—in scale, attitude, materiality. This combination of attitudes—slow/speedy, sympathetic/filled with hubris, humble/exalted—is evident in Ambasz's storytelling and in his projects, as they were in John Hejduk's work. In both cases, however, there is deliberate refusal to flesh out the whole picture, a picture that most architects flesh out with impunity. The architectural act is incomplete, restrained.

Ambasz's architecture indexes enclosure but habitually keeps it abstract and skeletal. His architecture refuses to take on the wholesome role—the absolute role of moral uprightness that posed no problems for the modernists—of supplying the positive presence that would close the site as a building, by definition, attempts to do. Ambasz's architecture belongs, instead, to a sixteenth-century world in which living structures (in a deliberate conflation of body and building) technically do not stand apart from their surroundings. The buildings grow mosses and other kinds of vegetation (not always wild) on themselves as if sympathetic with their (future) state as ruins (Private Estate, Montana; Nishiyachiyo New Town Center; Hortus Conclusus—Centre Georges Pompidou). Without conveying any information on the ecology, horticulture, or evolutionary system of the abstract form that is undergoing greening, the sculptural presence of this architecture in the landscape produces places where things might eventually bunch up: leaves, sand, life-forms. When things bunch up, in the natural world, it is not simply an accretion but a coalescence. Seeds that need a destination often find it in these kinds of bunched-up habitats. So we could say that, while highly abstract, the hospitality of Ambasz's structures to vegetation and animal life makes them fertile in a pre-technical way. Even the exquisitely designed machines and mechanisms in Ambasz's work seem to belong to a pre-technical world. The cars in the Mercedes-Benz Showroom are in fact like sheep on a hill. They are approaching some kind of border territory between their life as machines and their life as animals, made possible by the evolutionary ambivalence, the

vertical/horizontal ambivalence, the diagonal plane, of the architectural podium on which they sit.[9]

Examining Ambasz's architecture in relation to the history of life necessitates looking at different theories of how human beings can literally and figuratively be said to "architect" the world. This includes rereading Claude Lévi-Strauss's 1968 book *Totemism* and other theories of association between natural and human systems and rereading Foucault's 1966 book *The Order of Things* to revisit the early elaboration of his by now fully explicated "middle region" of inquiry, the region of the archaeologist. I believe the field of inquiry opened up by this and other work is related here, although I recognize that we are now, as a species, beyond the control of the critical oppositions and structures revealed by the horizontal section cuts of the structuralists. We are also, in some way, beyond the critique of structuralism and back on a surface of the gradient. The sixteenth century was an epoch of surfaces, and so is the early part of the twenty-first century. Developmentally fertile, the smooth green surfaces of Ambasz's landscapes might in fact be seen as a kind of sixteenth-century precursor to the flat fields of the digital surface, skipping the whole fraught in-between period of dialectical opposition, historiography, and poststructuralism.

However, it might be useful here to look back almost forty years to Claude Lévi-Strauss's *Totemism*. The "critical awkward" stance of buildings, projects,

79

and landscapes that interests me in architecture suggests, in addition to the unresolved quality mentioned toward the beginning of this essay, that a certain set of associations and references belonging to the pre-architectural state have not been fully exhausted in translation. "Associations and references" between worlds was the theme of Lévi-Strauss's field work. A totemic relation, Lévi-Strauss argues, elucidates a mythical relation between the animal world and the human world, between the infamous, and by now wearily oppositional, terms *nature/culture*. The relation is of course fully cultural, a place into which animals are drawn from the wild as needed. According to Lévi-Strauss, this kind of "associationism was

> a direct expression of the structure of the mind . . . and not an inert product of the action of the environment on an amorphous consciousness. . . . It is this logic of oppositions and correlations, exclusions and inclusions, compatibilities and incompatibilities, which explains the laws of association, not the reverse. . . . [There is] a homology of structure between human thought in action and the human object to which it is applied.[10]

Without revisiting the adventures of the *homology* per se, or even the still-remarkable insights of the structuralists, semioticians, and poststructuralists circulating in the philosophical atmosphere just prior to Ambasz's most productive period in the late 1980s, we could note that the "nature" of Ambasz's projects is, without question, a "mind" projecting itself into a world, rather than a world acting on an amorphous consciousness. No landscape in these projects is undressed. No tree or plant arrives accidentally by means of the wind. No water system is without its reflecting pool.

The way in which mind projects itself into the world is multiple and, as intimated above in a preliminary way, always engaged with problems of the technological, ideologically and/or materially. Architecture is, by definition, a mind and technology practice. Engaging both, Ambasz, like those structural anthropologists working in the 1960s and '70s, seems to imagine the world as an associational puzzle where one is in search of something like the famous coup de grâce of the structuralist analysis, extracting key operational structures from dense bodies of complex material. It is archaeological—submerged earth architectures, formal section cuts. The inclined plane proposed for the Grand Rapids Art Museum, although "of the air" rather than the ground, is just

such a cut into the Beaux-Arts architecture of the Federal Building. It reprograms the building and protects the entrance by reestablishing a "ceremonial staircase." The relatively simple move of inserting a giant inclined plane, on a horizontal mesh with water running down it, has massive consequences. It reverses the building because it is placed on the open, rather than closed, part of the U shape of the original building, and operates, in section, as a framing device. The plane is also a blade. And yet there is nothing oppositional or dialectical about this plane, and, finally, there is little that is "structural" about it either, in Lévi-Strauss's or Foucault's sense of the word. It does not draw its form or its metaphysics from the context; it does not use existing forms opportunistically; it is not episodic; it does not set up any form of transformational structural analogies that would keep us in oscillation between the old and the new. And, in spite of its, as always, meticulous engineering, and its sectional argument, the plane is all revealed surface. It has a minor interior.

The relation of structuralism to specific prior philosophical positions on "oppositionality"—Hegel, Marx, and, in different ways, Plato and Aristotle—is a complex one, and this is not the place for that longer discussion. But one of the most interesting points that Foucault made about the sixteenth century is that part of the epistemological relationship between things was based on "convenience," the proximity of things in space. Things that are next to other things produce more than a casual relationship. External affiliations of surfaces across space—surface resemblances—are the basis of sixteenth-century theories of causality, origins, description, life purpose. The plant is next to the animal, which is next to the rock, in a proximity that argues for an affinity of purpose, use, destiny. This is a radically different state of nature than the place we learn about in *Totemism*. The homologies that Lévi-Strauss tracks between animal species and human beings are structural and internal, not superficial. Animals, as manifested in a human cultural context, serve as models for human relations. As Lévi-Strauss writes, "It is because man originally felt himself identical to all those like him (among whom, as Rousseau explicitly says, we must include animals) that he came to acquire the capacity to distinguish *himself* as he distinguishes *them*, that is, to use the diversity of species as conceptual support for social differentiation."[11] Society and social relations, acts of social distinction, form the identity of Lévi-Strauss's man. No man, in this world of rampant distinction, is ever an island. It is, paradoxically, only in a world governed by resemblances across surfaces, the sixteenth-century world—not the world governed by differences, the eighteenth-century world—that man might be said to be an island.

Man is an island. Architecture and nature have a primeval relation—the rhetorical claims of Ambasz on the way to "eliminating architecture." There was no nature in the sixteenth century, or perhaps everything was nature. "Nature" per se was the invention of the eighteenth century, as was the invention of architecture as a formal discipline. Structure and the typology of structure are the newly manifested, documented, and historicized core of this architectural discipline. The ability to frame larger spaces with less mass, enabled by new forms of structure, brings with it a greater openness on the interior of buildings, or rather, the desire for the interior enlarges the interior, which in turn proportionally lessens the mass. Inside these spaces, forms of life that were previously amalgamated by means of resemblance are separated according to species.

The great nineteenth-century natural history museums were built to exhibit multiple forms of differentiated life, within the large open spaces of the architectural interior. A number of people, Fumihiko Maki among them, have noted the resemblance of Ambasz's "nature" to the half-mystical, half-scientific eighteenth-century sciences in which nature is reinvented as something simultaneously found and constructed. But there is yet another theory of science that we should examine in relation to Ambasz.

In many of the geneticist Richard Lewontin's discussions of contemporary genetics, he uses the word *construction* to talk about the relation of environment to organism and genetic process. Lewontin's argument is that organisms do not develop exclusively from the inside out. The crucial distinction made by Darwin between internal and external milieu, between the organism and its growth environment, made possible the necessary growth away from the "obscurantist holism"[12] of earlier periods, when life is lost in the plethora of its relations. But this theory also concentrated on the organism more than its surroundings. A Darwinian architecture would be a cool architecture; detached, impervious, developing along its own geophysical path. Lewontin's revision of this scene is to reactivate the environment, which, in turn, re-envelopes the organism. The environment, in contemporary genetics, is not "causally independent" of the organism. "Just as there can be no organism without an environment," Lewontin writes, "so there can be no environment without an organism." He continues:

> [An] "environment is something that surrounds or encircles, but for there to be a surrounding there must be something at the center to be surrounded. The environment of an organism is the penumbra of external conditions that are relevant to it because it has effective interactions with those aspects of the outer world."[13]

What began in Darwin as a heuristic device, enabling the theory of evolution to begin the task of locating similarities and differences in organisms, is restructured by Lewontin in the interest of bringing what is habitually external and internal to the organism into a more intimate set of relations. There is no preexistent ecological niche into which an organism enters and thrives or dies. Nothing can be called an environment that is not somehow mixed up with an organism. It is this sense of "environment" as something that is always already organic, and the attendant understanding of "organism" as something always already structured—each co-ordering the other—that brings the inside and the outside into a relation that is neither blurry (sixteenth century) nor distinct (eighteenth century). The digital architectures, to some degree, understand this new genetic model. They are opportunistic; they take advantage of inside/outside forces to motivate themselves; they believe in the power of motion to dissolve classical oppositional thresholds. Ambasz can be found here also. "Eliminating architecture" means, in this context, saturating the world with design. But this would not be possible if there were not elective affinities between organism and environment. The architectural environment, in Ambasz, is nothing if not a structure that, in advance, imagines its occupant; and the occupant is nothing other than a being who, in advance, plans his occupancy. Between the two there is never any inclemency.

So Emilio Ambasz, practicing in the twentieth and twenty-first centuries, takes a sixteenth-century idea of "man" and places him in an eighteenth-century "nature." He is an architect of the outside, often diagonal, surface, but also a virtuoso of the technical interior. His architecture believes in the mysticism of the basic orders: Foucault's order of signs and signatures, the marks by which we know that certain plants are medicinal for the disorders of the eye. At the same time, and in spite of his objection to the curtain wall—for Ambasz, an image of an impoverished and spiritually limited architecture—he believes in the imperial orders of architectural modernism. His architecture sustains movement on its surfaces, but also cultivates stillness, for example, the "granitical earth" of the mountains surrounding the Lugano project.[14] Ambasz's architecture/nature/man-as-island is, in effect, a complete organism/environment "circular plan" for the beginning of architecture. As he wrote in *Inventions*, "My quest for the essential in architecture is not about being simple and light, like a feather; it is about being essential and concise, like a bird."[15]

But part of architecture always strives to be "not-a-bird." "Inferno," as in Dante's *Inferno*, means "without birds,"[16] a place of the below, not the above. Architecture is never fully buried, because of its will to the upright, but it clings to the earth in literal and philosophical ways, not all of which are benevolent. Ambasz's architecture also occasionally reminds us of this more sinister aspect of architectures that mess with existential and ontological questions. "The first item I stored [in these alcoves]," writes Ambasz, "were my childhood toys, school notebooks, stamp collections and a few items of clothing to which I had become attached. Later, I started moving out of the house and into the second alcove gifts I had received while doing my military service, as well as my uniform. I became fond of traversing the water basin once in a while to dress up in it, to make sure that I had not put on too much weight."[17] About these architectural follies, the skeptical children are still wondering.

1   See Rietveld's very interesting essay entitled "Chairs," published in 1930 in the journal *De werkende vrouw* (founded in the same year), reprinted in *Gerrit Th. Rietveld, The Complete Works*, by Marijke Kuper and Ida van Zijl (Utrecht: Centraal Museum, 1992), 27.

2   Emilio Ambasz, *The Poetics of Pragmatic* (New York: Rizzoli, 1991), 24.

3   "I consider my architecture," writes Ambasz, "an alternative to prevailing architectural pursuits . . . finding ways of gracefully relating and juxtaposing the artificial to the natural . . . a return to the roots of a genuinely balanced architecture as a form of man-made nature." Ambasz, *The Poetics of the Pragmatic*, 27.

4   "The Vittel water bottle is based on water itself, and a merging of the bottle's practical requirements with the substance's sensual delights." The bottle is beautiful, easy to grip, feels "good in the hand," is not slippery, with a wavy texture that suggests the company's name and water simultaneously. "Like a perfume container for water, the bottle is designed to signal that something of real quality is inside." *The Poetics of the Pragmatic*, 282–83, 293.

5   Emilio Ambasz, *The Poetics of the Pragmatic*, 25.

6   Catherine Ingraham, *The Discipline of the Milieu: Architecture and Post-Animal Life* (forthcoming).

7   André Leroi-Gourhan, *Gesture and Speech*, trans. Anna Bostock Berger (Cambridge, Mass.: MIT Press, 1993), 19.

8   Ambasz, *The Poetics of the Pragmatic*, 28.

9   The diagonal plane is fundamental to Ambasz's architecture because it refuses the ideology of both slab and curtain wall. Several projects that use the diagonal plane explicitly: Marine City Waterfront Development, Otaru, Hokkaido Island, Japan; Worldbridge Trade and Investment Center, Baltimore, Maryland; Fukuoka Prefectural International Hall, Fukuoka, Japan.

10   Claude Lévi-Strauss, *Totemism* (Boston: Beacon Press, 1963), 91.

11   Lévi-Strauss, *Totemism*, 101.

12   Richard Lewontin, *The Triple Helix* (Cambridge, Mass.: Harvard University Press, 2000), 47.

13   Lewontin, *The Triple Helix,* 48–49.

14   Ambasz built a one-hundred-foot-long terrace to recreate the "view of mountains, sky, and clouds" at Residence-au-Lac, a resort hotel built in the 1950s. Ambasz, *The Poetics of the Pragmatic*, 192.

15   Ambasz, *Emilio Ambasz Inventions: The Reality of the Ideal* (New York: Rizzoli, 1992), 56.

16   Diana Wells, *100 Birds and How They Got Their Names* (Chapel Hill, N.C.: Algonquin Books, 2001).

17   Ambasz, *The Poetics of Pragmatics*, 162.

EMILIO AMBASZ: SOFT & HARD
James Wines

It is one thing to use the earth: it is quite another thing to receive the blessing
of the earth and to become at home in the law of this reception, in order
to shepherd the mystery of being and to pay attention to the inviolability of
the possible.
—Martin Heidegger

By his own admission, Emilio Ambasz wants to be remembered as a poet.
While this confession places his role as an artist above that of designer and
technician, he has also stated that his commitments are equally divided
between what he describes as the "Emilio" and the "Ambasz" sides of his
nature. Emilio is the visionary, acknowledging his preference for profusely
landscaped buildings, while Ambasz is the pragmatist, referring to his work as
an industrial designer. In the first capacity he proposes utopian visions, while,
in the other, he understands and applies the constraints of economy. As part
of this duality, he is equally at home in the company of artists and engineers,
idealists and politicians, theoreticians and bureaucrats. In his own words,
he "wants to please the angels with poetic design and please the people with
practical design."

Emilio describes himself as "cheerfully sad and sociably solitary," as a
person who is responsive to "myth/love and fear/furor." He even relates the
geography of his lifestyle to a dialectic, claiming, "If Emilio could not enter
Italy, he would feel as if he had been thrown out of Paradise. If Ambasz could
not return to New York, he would feel excluded from the capital of the 20th
Century." "Sometimes," he muses, "I fancy myself to be the last man of the
present culture, building a house for the first man of a culture that has not yet
arrived." Clearly, Emilio Ambasz has a penchant for dialectics. An endlessly
intriguing combination of romantic prophet and hard-nosed realist, he is a
contradictory genius who works simultaneously in two worlds, one soft and
the other hard.

Although Emilio and I have never specifically discussed his connection to
theories of opposites in the history of philosophy, I assume that Hegel must

have had a considerable influence on the development of his thought. Like Hegel, Ambasz sees reality as an undecipherable organic unity, an unstable and constantly changing phenomenon. He likewise seems to embrace Hegel's concept of the universe as an inaccessible condition of absolute idealism. "Justice," Ambasz explains, "whether social or moral, is a conceit of the mind. Justice does not exist in nature, but despite this cruel fact, I feel very strongly that it is our ethical imperative to pursue its implementation on earth. Even if we know it to be a delicate structure, held together by such ethereal material as abnegation and altruism, but destined to collapse at night, we must every new morning re-build it." In this statement, he appears to embrace Hegel's existential philosophy of conflicts—or, the Zeitgeist of mind and spirit, fused by time. This models Ambasz's exteriorization of internal conflicts (or, conversely, his outside as inside), the soft and hard qualities of his own persona, his dual roles as romantic messiah versus steely pragmatist and his search for a fulcrum to stabilize the shifting balance between ecology and technology. Emilio summarizes his position by confirming, "My existential wager is on poetry, and a commitment to justice is, for me, one of the necessary, but not sufficient, conditions to achieve such a high plateau."

In the thirty years I have known Emilio as a friend, advocate, raconteur, protagonist, and multidisciplinary colleague of Renaissance proportions, I have often thought about our controversial involvement in architecture (as designers who are frequently deemed "outsiders"), our areas of philosophical agreement, and our differences of approach to similar issues. Since we share a connection to progressive politics and concur on so many fundamental principles in art and design, I felt it would be helpful (for me, in writing this essay, as well as for readers) if I reviewed some of this history and its affinities and disparities.

Both of our architectural practices became well known in the early 1970s, as a result of being associated in the press with an international design movement referred to then as "Radical Architecture." While the term is generally attributed to the Italian writer Barbara Radice (who published the first "official" book on the subject), some of the pioneering curatorial work must be credited to the American landscape architect Jim Burns. In 1971 he focused on a group of artists and designers in Europe and U.S., assembling them under an umbrella title he called "Arthropods," which the dictionary defines as "a phylum consisting of articulate invertebrate animals with jointed limbs, the body divided into metameric segments." In Burns's view, this new category suggested an architecture that could expand beyond stationary shelter to include performance works, political actions, site-specific events, mobile living, public art, temporary environments, pneumatic structures, and a host of other manifestations not typically associated with doctrinaire building design. Burns's book included work by the American groups Ant Farm, Pulsa, Onyx, and Experiments in Art and Technology; the Austrian teams Missing Link, and Haus Rucker; Britain's Cedric Price and Archigram; Montreal's François Dallegret; and Italy's Archizoom.

By 1974 Radical Architecture shifted mostly to Europe. Although my memory is foggy, I believe Emilio and I were first introduced by members of the Milanese faction. In Italy, Germano Celant championed the movement; but, on more scholarly terms, it was refined by Paola Navone and Bruno Orlandoni, who published their graduation thesis, *Architettura Radicale*, in 1974 as part of a series called *Documenti di Casabella*, edited by Alessandro Mendini. This essay was one of the first serious evaluations of the new sensibility. Subsequently, various European design reviews responded to the *Casabella* lead, including *Architectural Design* and *Building Design* in England, *L'Architecture d'aujourd'hui* in France, and *Domus, In Inpiù,* and *Modo* in Italy. The press created an activist climate and, under the leadership of Mendini, proposed that only through a deep grasp of epochal awareness and nontraditional cultural values would architects ever hope to address the new world of social disorder and impending environmental catastrophe.

Ambasz, in addition to his role as a leader of Radical Architecture's environmental spearhead, was also a pivotal promoter of new design during his tenure as a curator at MoMA—a role culminating in the enormously influential exhibition of 1972, entitled "Italy—The New Domestic Landscape." This show had a powerful impact on the American design scene. It was perceived as a liberating force, as the predecessor to postmodernism and an endorsement of free-wheeling alternatives to orthodox modernism. In retrospect, many of the most advanced ideas exposed in "The New Domestic Landscape"—particularly those battle cries for social and ecological reform in architecture from groups like Superstudio, Archizoom, UFO, Ziggurat, and others—have lost their momentum over the past two decades, as the design world became pervaded by the neo-constructivist obsessions that still dominate the scene today.

Clearly, Emilio and I are both committed to a fusion of the visual environment with architecture. We see buildings as instruments of social/psychological communication and as extensions of their surrounding situations. We both emerged from the stylistic traditions of modernism and constructivism—rammed down our throats *ad nauseam* during our college years—and, in opposition to these traditions, our work represents a continuing search for alternatives. The common ground between us is integrative thinking and the desire to humanize the building arts by engaging all senses of the body—by incorporating user interaction and contextual feedback as sources of ideas for aesthetic solutions.

The divergence in our design objectives is sufficient to keep the dialogue between us feisty and challenging, but not so combative as to threaten our mutual respect and enduring friendship. In point, it was Emilio Ambasz (as design curator at the Museum of Modern Art) who first exhibited my drawings for SITE at MoMA. As a direct result of this support, he helped launch my international recognition. With corresponding advocacy, I have written about Emilio's work on numerous occasions over the past twenty-five years, including an essay crediting his seminal contributions to the environmental design movement in my most recent book, *Green Architecture*.

Our similarities grow from the fact that we both use architecture as a kind of philosophical matrix for exploring a wide range of ideas in multiple media—including visual art, critical writing and graphics, as well as furniture, product design, and landscape architecture. Our dissimilarities occur in certain areas of intent. For Emilio, the building art is a transcendental calling, where the combination of structure, vegetation, and their relationship to the environment is seen as part of an integrative utopia. In many cases his work is not unlike the Zen garden concept of "borrowed scenery"—the earthbound representation of a paradise beyond terrestrial boundaries.

Emilio and I interpret the fusion of architecture with context quite differently. Judging from his rather surreal portrayals of the environment in models and renderings—which often represent an austere and unpopulated Dalí-esque landscape—Emilio sees topography as a kind of *tabula rasa*, as the virgin receptacle for an architecture of incision, extrusion, and burrowing. While the physical characteristics of a site inform my buildings, I am less interested than Emilio in poetic readings and in the sculptural interaction between volumes and surfaces. I am more intrigued by the theatrical performance of people and by finding ways to include this kinetic interaction as an inseparable part of the architectural experience. Ambasz interprets environment as a metaphysical dream, while I view it more as a source of psychological implications and social messages. Described another way, I believe in going beyond the elements that actually exist in favor of thoughts about things whose existence is *implied*.

My own position with regard to the fusion of architecture with its environment has always been less idealistic than Emilio's; in fact, in many cases, my approach has been more about irony, humor, and a questioning of design-world values—more about architecture as a form of critical commentary on itself, rather than a visionary mission. Especially in my work of the 1970s and '80s, this critique took the form of a shift in aesthetic intention away from formalist design and toward an architecture based on inversions of meaning and the inclusion of information from a variety of outside sources. My conceptual direction grew out of the observation that wall surfaces, interiors, landscape and surrounding spaces can assimilate and reflect a broad range of social and psychological content. I saw the physical elements of architecture as "filtering zones" for reinterpretation and critique, for ideas that could be used to question many twentieth-century stylistic conventions. For example, rather than conceive of buildings as exercises in *form, space, and structure*, I shifted the emphasis to *idea, attitude, and context*; or, (like conceptual art) to the notion of architecture as a dialogue in the mind. I observed that many archetypes—office towers, shopping centers, civic buildings, suburban homes, etc.—are accepted by people as ubiquitous and unseen objects of reflex identification in their daily lives. By taking advantage of this subliminal level of recognition, I could use architecture as the subject matter of art, as opposed to the objective of the usual design process.

Emilio Ambasz—in my view—seems unconcerned with the kind of equivocal attitude necessary for irony and inversion; instead, he plunges fearlessly into the high-risk realm of fervent idealism in a cynical world. As a consequence of his courageous position, he has often been marginalized by the modernist/constructivist mafia as too romantic, chastised by the ecologically correct camp as not green enough, rejected by the landscape design profession as too controversial and thwarted by lost commissions at the hands of vacillating clients who have deemed him to be too risky or too impractical. Throughout all of these rejections, he has triumphed as an international presence who stands at the forefront of progressive thinking about architecture and its relation to the new Age of Information and Ecology.

Part of my assignment in contributing to this book on Ambasz is to place his work in the context of green design and sustainable architecture. Within a rigorous definition of green, he does not qualify as a mainstream contributor. His involvement with the latest environmental technology is minimal, his fusion of landscape with structure is not always responsive to regional ecology, his use of industrial materials frequently doesn't conform to LEED standards, and the energy demands of his buildings tend to exceed local recommendations. In summary, the "Emilio" aspects of his environmental buildings are evident in his lavish commitment to landscaped terraces, earth-sheltered roofs, and troglodyte living and working spaces. At the same time, the more pragmatic, or "Ambasz" features of his architecture—such as environmental technology and alternative energy systems—tend to be less resolved.

It should be mentioned here that the environmental shortcomings listed above could be attributed to the greenest of green designers today—including such self-proclaimed advocates of sustainable architecture as Ken Yeang, Fox and Fowle, Richard Rogers, Norman Foster, Cesar Pelli, and even a few of those doggedly hyperbolic messiahs of eco-centrism, such as William McDonough. However green the claims of these and many designers today, their decisions concerning building mass, industrial products, consumption of fossil fuels, invasion of land surface, and choice of architectural *imagery* have remained essentially the same—most often derived from the Age of Industry and only slightly modified to meet the requirements of recent environmental expectations. From the standpoint of an appropriate imagery for the current Age of Ecology, Emilio Ambasz has decisively influenced the standards. Whether strictly green or not, his work indelibly transmits the environmental message. In the iconographic tradition of Gothic churches, his vegetation-encrusted architecture serves the crusade with a persuasive, uncompromising, and billboardlike impact.

It is precisely this aesthetic identification with the romantic connotations of landscape—plus Ambasz's treatment of buildings as the embodiment of poetic fables—that has provoked some factions in the architectural establishment to bristle with resentment concerning his work. It is no secret that most of today's disciples of modernism and constructivism vehemently reject the notion that any shred of imagery in their architecture might be construed as referential or symbolic. Those perennial measures of design excellence, derived from the 1920s pioneers of abstract art, have ordained the virtues of formal relationships as preferable to what Robert Venturi once advocated as the "messy vitality" of popular culture and the psychological appeal of metaphorical imagery. From the perspective of today's architectural rules of decorum, God forbid that an association with communicative content might pollute the sanctity of the form-making/space-making process.

In point of fact, architects such as Peter Eisenman, Richard Meier, Dominique Perrault, Toyo Ito, Zaha Hadid, Daniel Libeskind, and a host of other high-design luminaries will jump through hoops to disclaim any connection to the untidy realms of allusion and narrative and, even more vehemently, to distance themselves from the ornamental aberrations of historicist postmodernism. What remains unacknowledged in all of this defensive posturing is the fact that the entire battle over formalist design was won ninety years ago during the earliest phases of the modern movement, when it was necessary to separate the progressive strategies of abstractionism from the decorative excesses of the Beaux Arts. To persist with these arguments in today's world of information explosions and environmental doomsdays has become quaintly anachronistic—or, what might be regarded now as a kind of Beaux-Arts redux. In this climate of outdated ideologies and stylistic redundancy, it is understandable that Ambasz's work is seen as a challenge to the status quo.

The tendency of Ambasz's detractors to dismiss his work as pastoral scenography opens up a number of intriguing issues concerning the relevance of the opposition and the inclination of mainstream architects to marginalize the green movement. It is a rule of thumb in environmental circles that one tree means four people can breath; so, based on this health argument alone, it raises questions about why plants and trees in architecture are reduced to the status of peripheral décor or eliminated altogether as superfluous intrusions. As mentioned earlier, part of the answer goes back to the earliest origins of cubism and constructivism, when the notion of architecture as a work of abstract sculpture became synonymous with good taste in design. Oddly enough, this stylistic baggage is usually dismissed by the art world as hopelessly old-fashioned—especially when it appears in the work of contemporary sculptors—while architects enthusiastically embrace these same influences as a source of cutting-edge emancipation. The most blatant evidence of this criterion is confirmed by design magazine presentations of prominent new buildings, in which people and vegetation are conscientiously avoided in photographs to eliminate any distractions that might interfere with the readership's appreciation of a pure sculptural experience. This hermetic view of architecture has also contributed to the frequent relegation of landscape around buildings to nothing more than charm bracelets of lollipop trees.

Based on this critique, I feel compelled to inject an observation here concerning the strange disconnection between Emilio's frequently voiced commitment to the humanization of architecture through poetic imagery, garden spaces, and people-comforts, and the models, drawings, and photos of his work that invariably depict an eerily unpopulated landscape—not unlike the haunting austerity of a De Chirico or Magritte painting. His buildings are usually designed as idyllic places to inhabit, yet he seems to prefer them to be seen as paradisiacal dreamscapes, undisturbed by the presence of occupants. For me, this is just one more example of the paradoxical Ambasz and the layers of contradiction in his work.

Another curious aspect of architects' resistance to change is their confinement of the use of computers to churning out drawings for buildings that persist in the traditions of labyrinthine formalist exercises and celebrations of industrial materials, while overlooking the fact that digital technology itself is the quintessential icon of the information revolution and the logical wellspring for a new architectural language. In reality, mainstream designers seem to steadfastly avoid a greater attention to the most potent sources of imagery associated with the twenty-first century. They tend to see landscape as a violation of sculptural form, social content as sentimental pabulum, sustainable design as a threat to modernist supremacy, and the computer as merely an illustrative tool.

The Age of Information and Ecology offers an incredibly fertile reservoir of ideas from science, popular culture, and nature—cybernetics, virtual reality, mass media, biochemistry, hydrology, geology, and cosmology, to mention a few—so the architecture profession's failure to access these sources is indicative of its continuing conservatism and apparent lack of epochal awareness. As I observed at the conclusion of my book *Green Architecture*:

Unlike the early Constructivists' works, which remained mostly unrealizable for the lack of computerized calculations and advanced construction technology, the CAD-equipped architect can easily describe and erect the most exotic configurations. Still, it seems oddly regressive to resurrect ideas from the 1920's, simply because they can be built today. And, finally, why have so few architects made the obvious conceptual and aesthetic connections between the integrated systems of the internet and their ecological parallels in nature? These questions point to the need for developing a visionary *eco-digital* iconography in architecture. By incorporating ideas from both informational and ecological sources, it suggests the development of an imagery that echoes the mutable/evolutionary changes found in nature and the fluid/interactive flow of data through electronic communications. In spirit, this seems to indicate something more like trying to capture the intangibility of the wind passing through the trees than expressing the cumbersome mechanics of construction technology. It seems more like the quest for an *invisible or virtual architecture,* as opposed to celebrating the weight and density of industrial materials.

This gnawing issue of designers' indifference toward (or fear of) the challenge of rethinking the conceptual foundations of architecture is, in my view, one of the most profound problems in the design world of the new millennium. As I wrote in a collection of essays entitled *De-architecture* of 1986, "The language of architecture should now be more psychological than formal, more cosmic than rational, more informational than obscure, more provisional than stable, more indeterminate than resolved, more narrative than abstract . . . . Architecture of the future will convey a meaningful message if, and only if, architects are able to perceive it differently." Ambasz reinforced the same message in an exchange of letters between us last year. "I have always been aware, and so have you surely, that architecture always has marched behind the other arts. Think back in time and you will always find that painters anticipated many of the concerns that later were taken up by architects. Architecture is a social art and the human material it utilizes is far more recalcitrant than oil paint." I feel the problem goes much deeper. As the result of their oddly insular psyches, designers seem smugly content with institutionalized definitions, aesthetically indifferent to the information revolution, politically passive toward environmental crises, and sociologically removed from the vitality and untidiness of the world for which they supply shelter. I don't agree with Emilio that architecture's conceptual deficits are caused by the restraints of a "social art"; instead, I view the gap as the result of architects' fundamental resistance to the kind of interrogatory process that Duchamp once described as, "teaching myself to contradict myself, in order to avoid conforming to my own taste."

The conceptual limitations of contemporary architecture—Ambasz's "social art" apology notwithstanding—are the consequence of an insufficient number of questions being asked and the misguided assumption that buildings are too physical, too burdened by function, budget, and gravity, to be about anything other than form, space, and materials. This limited perspective represents a peculiar detachment from the legacy of breakthroughs in the other arts and an unwillingness to experiment with new frames of reference. It is also the product of a century of architects' reflexive criteria and self-imposed limitations. There appears to be only one acceptable formula in the design process—drawn from that pivotal moment when the disdained nineteenth-century notion of sculpture as merely a form of décor *on* a building was exchanged for the concept of the whole building as a piece of sculpture in itself. But this is only one revolution, crystallized in the early 1900s. In contrast, the visual arts have been convulsed by innumerable revolutions over the past hundred years.

Contrary to Emilio's excuse for architectural inertia (a building is "more recalcitrant than oil paint"), I want to emphasize that major changes in art have not been wrought merely as the result of an ease of execution or a less expensive overhead. For example, when Duchamp laid the foundations for conceptual art, he spoke of his work as "non-retinal"—announcing his lack of interest in the academic traditions of illusory representation and the seductive surfaces of, say, an impressionist painting or a cubist collage. His designation of the non-retinal did not refer to invisibility—obviously, all forms of art and architecture are embodied in a visual presence—but instead he was staking out a claim for art as "the idea of art," art as more mental than physical. The conceptual artist Joseph Kosuth explained this attitudinal position in a seminal essay of the late 1960s entitled "Art after Philosophy": "Being an artist now means to question the nature of art. If one is questioning the nature of painting, one cannot be questioning the nature of art. Painting is a kind of art. If an artist accepts painting, he is accepting (and limited by) the traditional baggage that goes with it." Architects rarely initiate this type of critique and tend to resist any comparable level of reevaluation of their profession.

To Ambasz's credit, he understands the value of conceptual change and alternative sources of content—especially terrestrial and cosmological references—as a far more fertile basis for artistic expression than scavenging the timeworn language of the Industrial Revolution. In particular, he has consistently explored the uses of vegetation as intrinsic elements in architecture by integrating trees and plants to a point where they become as much a part of the fabric of buildings as glass, steel, concrete, and brick.

Returning to Ambasz's dialectical persona in relation to his philosophy of architecture, sometimes this interface between soft and hard is difficult to reconcile. For example, following a charismatic presentation of his work at a recent conference on green architecture in Costa Rica, Ambasz startled an audience of fervent eco-advocates by declaring that the success of the environmental movement in the future will depend on corporate profits—in short, if green design doesn't make money, it won't stand a chance of survival. After assuaging the symposium attendees with a PowerPoint presentation of idyllic, landscape-encrusted buildings, reinforcing his role as Emilio the poet, he wrenched them back to reality with Ambasz the banker (leaving the crowd speechless). Certainly every designer acknowledges that buildings cannot exist without the support of wealth; but, in the context of an environmental conference, Ambasz owed his audience a more measured evaluation of the corporate relationship to ecology and some productive recipes for the education of patronage.

While Ambasz's broad-based credentials and ease of access to the fraternity of haute finance are impressive, I don't think students and colleagues in Costa Rica embraced his profit-or-perish prescription for the green movement—mainly because, as every environmentalist knows, corporate bookkeeping rarely acknowledges the destruction of nature and the waste of resources as financial deficits, and it certainly doesn't accept the responsibility for reparation as overhead. Since it is precisely this profit-driven scenario that has created our global environmental disaster in the first place, I think the audience was waiting for Emilio to elaborate his argument more fully. I am sure that he tries to guide business clients into paths of ecological accountability; still, it would have been interesting to hear a fleshed-out version of how he addresses a challenge of this magnitude—especially in the light of the U.S. government's current political philosophy of drill for Dubya and shed blood for oil, which certainly has an impact on international corporate policies.

In all fairness to Emilio Ambasz—along with all architects dedicated to the environmental cause—there is very little the green designer can actually accomplish, given the accelerated demands of contemporary living over the past three decades. The plugged-in societies' thresholds of expectation, in terms of food, shelter, climate control, transportation, electronic communications, and so on have placed such unreasonable demands on the natural environment that nothing short of a decade-long shutdown of the entire superstructure we regard as "normal" would even begin to solve the impending Armageddon. One ultimate question looms larger every day: Which countries, now benefiting most from globalization, are really prepared to forfeit any significant degree of physical or economic advantage in favor of ecological salvation? The list would certainly not include the U.S., with one-twentieth of the world's population and presently consuming 25 percent of its resources. Some nations have created doctrines and signed agreements supporting a sane environmental policy—for example, Germany, Holland, Finland, Sweden, Costa Rica, and others—but the bottom line in highly developed economies, with their irrational levels of comfort requirements, translates into the fact that the construction of human shelter now consumes nearly two-thirds of the world's resources. Architecture is a major part of the problem.

In looking at the relationship of Ambasz's work to the broad spectrum of green design today, it is important to bear in mind the key environmental issues of the twenty-first century, which continue to be used as criteria for the evaluation of designers' varying degrees of ecological responsibility. The obligatory checklist includes:

— **Construction of smaller buildings**
   (fewer than six stories and confined to clustered configurations)

— **Maximum use of recycled and/or renewable materials**

— **Use of materials with low embodied energy and a minimum of toxic waste expelled during production**

— **Use of harvested lumber**
   (except when it is necessary to transport wood products from great distances)

— **Conservation of water supplies**

— **Low maintenance and energy efficiency for heating and cooling**
   (which suggests a variety of alternative energy sources, in addition to passive solar)

— **Recycling and adaptive reuse of existing buildings**
— **Reduction of ozone-depleting chemicals**
   (related to all aspects of construction and maintenance)

— **Maximum preservation of the existing environment**

— **Encouragement of public transportation as an alternative to the use of private vehicles**

In this brief overview of Ambasz's work, I want to review the innovations that combine environmental responsibility and conceptual significance, as well as those ideas that appear to have exerted an influence on international architecture. As Emilio rightfully observed in a recent interview: "I have begotten children, grandchildren and not a few little bastards. To see Renzo Piano, Jean Nouvel, Tadao Ando and many others utilize vegetal matter in their projects makes me feel my mission is beginning to bear fruits." At the same time, I think this statement shortchanges some of his more significant accomplishments. Innumerable architects throughout history have fused landscape into buildings, with Frank Lloyd Wright as the most significant progenitor of organic architecture in the twentieth century. So I prefer to focus on Ambasz projects where I see a significant departure from the stylistic mainstream, a successful communication of the green message and a maximum integration of nature and technology.

I recall, particularly, how impressed I was when *Progressive Architecture* first published Emilio's 1976 Cooperative of Mexican-American Grape Growers project for California. The concept seemed to focus on every relevant issue—ethnic identity, integrative landscape, humble technology, adaptive reuse, and regional weather conditions—that conventional architecture was barely beginning to address. By means of an overhead shelter of grape vines and canopies of leaves, he created an enclave for communal living and user access to an increased amount of shaded land surface for alternative agriculture. I was also intrigued by Emilio's courageous venture into the realm of romantic landscape and his convincing proposal for a "non-building." In the early 1970s, the Grape Growers' Cooperative confronted high-tech chic, then so popular in AIA circles, with a head-on collision of ideology and interpretation.

The next projects that riveted my attention were Ambasz's 1975 Center for Applied Computer Research in Mexico City and the Lucille Halsell Conservatory of 1982 in San Antonio, Texas. In both cases, I was fascinated by his engagement of the building with the site (not just an object sitting on a base) and his propensity for troglodyism and molelike burrowing into the land surface. In designing the computer research center, he anticipated the impending dreariness of the digitally driven workstation—a prophetic view of the corporate environment that has become a universal reality—by floating the offices like lily pads on the surface of an artificial lake. This novel choice compensated for Mexico City's sinking volcanic soil by allowing the architecture to seek its own stabilized position on the surface of water. As an additional feature, these office pods could be moved around and expanded in number, depending on how many people were employed on-site, versus those connected by home workstations. This points to another example of the perspicacious Ambasz predicting, as early as 1975, the inevitability of an escalating number of office workers who would prefer a lifestyle centered around the home-based computer, with only occasional visits to headquarters for strategic meetings.

The research center's combination of vertical and inclined walls, enclosing a central lake, is reminiscent of the imposing mass of a Mayan temple. This interpretation also evokes the sense of an interface between two gigantic computer screens—like an archeological ruin left over from the space age—

which then provides an appropriate imagery for both the technological function of the building and the ambient identity of Mexico City. Ambasz extended his refined sense of epochal cross-referencing to the Lucille Halsell Conservatory. In this case, the entire complex of greenhouses appears to have erupted from underground and, in contrast to the flat terrain, resemble Martian biolabs for cosmic agriculture. The land-surface incisions and earth mounds add to the ritual-like character of the site. In reality, the buildings shelter plants and flowers of the most delicate kind, protecting them from the heat of a hostile desert climate. The partially underground greenhouses offer the advantages of both adequate shade and humidity control for a wide variety of vegetation.

Another early work—the 1978 Casa de Retiro Espiritual—is one of the designer's personal favorites and was only recently built, after twenty-seven years. It is pure "Emilio," expressed as a love affair with Andalusian architecture and local terrain. As in the Mexico City and San Antonio projects, his strong affinities for Spanish culture filter through the design of this private house. The configuration is clearly inspired by historic regional dwellings—bleached white, coolly geometric and wrapped around an inner courtyard—designed to cut out the relentless sun and capture the prevailing winds. But while postmodernist architecture often has an artificial historicism, Ambasz manages to avoid the temptations of referential décor by imposing a restrained agenda (an "Ambasz rigor," by his own definition), which saves his architecture from the cloying preciousness of po-mo design. In the Casa de Retiro, these elements include a courtyard cut into the land surface and a monumental freestanding facade, asserting itself on the horizon like a surrealist beacon for regional culture.

Emilio has a somewhat different view of the building. He describes his intentions as wanting to "eliminate architecture." He sees the design as "a facade, which would be like a mask—a surrogate for architecture. The architecture would disappear. You would only see the earth. You might say that by this device I rhetorically sought to eliminate architecture as a culturally conditioned process and return to the primeval notion of abode." In my opinion, the structure is saturated with "culturally conditioned" references; Emilio's skillful orchestration of these associations is most responsible for the villa's artistic success as an Andalusian icon.

In some ways, the "Emilio versus Ambasz" opposition is consistent with the classic dialectic of his Spanish heritage. For example, in the case of Cervantes's greatest novel, the conflicting personalities of Don Quixote and

Sancho Panza—idealist versus realist—are widely seen as symbolic of the Spanish character. This portrayal also includes a dark side, an "apocalypse/ utopia" conflict that infuses the work of Cervantes, as well as culture heroes such as Goya, García Lorca, Picasso, Neruda, and Almodóvar. Unlike the excoriating irony and radical politics associated with this legacy of torment, Emilio's work has a gentle melancholy and solitude, a kind of Hispanic *Weltschmerz* that is best illustrated by the feelings of isolation in his architectural models and renderings and his designs for public space.

His "cheerfully sad and sociably solitary" self-characterization is reflected in two public space designs: his Plaza Mayor of 1982 in Salamanca, Spain, and the 1983 Grand Rapids Art Museum renovation. In both cases, he dealt with stylistically assertive existing architecture, confronted by bleak slabs of pavement. His job was to enliven the public areas but maintain the classical character of both environments. The Salamanca plaza is enclosed by Alberto Churriguera's masterpiece, an assembly of Baroque civic buildings, so there was a special need to honor and integrate with the context. Ambasz's solution was an ingenious sunken plaza, where pedestrians would descend a stairway into a restful sanctuary covered by welcome shade trees in the warm climate. In order to honor the Churriguera facades, these trees are a regional variety that only grows to a certain height; therefore, at grade level, when the viewer looks across the total public space, the panoramic view of the facades is not blocked by vegetation.

For the Grand Rapids Art Museum renovation, Ambasz transformed the grand stairway of the 1908 Beaux-Arts structure by creating a "stairway over a stairway" in glass, activated by flowing water. This is one of Emilio's most poetic and site-specific projects, since it brilliantly transformed a ponderously weighty entryway into an information-age floating fantasy, using the same visual vocabulary and creating two covered plazas that didn't previously exist.

In the public space category, I have always admired Emilio's small 1983 entry plaza for the Résidence-au-Lac in Lugano, Switzerland. Rough-cut granite slabs emerge vertically from the plaza surface, overlapping in space as a metaphor for the surrounding mountains. By means of a series of successive partitions—with identical layers interpreted in silk on the ceiling—he created the impression of a metaphysical landscape, where inside and outside have merged with the regional environment. This project is also a example of the "sociably solitary" aspect of the architect at its best.

Even though Ambasz's most inventive public project—the 1986 master plan for Expo 92 in Seville, Spain—was not realized, his proposal is a representative embodiment of his Spanish sensibility, Quixotic nature, and commitment to the humanistic city. Since I was deeply involved in the World's Fair (working with SITE on the main pedestrian artery, Avenue Five, and the Saudi Arabian Pavilion), Emilio's contribution to the exposition has always been of particular interest to me. Honoring the Expo's Columbian Anniversary theme, Ambasz's concept called for the development of three large lagoons, with clusters of floating national pavilions. The water feature was intended to symbolize the routes of the original Portuguese and Italian explorations in the fifteenth century. The series of islands, like explorers' ships, supplied the nautical connection between Spain and the New World. For a myriad of reasons (mainly Expo politics) the Ambasz plan was scrapped—much to the disappointment of many international architects (including SITE) who had begun to develop imaginative ideas for the various floating pavilions.

Emilio's master plan combined the multiple purposes of a true exposition at a moment when the communication advantages of the Internet and the meteoric rise in global tourism were in the process of relegating the entire conceit of a world's fair to the dustbin of history. He offered a "theme park" vision—not unlike the great expositions of the nineteenth century—predicated on an idealistic faith in the value of communal celebration and the sharing of ideas in a destination attraction. As a designer who has worked on five expositions, I continue to believe that periodic global parties have significant value in fostering international relations. Expos offer a level of personal engagement that messages on a screen can never supply. Also, as civically sponsored vehicles for city revitalization, expositions generate an urgently needed focus on new ideas for urban design. As Emilio's has noted:

> You ask what relevance the concept of "theme parks" may have for urbanism. If it is now possible to live anywhere in the countryside, cloud deep in the belief that one is connected with everything and anyone via the Internet, how can an urban planner refer to such an elusive and amorphous socio-cultural system as a guide to creating urban forms? Unless he is stiffened by strong ethical beliefs, he will opportunistically offer himself to design the palaces and temples of the emerging powers and their manipulated beliefs. That is the goal this season's prophets propose as urbanism's task: to return to its old profession of glorifying the masters and mystifying reality.

Ambasz's Expo 92 plan set the stage for rethinking urbanism as a mutable and evolutionary process, in which a flexible matrix (in this case, bodies of water, ample landscape, and movable/convertible/exchangeable buildings) would encourage the organic development of future growth. Emilio's concept is the polar opposite of that manic modernist paradigm still dominating the so-called new urbanism. Within this trendy school of planning, the designation "new" is the equivalent of dangerously "old," since its motivating philosophy reinforces the environmentally catastrophic illusion that current models for economic expansion can continue in perpetuity. From the perspective of design solutions, this escalating growth factor is invariably manifested in those claustrophobic street grids, mega-malls, and canyons of curtain-wall towers.

One of the reasons that Ambasz's Expo 92 proposal failed to be implemented was based on the Seville planning commission's observation that, by floating the national pavilions, with only bridges for access, the program was not flexible enough to accommodate the massive crowds of people expected to attend the event. In all honesty, having designed one of the grand-scale pedestrian arteries and its adjoining restaurants, I would have to agree in part with this criticism. The attendance at the exposition exceeded expectations; so Emilio's floating pods would probably have sunk under the sheer volume of visitors, even if the accessibility issues had been resolved.

These shortcomings notwithstanding, the Ambasz master plan laid down a set of principles in Seville that continue to have relevance for cities in the Age of Information and Ecology. For example, after the terrorist destruction of the World Trade Center, it became clear to a generation of 9/11-sensitized architects that the archaic blast-out-a-hole-and-build mentality of the Robert Moses generation of urban planning in New York was, in itself, a camouflaged form of terrorism. As might be expected, the usual suspects in the real-estate cabal have rammed through a "new" World Trade Center that includes the same ensemble of skyscrapers, parking garages, and enclosed malls as the original version—all conventionally mounted on vast acreages of paving, which are conciliatorily referred to as "people spaces." As every sane urban planner who protested the first WTC plan knew, Port Authority's cannibalistic intervention cut off a number of important Lower Manhattan street connections—including the east/west extension of Fulton, Cortlandt, and Dey Streets and the north/south continuation of Greenwich and Washington Streets. These intrusions physically isolated and economically disrupted five neighborhoods. And, in an area equivalent to the size of Tribeca and Soho combined, hundreds of historic buildings were demolished to make way for the Twin Towers.

Returning to Ambasz's Seville master plan, in relation to the development scenarios for the new World Trade Center, the principal value of his scheme was to offer a compositionally unified system, specifically designed to encourage incremental growth. In downtown Manhattan, this approach would suggest a reconnection of all the streets that formerly linked the neighborhoods, a heightened stimulus for mixed-use development, the abandonment of mega-skyscrapers in favor of smaller, clustered buildings by a variety of architects, the promotion of a sustainable-design agenda, the designation of major areas for parklands, and the inclusion of a strong representation of New York's ethnic and cultural diversity.

From the perspective of urban design, Ambasz's Fukuoka Prefectural International Hall of 1990 is a major contribution to the integration of landscape and architecture, built as part of a politically and socially endorsed enhancement program for community life. The vertical stair-step configuration of the building includes fifteen terraces of lateral and cascading vegetation, with an adjoining public park at grade level. Prior to the completion of this civic center, the citizens of Fukuoka had raised a vociferous protest against the construction of a building that would remove the community's last remaining park. In response, Ambasz doubled the size of the green space, gave civil employees a unique working and recreational environment, and added a "Hanging Gardens of Babylon" attraction to the cityscape. In a unique way, he also achieved a viable twenty-first-century adaptation of the Gothic/Renaissance communicative facade. Instead of depending on the fourteenth-century convention of stationary walls, with narrative sculptured images, Emilio's Fukuoka facade offers a living iconography of organic growth and human interaction. As confirmation of his own philosophy, he sees this structure as the embodiment of "green over gray" in the urban environment. "This building is for me," he writes, "very strong evidence that the prevailing notion — the cities are for buildings and the outskirts are for parks—is a mistaken and narrow-minded idea, only favorable to commercial architects hell-bent to their not so well rewarded task of enriching developers."

I have tended to dismiss Emilio's complaints about the neglect of his work in the American design press as merely indicative of his professional paranoia; but, in the case of the Fukuoka project, I would have to agree that the media blackout has been disgraceful. I simply cannot grasp why our leading design reviews — poverty-stricken for truly original work to feature—steadfastly avoid publishing a building of this significance and visual power. These are the same magazines that provide endless exposure to pallid rip-offs of Chernikov, Melnikov, Tatlin, Mies, and Aalto, or that lavish undue praise on those equally derivative scultural configurations reminescent of Henry Moore and Jean Arp, which are now proliferating as part of the "amoebic form" movement. Unexplainably, although the project is profusely published abroad, I am not aware of a thoughtful analysis of Ambasz's International Hall in a U.S. magazine.

In summarizing my observations concerning the architecture of Emilio Ambasz, I want to mention a few of his recent ideas and images from certain works that have arrested my attention and gained my admiration as significant contributions to progressive thinking in architecture for the new millennium. In the category of community design—using landscape as the main iconographic ingredient—Emilio's 1989 New Town Center in Chiba, Japan, created an entirely new suburban nucleus while taking advantage of a high-speed rail system. Through a combination of vertical tiers of potted trees and glass-enclosed elevated train stations, he changed what could have been just one more anonymous stretch of suburbia into a township of memorable identity. With similar transformational instincts, in 1990 he proposed the adaptive re-use of a series of old industrial buildings by converting their barrel-shaped roofs and most appealing industrial features into the Focchi Shopping Center of Rimini, Italy. As a shade provision, he wrapped the structure in a series of massive ivy-covered screens that mask the unattractive concrete walls with an enveloping greenscape. In many respects, this project has become the most visible example of his green-over-gray design principles.

In a similar way, Ambasz's 1997 Environmental Park Research Laboratories in Turin, Italy, achieve green over gray by integrating twenty-million square feet of enclosed space and the surrounding site as one total landscape experience. Although the ensemble of facilities presents a factorylike appearance, all of the roofs are covered with grass and vegetation; also, the adjacent Dora River is respectfully acknowledged by means of inclined and embankment-like grass walls that appear to emerge from the laboratories themselves.

My main reason for including the three projects above is to credit Emilio's skill in converting normally mundane circumstances into vastly improved living and working environments. This sounds like the most obvious responsibility of any competent architect; but, as I noted before, most designers reject the inclusion of landscape as a remedial and humanizing ingredient in their buildings, while remaining oblivious to the symbolic and socially referential power of trees and plants.

The last two projects I want to discuss are recent and strangely removed from the idealistic imagery one associates with Ambasz's work. While these buildings are polar opposites in terms of category, both structures seem to indicate a few hitherto unrevealed and conflicting elements of irony, humor, and aspirations to penetrate the establishment. In the beginning of this review of Ambasz's oeuvre, I mentioned that I felt the main differences in our approach to architecture were based on the fact that Emilio took the design mission very seriously and I treated it mainly as a supply source for art ideas and/or a means of commentary on cultural phenomena. Obviously, given the signals emitted from some of his most recent works, the complexity of the Ambaszian dialectic continues to unfold.

The truly odd project is Emilio's Barbie Knoll of 1995 in Pasadena, California. The fact that he has pursued this endeavor as a reverential monument to a pop icon—trying to create a Taj Mahal for America's quintessential symbol of chic immaculacy—lends his proposal an edge of farce. On the other hand, it seems to be conceived in total earnest—Emilio calls it "the ecological embodiment of Barbie"—but with the bothersome inference that it can't be serious. No eloquent missionary of the transcendental in architecture would build a Greek forum for a Mattel doll. Yet, here it is—pastoral, elegant, and site-specific, with such participatory features for children as a playground that spans the undulating surfaces of a giant and chastely virginal Barbie, reclining in the desert.

One final project that has intrigued me ever since I first saw it three years ago is Ambasz's massive Monument Tower Offices, designed for Phoenix, Arizona, in 1998. In general configuration and sheer sculptural mass, it seems to be the antithesis of the philosophy he has championed in all of his other work. The building is a thirty-four-story monolith, with layers of horizontal fins that are designed to deflect sunlight and help cool the structure during hot periods in Phoenix. As a result of its truncated forms, the building reflects the craggy severity of the surrounding mountains. According to the plans, the office includes a flexible interior, open to changes that provide tenants with an opportunity to personalize their own spaces. A central plaza opens into the street, while canyon-like atria and double-height elevator lobbies are offered to major tenants.

This is an Ambasz project that definitely awaits completion before there can be any fair critical assessment. Based on the model, I have my own list of questions. Although the sculptural features of the building are admirable, the overall effect is a little too close for comfort to those Baroque excesses now identified with the work of Eisenman and Gehry (and I thought Emilio didn't want to be a 1950s abstract sculptor!). Additionally, I wonder about the quality of inside vistas, as seen through all of those thinly sliced windows. Given Ambasz's environmental commitments, I also sense that the sustainability rationales for such a massive structure may be as problematic as those of Ken Yeang and Norman Foster, when they display labyrinthine air-flow charts to justify some fifty-story tower in glass and aluminum. And, finally, a few of my aesthetic reservations concerning the Phoenix Tower are based on my own method for evaluating sculptural buildings—in particular, how does it meet the "pedestal test"? I developed this means of assessment a few years ago, describing it as follows: "The pedestal test confronts that endless twentieth-century debate concerning the differences between *art* and *design* and helps to sort out *object,* versus *contextual,* sensibilities when applied to buildings. This evaluation proposes that good buildings (in model form)—particularly those with proclaimed environmental ambitions—can be weeded out from the bad examples, based on whether they look more convincing installed on their intended sites, or mounted on exhibition plinths. In architecture, the pedestal test seems to indicate that if a building looks better as a model on a base, there is a good chance it should probably stay there."

It isn't my intention to close these remarks on Ambasz's work with a negative critique or litany of questions concerning the consistency of his philosophy. It is my purpose to conclude with a balanced review. Admittedly, my apprehensions concerning the environmental implications of his Monument Tower Offices may be nothing more than my own failure to understand Emilio's mercurial personality and diversionary experiments. Also, given the level of environmental aberrations associated with architecture during the past decade, Ambasz stands out as a hero of green. His range and quality of innovation bears witness to his commitment. To mention just a short list; he is at the cutting edge of:

— **Integrating architecture with context**
— **Incorporating earth-centric and cosmological references as imagery**
— **Challenging the status quo of neo-modernism**

— Exploring the realm of invisible architecture
— Designing for a postindustrial era of home computers and verdant suburbias
— Encouraging the adaptive reuse of existing buildings
— Setting new standards for incremental growth and change (including "contraction") as the foundation for a new agenda in urban planning

At a time in history when environmental alarms have reached the highest decibel levels (a pinnacle of warning, that is, before a silencing disaster takes control) the work of Ambasz and many other green designers is providing some hope for the cause. Planting gardens and fusing buildings with their contexts is only a small fraction of the ecological challenge; but it is at least productive, healthy, symbolic, and persuasive as a reminder for the public. At the opposite extreme, the urgency of sane environmental policies, the search for alternative sources of energy, a greater investment in conservation technology, and the maintenance of ecological diversity cannot be overestimated. The crisis is real. Harvard biologist E. O. Wilson has reported: "If present measurements of habitat destruction are accurate, the world may be losing 18,000 species a year, many of them unclassified and unexamined by scientists. Others put the figure as high as 40,000 per year. But whatever the exact number, species fallout is expected to rise dramatically as plant and animal populations are forced into dwindling islands of habitat in a sea of human industrial and agricultural development." With a similar message in 1970, biologist Barry Commoner told an audience of students at Northwestern University, "We are in a period of grace, we have time—perhaps one generation—in which to save the environment from the final effects of the violence we have already done to it." His reference to a generation of grace has now long passed.

Within the perilous scenario described by these leading biologists, it is tactically and intellectually questionable to credit architecture with any environmental virtues. It is particularly ironic that, from the beginning of Barry Commoner's "grace period," starting in 1970, the design of buildings by leading architects has never been more wasteful, bombastic, egocentric, and impractical. In general, the construction of human habitat—as much as flooding our rivers with industrial wastes and drilling for oil in Alaska—is as far from an ecologically favorable enterprise as any profession can get. For this reason, Emilio Ambasz's combination of dialectician, pragmatist, and poetic idealist is well positioned to help lead a new generation of designers to face the environmental challenge head-on.

Throughout the many years I have known Emilio, he has valiantly maintained the courage of his convictions. In a letter to me last year he wrote, "I always knew that my pursuit of alternative models for a better future would be rejected, mocked, or, at best, I would be left alone to bark to the moon. But I always remembered that the madman who threw stones at the moon never hit her, but, at the end, no one else in the village could throw these as high. I still feel idealistic. I cannot say that I am hopeful because by nature I'm a pessimist. (I have been treated for congenital depression since I was fourteen. I come, on the maternal side, from a documented long line of these sorts.) Whenever I go forward and fight on, I have to also fight within myself a pervasive awareness of the pointlessness of it all. But I devotedly believe that the task of inventing better futures may stagger the imagination and may paralyze hope, but we cannot relinquish this holy call."

If anyone can succeed in so daunting a mission, Emilio will pull it off and realize his dream to "build a house for the first man of a culture that has not yet arrived."

ITALIAN DESIGN &
THE NEW POLITICAL LANDSCAPE
Felicity D. Scott

The question was gaining urgency in the late 1960s: is there, or could there any longer be, a utopian dimension to contemporary architecture? Faced with the increasingly totalized condition of late capitalism, how could architecture, already so immersed in the extant socioeconomic and political apparatus and its technical correlates, maintain any semblance of a critical and transformative capacity in postindustrial society?[1] How, with the emergence of the third machine age—the information age—and rapid changes in conditions of production as well as social and urban relations, could the discipline continue to project an image of a better future? Transformative aspirations had motivated the oppositional strategies of the historical avant-garde and the progressive ideals of its modernist counterparts. But by the end of the 1960s, as disenchantment grew with the capacity of recent oppositional tactics—from megastructures and inflatables to student insurrections—to effect structural change, any critical or utopian vocation began to seem not only idealistic but nearly entirely foreclosed by the machinations of a society of consumption and control.[2]

Such questions were historically pressing and continued to haunt contemporary radical European practices in the late 1960s and early '70s, notably those known in Italy as Architettura Radicale.[3] However, they were not at the center of American architectural discourse at that time, which had taken a distinctly post-utopian turn, focusing instead on another, related set of problematics: that of architecture's integration into, versus autonomy from, the prevailing social, economic, technical, and aesthetic forces of late capitalism.[4] It is as a strategic counterpoint to this context that Emilio Ambasz's work at the Museum of Modern Art from late 1968 until July 1976 emerges as of particular interest.[5] Transgressing dominant discursive and institutional demarcations within the U.S., Ambasz's curatorial work pointed to prospects for a politically engaged mode of design, prospects that, like those of his radical European counterparts, remained haunted by a utopian conviction, albeit significantly recast from earlier-twentieth-century precursors.

Ambasz arrived at MoMA having recently graduated from Princeton University's School of Architecture, where he had also taught briefly. He was, additionally, a fellow at the Institute for Architecture and Urban Studies (IAUS) in New York. Yet if his work was not easily situated along the axis of integration-or-autonomy on which contemporary American polemics were aligned, the underlying problematics of that work *were* related to the discursive frameworks and institutional politics informing those debates (which I will outline below). Ambasz approached the increasingly totalized, if fragmented, historical condition—which would come to be known as postmodernism—via an investigation of nondeterminist models of social and institutional transformation. Nowhere was this recasting of the role of the architect more evident than in his 1972 exhibition *Italy: The New Domestic Landscape,* which presented an array of design objects and specially commissioned "environments" within a field of highly articulated and politicized discourses. These objects and environments—work by Italian radicals—thus emerged as a critical alternative to the mainstream.

It is beyond the scope of this study to do justice to Ambasz's extensive work at MoMA, let alone the complex intersection of institutions at which this work was situated.[6] But we can understand many aspects of his contribution to American architectural discourse in the 1970s by focusing on *Italy: The New Domestic Landscape.* The critical stakes of this show are perhaps best demonstrated through a "dialog" with Marxist historian Manfredo Tafuri. Tafuri contributed an essay to the exhibition catalog, and he mentioned the MoMA show and the visibility it lent to Architettura Radicale many times during the 1970s. When his *History of Italian Architecture, 1944–1985* appeared in 1986, however, little over a page addressed the work of the radical practices included in the exhibition.[7] While he had always been critical of the work of groups such as Archizoom and Superstudio, Tafuri's decision to minimize the work's place in his history was symptomatic of a larger set of concerns and throws into relief the stakes of the political and architectural paradigms at play.

If utopian questions had ceased to haunt the imagination of many American architects in the 1970s, this was not (as demonstrated by Architettura Radicale) simply the product of their proximity to late capitalist forces.[8] Moreover, the poles of integration and autonomy, although indicative of how architects were positioned relative to each other, were not accurate measures of each side's critical and political engagement with that historical condition. Neither pole forged models of transformation. What they demonstrated more effectively were alternative lines of escape from the recent legacy of modernist strategies. Some background is relevant: Although late modernist orthodoxies retained a stronghold on mainstream practice in America during the 1950s and '60s, theoretically minded architects began to turn from earlier functional-ist paradigms and to discourses and techniques of the behavioral and social sciences, systems theory, and operational research. From the work of Kevin Lynch to that of Christopher Alexander and beyond, this new generation of functionalists sought models, or rather design methodologies, for regaining control over this increasingly complex historical condition.[9]

By the end of the sixties, however, such positivist inquiries were eclipsed by investigations into other modes of communication, what George Baird and Charles Jencks identified as "meaning in architecture."[10] Their 1969 anthol-ogy of this name marked a turning point, soon after which vanguard architec-tural debates no longer revolved around technology, information theory, and design methodology but around European discourses of semiology and struc-turalism. The American encounter with semiology was quickly divided: the revival of historicist, popular, and vernacular referents marked one side and the embrace of linguistic theory, and correlate investigations of architecture as an autonomous language (a closed system) marked the other.[11] This division was encapsulated in the decade's most visible polemic—the "Grays" versus the "Whites." It was in response to this Gray/White nexus that Tafuri advanced his melancholy summation of American architecture in the mid-1970s: even if the Whites' pursuit of autonomy involved an oppositional refusal of the present, a continuation of avant-garde negation, both sides of this dialectic—capitulation and withdrawal—remained caught within the now-inescapable vicissitudes of capitalism. Both were, according to Tafuri, symptoms of an ever more pernicious alignment with those forces.[12]

Ambasz recognized similar symptoms in the poles of the Gray/White debate, yet his response was quite different. Central to his work at MoMA during this period was inquiring how designers might act as agents of transformation *within* what he referred to as the "technological milieu," how they might forge a critical practice not autonomous from, but somehow inside, a dispersed system that was inextricably connected to the pervasive administrative and commercial apparatus. In this risky alignment with the forces of capitalism, the stakes of such an engagement were high: for without some notion of architecture's capacity for active critical encounter with historical forces, the discipline faced an unprecedented impasse. Such an impasse was the source of Tafuri's melancholy and betrayed, as Fredric Jameson argues, "some kinship with Adorno's late and desperate concept of a purely 'negative dialectic.'"[13] Jameson pointed to the "paralyzing and asphyxiating sense of the futility of any architectural or urbanistic innovation" in Tafuri's thinking, a situation in which the "increasing closure of Late Capitalism" left only the unlikely prospect of total social revolution as a solution to the crisis of aesthetic practice.[14] In search of an alternative to Tafuri's resolutely negative position, Jameson turned to Antonio Gramsci as the author of a "positive" or "anticipatory" strategy that was not simply reformist, noting parenthetically that the institutionalization of Gramsci's thought in the Italian Communist Party (ICP) might have made it unpalatable to Italian radicals. Ambasz, however, found an alternative anticipatory paradigm in the diverse and often irreconcilable discourses and strategies of Architettura Radicale, strategies that—following a key formulation of the Italian Autonomia movement—were frequently predicated on a relation to capitalism that was "inside and against." As opposed to Tafuri, who saw the risk of engagement as too great, simply producing an ever more effective moment of technological integration into the commodified landscape, Ambasz saw it as a necessary wager.

Ambasz had begun to theorize a model of anticipatory structures for the postindustrial era prior to *Italy: New Domestic Landscape*, most notably in "Manhattan: Capital of the Twentieth Century." Written in 1969, the article appeared in a number of prominent publications in 1971 and was included in the "Design Program" sent to participants of the Italian show.[15] The title made reference to Walter Benjamin's famous exposé of 1935 from the *Arcades Project*, "Paris: Capital of the Nineteenth Century," a translation of which had appeared in *Perspecta* along with Ambasz's "Formulation of a Design Discourse."[16] Indeed, the epigraph to Ambasz's Manhattan text was taken from Ben Brewster's introduction to that translation.[17] Benjamin's text addressed the nineteenth-century conjunction of the emergence of iron construction, commodity display, and the ascension of the bourgeoisie, with reference to architectural sites such as the Parisian arcades and the increasingly privatized domestic *intérieur*. Ambasz would revisit Benjamin's structures of mediation by looking at the impact upon architecture and design of economic, technological, and social relations forged within a later stage of capitalism.[18]

Ambasz described Manhattan as symptomatic of the postindustrial age: "Unencumbered by permanent memory, and more interested in becoming than in being," Manhattan, he wrote, could "be seen as the city of that second technological revolution brought about by the development of processes for producing and controlling information rather than just energy." Beyond being a product of information technology, Manhattan, Ambasz argued, manifested a cybernetic organizational structure: it could thus be read, allegorically, as a series of interconnecting "networks":

> If beheld as an infrastructure for the processing and exchange of matter, energy, and information, Manhattan may be seen, either as the overwrought roof of a subterranean physical grid of subway tunnels and train stations, automobile passages, postal tubes, sewage chambers, water and gas pipes, power wires, telephone, telegraph, television and computer lines; or, conversely, as the datum plane of an aerial lattice of walking paths, automobile routes, flight patterns, wireless impulses, institutional liaisons, and ideological webs.[19]

Along with this network structure came a level of indeterminacy and an inherent, systematic capacity for transformation. The networks, Ambasz explained, had "been repeatedly charged, on and off, with different meanings." This reconceptualization of the city had a paradigmatic value: "Manhattan's infrastructure would emerge—in all the complexity of its physical organization, the capacity of its input-output mechanism, and the versatility of its control device—as the most representative urban artifact of our culture."

Ambasz's tale did not end at the analytic level, but as with much of his work at MoMA, it harbored a "prospective" function. Manhattan, Ambasz proposed, was not only a physical urban artifact but could be conceived of (and even deployed) as an abstract diagram of open-ended relations. Imagining the city's infrastructure freed from the constraints of geographical location, he proposed that such a diagram could be "transferred" to other locations, from the San Francisco Bay, to the African plains, to the Great Wall of China. The city thus had the status of what Ambasz termed a "structure." Following the semiotics of Charles Sanders Peirce, Ambasz's interest in such a structure was that it operated at the level of the "icon," a semiotic figure that functioned through a relation of similitude between signifier and signified, thereby distinguishing it from the fixed meaning or conventional rules of a symbol. According to Ambasz's rather idiosyncratic reading of Peirce, this meant that such a structure functioned at an open-ended and pre-symbolic stage of meaning and could thus act as a "new beginning," one that implicitly challenged the notion of a fixed norm or transcendental signified.[20]

Having posited this capacity for Manhattan, Ambasz went on to speculate on the form of an actual city created out of such a transfer operation. Taking considerable license with Marxist terminology, he pondered how the "super-structure" of this Manhattan Transfer might be supplemented in order to provide spaces and programs that would themselves be subject to a continual process of transformation.[21] As he explained, "The outcome of such an under-taking may be agitational, and render, if not actual proposals of superstruc-tures, at least an explicit Inventory of Qualities of urban existence toward a yet-to-be-defined 'City of Open Presents.'" He specified two types of elements that might give rise to such qualities: first were "surviving fragments of mem-ory" and second were newly invented (designed) attachments to the infrastruc-ture. The first category included Bologna's arcades, Ludwig Mies van der Rohe's Barcelona Pavilion, John Soane's house, Baudelaire's "fleeting instants," Michael Heizer's "land marks," and Joan Littlewood's Fun Palace, designed with Cedric Price. Even if initially having the status of personal creations, such "irreducible fragments" of cultural memory had, Ambasz proposed, produced collective or transindividual values that fed back into the cultural system. Moreover, this process, in which the artifacts were torn from their contexts and grafted allegorically into new ones, would open those fragments up to "new meanings." [22] That is, it would open them up to difference.

The second category, invention, accorded with Ambasz's belief that the designer's role was to forge new icons, transactional devices that would be set out in a provisional state in order to create a similar process of evaluation and feedback. With regard to the "constructive powers" of such designs, he explained: "Insofar as they question the context of the Present, they assign it new meanings; insofar as they propose alternative states, they restructure it."[23]

Ambasz's formulation was critical of futurology. The City of Open Presents was not identical to the already existing "emerging city"—of which Manhattan was an instance—since it would "not merely unfold from the present" but had to be created. Even if it was changing, the emerging city, as with any reformist ideal, remained tied to extant institutions and systems of thought. Indeed, as Ambasz argued, its structure and processes were "isomorphic" with them. An "open present," in contrast, would arise only when that emergence across time was altered by "structural transformations" forged through new interdisciplinary institutions. In this sense, those structural transformations required what he was then formulating under the title *Institutions for a Post-Technological Society: The Universitas Project*, and they would only arise when design did not determine a final form but merely set forth an open structure.[24] What becomes increasingly clear is that the Manhattan text (as with other of Ambasz's fables) aimed to serve as an indeterminate and multiplicitous mediating structure, hence its inclusion in the Design Program. In this sense it can be read as having affinities with a Bergsonian or even Deleuzian virtuality. For it is precisely from such a virtual structure or multiplicity that numerous, differentiated actualizations might be created without being predetermined. The City of Open Presents was to be a city unfolding in duration through a process of "creative evolution."[25]

Ambasz's model of immanent transformation was at odds with theoretical formulations then impacting American architectural discourse, notably through the IAUS and later its journal, *Oppositions*. Ambasz had been involved with the institute from its founding as an independent research body in New York in 1967 and, as mentioned, was a fellow at the time of his appointment to MoMA. When "Manhattan: Capital of the Twentieth Century" was republished in *Oppositions* in 1974, differences between Ambasz's intellectual framework and those of the editors were marked. Although included in the Theory section of the journal, Ambasz's "Working Fables," according to Mario Gandelsonas's introduction, were not theoretical. They "neither aim[ed] to be part of the creative process nor to be a theoretical explication," and their inclusion was to be understood, rather, as revealing their false consciousness through "the ideological use of poetics."[26] When viewed through the lens of a structural analysis that read architecture as a closed, autonomous system, Ambasz's fables seemed to play into an ideological and political trap. From Gandelsonas's perspective, the texts operated at the level of metaphor, and since Ambasz had not articulated architecture's autonomy from the existing capitalist system, they served merely as a "mask by which to facilitate the consumption of [society's] economic, political or ideological products." Moreover, they seemed to Gandelsonas deterministic, ultimately implying a "general principle of conduct."[27]

Gandelsonas was, of course, correct in arguing that Ambasz had not forged a critical distance from the capitalist milieu. For Ambasz, this was precisely the point. His fables aimed to point to other strategies of negotiating and even of transforming the capitalist system from within. Furthermore, his approach cannot easily be subsumed into what Gandelsonas read as "ideological utopias developed in the sixties, be they formal, communicational or related to a systems approach." Aspects of those ideological utopias, especially those forged through communications and systems theory, *had* informed Ambasz's eclectic mix of interests. Yet his theoretical apparatus was also marked by critical tropes that problematized the organicism, and even the logic, of assimilation that Gandelsonas found troublesome in earlier experimental engagements with communication technology. These were of course practices that *Oppositions* refused, as evidenced in Peter Eisenman's parodic introduction to Martin Pawley's 1976 article on Archigram.[28] If much of the techno-optimism of the 1960s had rightly been revealed as aligned with the controlling forces of capitalism, not all experimental investigations assumed the same relation to new technologies, and not all remained blind to the dystopic counterpart of technological progress. That Ambasz believed it was somehow possible to operate through such an immanent paradigm without simply preserving the status quo would be the wager of his 1972 exhibition of Italian design. Not only was Manhattan offered to Italy as a model of transformation in his fable, but Italian paradigms would feedback into Manhattan with quite an impact.

Designed and curated by Ambasz, *Italy: The New Domestic Landscape* opened to the public on May 26, 1972, and remained on view until September 11.[29] Two years in the making, it included 180 domestic objects exhibited in the MoMA garden, along with eleven specially commissioned, gallery-installed Environments. In addition, as Adolfo Natalini noted when reviewing the show, there was an abundance of "information" on display.[30] Pointing to the exhibition's allegorical character, Ambasz argued repeatedly that although it focused on Italian design, the issues raised by the work were of concern to other industrial societies. Italy was being presented as a "micro-model" of a universal condition then impacting design and its relation to production, a condition that had led to a "growing distrust of objects of consumption."[31] Italy provided a poignant case study not only as a "dominant product design force" but as a critical and theoretical force as well. The Italians, Ambasz contended, "have a high level of critical consciousness as to what design activity means in terms of the design profession and in terms of society. Nowhere else is this discourse so explicit, is it so well articulated, and is the situation so well crystallized."[32] That discourse—what Natalini referred to as information—was in fact very much part of both the curatorial ambition and the display leading one reviewer to note that the "Supershow" was "uncomfortably didactic."[33] The exhibition was even structured according to the discursive factions of the Italian scene, and substantial space was dedicated to audiovisual presentations in an attempt to explicate their positions for the visitor.

On the occasion of his appointment as curator of design in 1970, Ambasz explained that along with certain forms of experimental design, architectural theory had all but eclipsed traditional modes of practice as the most cogent site of advancing the discipline.[34] Bringing together the critical, retrospective function of his newly founded Program on Environmental Design—a program he directed under the umbrella of the Department of Architecture and Design—with a postulative or prospective one, he also announced a book series entitled *Prospectives of Design* that would publish "the most important theoretical writing of the last decade."[35] While this book series did not ensue, we can see the anthology of historical and critical articles in the *Italy: The New Domestic Landscape* catalog as demonstrating the importance Ambasz attributed to theory.

The remarkable presence, even excessiveness, of discourse found both throughout the catalog and in the exhibition itself was an important component of the show. It was almost as if Ambasz were curating the texts in the extensive audiovisual displays, treating them like objects of exhibition and translating them into fictive, often spectacularized images. At the same time, the "material" exhibits were saturated by texts.[36] In a Benjaminian turn, one not unlike that he visited upon the "surviving fragments of memory" in his Manhattan text, Ambasz strategically appropriated both the objects and texts. If such an operation was to a degree the product of suspending such objects within the institutional framework of a museum, Ambasz mobilized those

Shipping and displa
containers for Obje
section of *Italy: The
Domestic Landscap*
designed with Thom
Czarnowski. On dis
the MoMA garden.

objects, removed from their functional context, to distinct ends. As we shall
see, this powerful allegorical procedure can be traced throughout the exhibition, from the image/text relations of the audiovisual sessions to the installation strategies and beyond, recasting curatorial and institutional practices with
a political force not to be repeated at MoMA. Before we turn to its reception
and to an explication of Ambasz's critical project, the show itself warrants a
detailed description.

Interpretation began prior to entering the exhibition proper. An Orientation
Gallery offered a 3-D model of the exhibition to incoming visitors, supplemented with wall text and even a leaflet demarcating the groupings within
exhibition areas. Then, before entering the garden, visitors were presented with
a small, triangular screening room in which a twelve-minute rear-projected film
faced onto rows of luminescent white seats.[37] Written and directed by Ambasz,
the film had a dense voice-over outlining the intentions and premises of the
Objects section of the exhibition, accompanied by images of "elaborate scaf-
folding and out-of-context objects arranged in an Italian shopping arcade—
the Galleria Vittorio Emanuele, Milan."[38] The overtly contemporary design
objects seemed strangely out of place in the nineteenth-century arcade, but
Benjamin's earlier allegorical reading of these industrial structures as emergent
capitalist spaces would find a twentieth-century counterpart in Ambasz's subsequent installation.

ipping and display
or Objects
taly: The New
andscape. 1972.
th Thomas
. On display in
garden.

The design objects, including furniture, lighting fixtures, flatware, china, electrical goods, and so on were installed in pine and Plexiglas crates designed by Ambasz and Thomas Czarnowski as vehicles for both shipping and display. The sides were hinged and could be lowered for transportation or stabilized in an upright position to create tall towers, revealing Plexiglas windows through which objects and their grainy backdrop of photographic blowups could be seen. Colored, hemispherical Plexiglas lights were affixed to the outside. Approximately forty crates were arranged as a grid on the upper terrace of the garden, with eight others organized more loosely on the lower level.

Although the crates formed a stunning installation in the MoMA garden, many reviewers were critical of their formal and organizational associations.[39] Ada Louise Huxtable, critic for the *New York Times*, described the effect as "a military array of monumental 'shipping cases,' row on row."[40] By far the most common associations, however, were to sites of commerce. "According to one opening-night visitor," Huxtable recalled, silently citing Arthur Drexler, the arrangement resembled "a supermarket at Karnak."[41] Writing for *Print* magazine, Rose deNeve pointed to a more proximate referent. To her, the crates "created the illusion of a giant and grotesque Fifth Avenue of Italian design," an effect that led to the suspension of their "historical and philosophical" import in favor of visitors "simply be[ing] dazzled by their colors and forms."[42]

For art critic Gregory Battcock, too, the serial arrangement resembled nothing so much as "rows of shop windows." This gave rise to "the feeling that, though one has paid to enter the store (the museum) one is back out on the street again." This collapse of institutional space with the space of commerce was a practice hardly new to the museum's presentation of design, yet for Battcock it had a particular effect.[43] Although making the objects appear more accessible, it in fact led to "a kind of distance between object and viewer," since the arrangement did not produce a sense of immersion but rather protected the museum visitor from "a realistic confrontation with the radical design."[44] In Benjamin's analysis of artwork, such a prophylactic distance is characteristic not only of the aura given off by authenticity but also of the false auratic quality given off by commodities.[45] Doubly mediated by the museum and the Plexiglas windows, Ambasz's arrangement extended the dialectical structure Benjamin had read into the arcade—in which the relation of interior and exterior was confused—to the twentieth-century shop window.

While reviewers seemed either bemused or troubled by this connection to commerce, the commodification of the social realm was at the nexus of critical questions Ambasz hoped to raise. He later pointed unapologetically to this affinity, noting that beyond the functional aspects, "on a second level, the crates created a micro urban environment, providing the public with shopping avenues that seduce with their views of designed artifacts."[46] As Huxtable acknowledged, this was not simply a reiteration of MoMA's earlier program of selling good design to the American public but a "complete departure": "The objects in the garden are not merely enshrined," she argued. "They, too, have meanings."[47] While the objects were avowedly seductive, the curator had both captured the visitors' attention and suspended viewers within a critical discourse (what Huxtable referred to as "meanings").[48] The arrangement foregrounded relations between commodity fetishism and contemporary domesticity, situating those relations as integral to the technological milieu and also an arena requiring scrutiny.

Natalini offered another reference to commodification. Invoking the mausoleal quality of museums, he referred to the crates as "pharaonic chambers." He then shifted metaphors to suggest that Italian design had been "shut up in the wooden towers of a parody of Manhattan." It was a specific parody to which he no doubt pointed—The Eleventh Ideal City: The City of the Splendid Houses by his own group, Superstudio. A caricature of the commercialism and superficiality of contemporary urban domesticity, this was published as part of

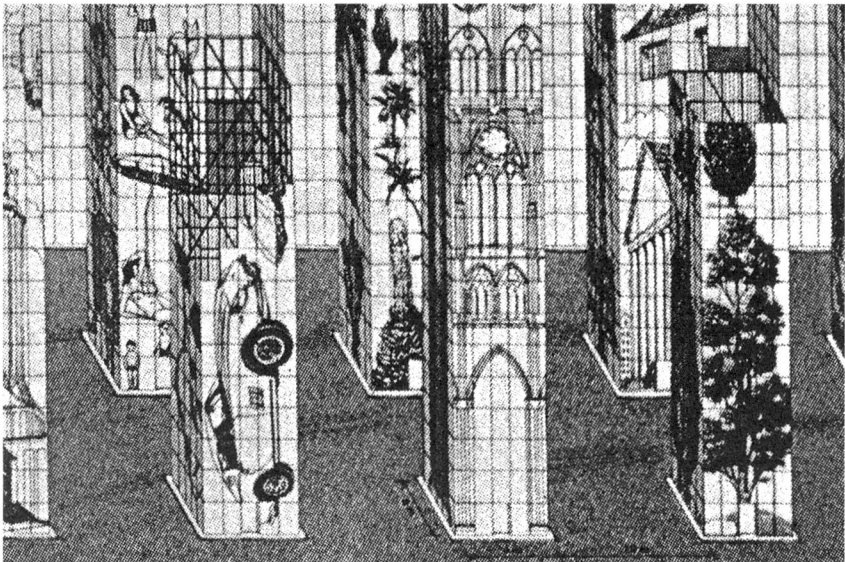

"Twelve Cautionary Tales for Christmas: Premonitions of the Mystical Rebirth of Urbanism."[49] A vivid precedent for Rem Koolhaas's own "retroactive" City of the Captive Globe, the parable was comprised of a Manhattan-like grid of tall towers each asserting their commodified difference through the panels in which they were sheathed. As the accompanying text explained, the citizens labored in factories, producing the metal components and silk-screened plastic panels that were continuously brought and fed back into the decoration of their houses in a delirious drive to consume and embellish.

Within Ambasz's grid, the objects were distributed "to illustrate the various intellectual design positions which have evolved in Italy in the last 10 years."[50] (This also resonated with the distributive logic of Manhattan in which particular programs congregate to create points of density.) There were three primary, if rather enigmatic, categories: Conformist, Reformist, and Contestatory, each responding differently to the condition of design within postindustrial society. This mode of classification was not entirely self-explanatory and, despite the audiovisual presentations, many critics, and we might assume other visitors, remained puzzled.

The conformist category covered the vast majority of exhibits, including "objects chosen for formal, technical or typological reasons."[51] Such explorations, Ambasz argued, did not question the status quo or engage the sociocultural context and as such offered no critique. Their aims were, rather, confined to "exploring the aesthetic quality of single objects—a chair, a table,

a bookcase—that answer the traditional needs of domestic life."[52] In the catalog Ambasz polemically referred to "designers who conceive of their work as
an autonomous activity responsible only to itself," therein implicitly extending
the dialogue between Italy and New York. If some members of the IAUS had
mobilized the notion of autonomy to claim a critical space for architecture, a
space outside of the vicissitudes of commercialism, Ambasz (like Tafuri) cast
this as conservative form-making.

The reformist category included objects whose forms were "derived from
or motivated by semantic operations upon established socio-cultural meanings,
such as 'back to nature,' pop art, anthropomorphism, etc."[53] These designers
were "motivated by a profound concern for the designer's role in a society that
fosters consumption as one means of inducing individual happiness." Yet
rather than attempting to transform social and institutional paradigms (as
would utopian projects), these designers had turned to rhetorical operations

on sociolinguistic codes—revival, ironic manipulation, kitsch, recycling, the embrace of ritual, formlessness, etc.—to comment on that condition.[54] While the conformist position was aligned with the Whites, the reformist position resonated strongly with the polemic of the Grays. Thus articulating the divide of American debates, Ambasz's descriptions of reformists ironically pointed to the pop architecture of Robert Venturi and Denise Scott-Brown as well as the postmodern sensibility of Charles Moore and the Yale school.

For Ambasz, neither the conformist nor the reformist attitudes were up to the task of transforming consumer society; both were merely "enacting the role of voyeurs of the technological dream."[55] The third category, contestatory, entailed two further attitudes that did not point to American counterparts. The first was "a 'moratorium' position and an absolute refusal to take part in the present socioindustrial system." Adopting an anti-object position, these designers recast their role as political action, philosophical postulation, or total withdrawal from design. For Ambasz, such a response ultimately fell into a trap of "passive abstention," and he distinguished it from a second form of contestation, one closer to his own ideals of active critical participation. Here were to be found objects conceived in close relation to their users as "an ensemble of interrelated processes, whose interaction results in constantly changing patterns of relationships."[56] Providing an "open-ended manner of use," such objects could "be offensive, because they refuse to adopt a fixed shape or to serve as reference to anything." Examples included the Sacco beanbag chair designed by Pierro Gatti, Cesare Paolini, and Franco Teodoro (1969), Joe Colombo's "tube chair of nesting and combinable elements" (1969), and Bruno Munari's *Abitacolo* [Cockpit] "habitable structure" (1971), each of which included a set of adjustable or transformable parts. Ambasz understood the nonformal attributes of these new objects as tied to transformations in the social realm: "Imagine trying to be stuffy," he remarked in 1970, "while slouching in a bean bag chair."[57]

The form of contestation in this context might well have remained opaque to most visitors. The catalog, however, offered further clues, indicating that the term *contestatory* most likely came from Henri Lefebvre, a speaker at Ambasz's Universitas symposium the previous year. Ambasz quoted the following remarks from Lefebvre's book *The Explosion, Marxism, and the French Upheaval*: "Contestation . . . rejects the ideology which views the passive acts of consumption as conducive to happiness, and the purely visual preoccupation with pure spectacle as conducive to pleasure."[58] Within Ambasz's project this was taken to mean that objects of daily consumption might also no longer just be passively consumed. Rather, the domestic realm was positioned as a site of introducing "forms and scripts" from the larger public realm, a space able to respond, given the right equipment, to "our desire for continuous participation in the self-shaping and self-management of everyday existence." The "environmental ensembles" on display were believed to enable such forms of participation, as distinct from passive consumption, and they provided the model for the commissioned—or, in Ambasz's words, the "provoked"—environments.[59]

Prefaced by another audiovisual presentation, the entrance to the environments was "marked by a letter-by-letter, teletype message, videotaped and projected on a screen above the viewer."[60] The four-minute text sequence presented the Specific and General Considerations of the design program initially sent to participants which, Ambasz argued, would have been overlooked if presented at the exhibition in ordinary written format.[61] Citing a spectacular precedent, he noted that the aim was "to present it letter-by-letter in lights, like the Allied Chemical news bulletin at Times Square." Ambasz thus appealed to the visual training of the contemporary observer and while so doing recast the nature of the message such a billboard might have offered.

The design program set out both physical and conceptual parameters for the installations, from overall dimensions to the requirement of a four-to-five-minute film (to be shown on a television set) that depicted "the ceremonies and the modes of use contemplated" by the designers for their environments.[62] Staged as a departure from the "prototypical solutions" of the so-called heroic period of modern architecture, the installations were called upon to propose "microenvironments" that facilitated "microevents," the latter understood as "the succession of constant and new experiences, conceptual and perceptual, that occur and recur between today and tomorrow."[63] The general considerations of the design program took their intellectual coordinates from the Universitas project (and even some of the texts, such as Ambasz's reading of Manhattan) and recast them to address domestic, rather than pedagogical, institutions. Avowedly eclectic, the brief, he claimed, was "not part of a precise ideological sequence, but rather a collage of related thoughts."[64] That collage reiterated Ambasz's strategy, already staged in the Universitas project, of bringing together distinctly Anglo-American forms of behavioral psychology, systems theory, and semiotics with a heterogeneous mixture of European philosophy. It was accompanied by an anthology of writings on behavioral and environmental psychology, which also included Aldo van Eyck's contribution to the ninth CIAM and Martin Pawley's essay "The Time House."[65] In addition to being sent to invited participants, the design program served as the basis for a competition for designers under the age of thirty-five.[66] Ensuring the textual foundation of the environments, the design program exemplified the curatorial strategy.

Like the objects, the environments had their own taxonomic system: Commentary, Pro-Design, and Counter-Design. Functioning as a prologue and situated in its own category—Commentary—was Gaetano Pesce's *Archaeological Environment*. The brown-plastic-surfaced environment was installed in a liftwell and ironically staged as the postapocalyptic discovery of a small subterranean city from a previous millennium (from "The Period of the Great Contamination"). Also on view was a fragment of film supposedly found at the archeological site that conveyed images of "family life." Opening-night reviews recounted the installation's popularity, noting long lines of visitors waiting to put on special soft shoes to enter the surrealistic space.

Next came seven Pro-Design environments that demonstrated "a commitment to design as a problem-solving activity, capable of formulating, in physical terms, solutions to problems encountered in the natural and socio-cultural milieu."[67] Included were three House Environments and four Mobile Environments, each of which, we are told, responded to new notions of privacy and territoriality. The House category included Gae Aulenti's molded red plastic architectonic elements, which could be multiply rearranged; Joe Colombo's compact *Total Furnishing Unit*, made up of four independent, reorganizable, and predominantly plastic components; and Ettore Sottsass's serial system of gray plastic container units on wheels, intended as neutral, pre-prototypes that could be filled in with a domestic program and rearranged. Participating in a rhetoric related to the Counter-Design section, Sottsass claimed that the "uncute" forms provided a type of resistance to the commodity fetishism of postindustrial society, that they were "a kind of orgy of the use of plastic taken as a material which allows an almost complete deconditioning process from the interminable chain of psycho-erotic self-indulgence concerning 'possession.'"[68]

The Mobile category included: Mario Bellini's green *Kar-a-Sutra*, a mobile environment of sensorial pleasure; Richard Sapper and Marco Zanuso's aggregational, transportable, recycled, and refitted freight containers which, they claimed, were suitable for provisional living quarters (for mobile workers,

tourist colonies, or "communities of rescue workers carrying out first-aid operations in areas struck by catastrophe"); and, finally, Alberto Rosselli's *Mobile House*, a gray and blue aluminum capsule, expandable in four directions.

In contrast to these Pro-Design environments, the Counter-Design proposals harbored a distinct refusal of the fixed, prototypical solutions cast as the aim of modernist design. Although providing installations, each group took the opportunity of exhibiting at MoMA "to emphasize the need for a renewal of philosophical discourse and social and political involvement as a way to bring about structural changes in society."[69]

Archizoom presented an empty room in the middle of which hung a microphone acting as a speaker. Emanating voices alternated between dystopic accounts of the end of objects and individuated notions of utopia. "Not a single utopia, then, but an infinity of utopias, as many as there are listeners," the text proclaimed, indicating the refusal to project a normative ideal. They also made reference to their "scientific study of the problem of the house and of the city," famously articulated as the *No-Stop City* project and published the previous year.[70] Superstudio too offered a "reappraisal of the possibilities of life without objects." The main volume of their environment was darkened, and the black felt that lined the gallery continued inside to cover the floor and ceiling,

Installation shot of environments in *Ita[Domestic Landscap[* In the photo on the[Marco Zanuso and [Sapper's project is foreground, Alberto *Mobile House* is on Mario Bellini's *Kar-a[* at rear.

with corners demarcated by luminescent lines. Raised on a platform within this space was a smaller cube fabricated from one-way mirrors, its floor lined with a checkered grid of laminated plastic representing a continuous infra-structure network of energy and communication systems. Looking inside, one saw the interior space of that cube infinitely reflected. Out of this continuous grid emerged a set of life-support terminals—air, heat, water, food, communication—including a television monitor presenting *Superface*, a short film containing images of a technologically enhanced life in a continuous state of nomadism, a life entailing the "reduction of objects to neutral, disposable elements."[71]

Ugo La Pietra presented a "didactic box." Triangular in section, it was constructed of plastic laminated panels and mesh screens onto which was projected, using "stylized present-day electrodomestic and cinema/photographic equipment," his proposal *The Domicile Cell: A Microstructure within the Information and Communications System*. The domicile cell was to operate as what he termed an unbalancing system within the larger network, transforming existing one-way audiovisual technologies into feedback loops that, he argued, would restructure public/private relations as well as formal principles, acquired typologies, and domestic norms.[72] Gruppo Strum (Group for

free distribution
of "fotoromanzi"
to the visitors

Instrumental Architecture) used their allotted space to distribute three
newspaper-format "photo-stories with documents." First, a white one, *The
Struggle for Housing*, illustrated how contestations "continually reshape cities,
by attacking and defeating the capitalist organization of territory together
with the symbolic values that formalize it." Second, a green pamphlet entitled
Utopia proposed "rediscovering UTOPIA as an act of provocation, and as
a negation of the objectivity of the present-day system of production." Third,
a red one entitled *The Mediatory City* addressed the development of revolutionary organizations.[73] A final Counter-Design project by Enzo Mari, the
response to an invitation not to design an environment, appeared in the catalog
only.[74]

Presented under strong spotlights in a darkened space with black felt
floors, black walls, and a ceiling (an arrangement that gave them a quality of
floating in space), the Environments section had an ambience that stood in
strong contrast to the objects presented in the garden. One commentator
explained, "Ostensibly this destroys the reality of the familiar here and now,
and aids one's perception of the TV films." In actuality, she contended, it gave
rise to an ominous feeling, the sense that the environments were "displayed in a
purgatory-like interior blackness." Exacerbating this sense of threat was the

LEFT: Strumm, *Utop*
phlet from *Italy: Th*
Domestic Landscap

RIGHT: Ugo La Piet
Cell from *Italy: The*
Domestic Landscap

corresponding assault of discourse. She recalled: "Voices from the TV films send a confusing cacophony from all sides. One can't wait to get out, back to the fresh air, sunshine, and that fascinating bazaar."[75]

Leaving this archipelago of environments, the visitor was faced with one more didactic display, a fifteen-minute audiovisual program presenting Ambasz's historical and critical assessment of both the work and its utopian vocation. Even more spectacularized than the preceding information sessions, the slide program consisted of thirty-two simultaneously changing sequences and was rear-projected onto the walls of a space lined with specially treated mirrors. Olivetti, which had been responsible for graphics throughout the exhibition, used their Implicor system to coordinate the 2,500 slides, which were synchronized with the sound through a stereo-tape unit, "one track regulating the slide feed, the other carrying the audio portion to the amplifier and speaker."[76]

If the earlier audiovisual information sessions had functioned along the lines of prefaces, introductions, and the republication of the design program—that is, had mimicked the structure of the didactic catalog—this final section stood in for the summary of the historical and critical articles the catalog also included. Recalling Benjamin's strategy for the Arcades project—that of "literary montage"—Ambasz's summary reiterated key points found in many of the articles, in particular those by Vittorio Gregotti, Filberto Menna, and Tafuri. As Benjamin explained of a method of composition in which "everything one is thinking at a specific moment in time must at all costs be incorporated into the project then at hand": "This work has to develop to the highest degree the art of citing without quotation marks."[77] Ambasz's strategy with regard to the complex of discourses he was citing could be traced in other parts of the show, but nowhere was it more evident than in the manner in which he drew upon these texts.

After reiterating that the exhibition had set out "to honor the accomplishments of [Italy's] gifted designers and incisive critics," Ambasz offered a historical summary of the sociopolitical, technical, and economic conditions that had led to the phenomenal rise of postwar Italian design. Italian design retained a problematic relation to consumer society, he explained: it had been ineffectual at facilitating mass production of domestic goods and yet had outshone architecture in terms of "formulating hypotheses for change."[78] There was also an inherent contradiction that had led to a "pervasive sense of crisis": the avant-garde was both structurally alienated from industrial processes and administrative power and at the same time closely allied with private capital. Caught between social responsibility and a "self-doubt regarding their own role," designers were captured in a predicament that, Ambasz argued following Gregotti and Tafuri, had given rise to the proliferation of an articulate and critical discourse.[79] While the synchronized presentation of images and the enclosing nature of this multiscreen, multimedia installation would imply a totalizing logic at work, Ambasz's text, as we shall see, offered a fragmented and melancholy yet also prospective sequence of reflections on the capacity for design to maintain a utopian prospect in the postindustrial age.

That Ambasz's polemic was operating through a different set of terms than those in traditional Marxist or ideological critique was registered in the reception of the show. In a review published in *Artforum*, Robert Jensen condemned the environments as "an attempt to beat us into submission before some of the most powerful forces in our culture," forces including science, technology, modern psychology, and corporations.[80] The environments to him represented a form of conditioning, not liberation. In fact, he wrote in this "postmortem" to the show, they were "just the opposite of revolutionary." Far from providing modes of participation, as proposed by Ambasz, the designs were read by the critic to assert "aggressive polemics for the techniques of living implied by the forms," techniques that simply exacerbated a pervasive condition of human alienation. Moreover, what was particularly disturbing to Jensen was that, despite all this, the designers shared certain radical leftist convictions: they were against the current organization of cities, they opposed the inegalitarian class structure of Italian society, and they rejected the society of consumption. Yet unlike the historical avant-garde, their work did not make claims to a "revolutionary impact" or to any oppositional or utopian vocation. Implicitly rejecting the paradigm of immanent transformation, Jensen saw the work as mimicking the "irrationally organized present" rather than offering any strategy of overcoming it, as would have been the aim, he posited, of Hegel, Freud, or Marcuse. Without an appeal to opposition, and to a class subject with historical agency intact, for Jensen there remained no prospect of transformation, only a dystopic submission. "The images grip us like polished steel," he retorted, "and we become limp seeing the forces around us, not only unbroken but reinforced."[81]

An equally critical, albeit more nuanced, understanding of Italian design was presented by Tafuri in "Design and Technological Utopia," his contribution to the exhibition catalog. Tafuri traced a historical dialectic of aesthetic autonomy and engagement with technology in twentieth-century Italian design and divided into two camps what he referred to as a postwar "farewell, even though a retrogressive one, to utopia." Modernist ideals, he explained, had been rejected on the one hand by those turning to semantic strategies, who had adopted the modality of "spectators inclined to mockery and irony." On the other hand was to be found a perhaps more disturbing modality: "actors engaged in contradicting reality precisely in order to assume, like a chameleon, its outward semblance."[82] Moreover, for Tafuri the two poles were connected, even reconciled, through another set of tools recently adopted by design: structural and semiological theories of communication. Remaining divorced from actual production, Italian designers, he argued, had adopted theoretical tools developed for the third machine age, but they had done so for the purpose of purely formal exercises, finding a particular (and for him particularly disturbing) interest in the "relation between entropy and the semantic ambiguity of aesthetic information."[83] That ambiguity contradicted the architectural logic of the project and the modernist logic of the plan.

Tafuri read this anti-utopian semantic play as a neo-avant-garde embrace of, or compensation for, design's disengagement from actual relations of production. Even in the prewar period, he argued, the "revolt of the object" had come about not as a mode of active opposition to conditions of production but "because of the alienation of the object from its context."[84] That context was always political, economic, and industrial, and the separation of design from this system had again left the discipline bereft of any response other than a turn to allusion, ambiguity, and irony through the recovery of what he termed the "representational character of the object." Tafuri referred to this neo-avant-garde repetition as "a 'theater of utopia' in which pure 'plays of anticipation' are performed with conscious detachment."[85] The structural detachment—which he saw in the work of Superstudio, Archizoom, and La Pietra—paradoxically functioned as both the precondition of claims to being utopian or avant-garde and at the same time as that which determined architecture's inability to effect any social or institutional transformation.[86] Tafuri argued that this disengagement from processes of mass production had an additional effect, that of maintaining the traditional value of "the 'quality object' produced by craftsmen." An anomaly in an age of mass production, let alone mass reproduction, the paradigm of authenticity associated with the craft object was anathema to the politics of radical aesthetic practice in mass culture.

Being structurally detached from traditional sites of revolutionary praxis—labor power associated with mass production—the work fell on the side of quietude for Tafuri. Jameson argued that Tafuri's critique remained confined to a high-modernist utopian framework: "The dawning of some new postmodernist moment or even 'age,'" he wrote, "is utterly alien to Tafuri."[87] Yet Tafuri understood all too well that capitalist forces had undergone some sort of mutation under the regime of new technologies, and that the state was becoming increasingly variegated in its co-optive operations as a result. He did not, however, completely acknowledge forms of political struggle associated with new sites of productive labor, and with new social subjects (hence new forms of surplus value) now infinitely more singular and dispersed than the white male working-class subject at the center of the industrial paradigm. As recognized by the Italian Autonomia movement, to which we shall turn, the battle lines had been redrawn and political struggle no longer took place at the mass level but through micro-revolutions, through multiplicitous strategies of resistance that were anti-hierarchic, anti-dialectical, and which refused to congeal into a "general line."[88]

Tafuri articulated this detachment of Italian design from conditions of mass production in relation to technology. He spoke of "a veritable 'theory of technological integration'" in the work, and of "a synthetic kind of design in which the control of the irrational becomes 'productive' on the basis of its systematic adoption of the principles of the cybernetic universe."[89] If Archizoom and La Pietra sought alternative strategies through which the subject might occupy the contemporary metropolis, strategies that engaged the logic of that cybernetic universe, for Tafuri the feedback systems upon which they were based worked simply as a model of integration of that subject into the capitalist city. For Tafuri the environments at the center of *Italy: The New Domestic Landscape* in fact simply provided "shock therapies" that acted to reconcile the subject with that historical condition, thus retooling, in Benjaminian terms, their perceptual apparatus. But marking a contrast with Benjamin's reading, Tafuri believed that this facilitated not survival but merely integration.[90]

Tafuri never explicitly discussed the contents of Ambasz's exhibition in his essay (although he would shortly afterward), but he pointed to problematics in which the environments participated. For instance, while not mentioning Olivetti's extensive role in the exhibition, he implicated the company and its products in this dynamic of integration. With *ad hominum* reference to Olivetti's advances in automation, and in reference to the forces of multinational capital, Tafuri noted the irony of a situation in which the technologies put forward by the architects as advancing models of participation were exactly those that, in their ever increasing levels of control, served to foreclose any such creative (in Tafuri's terms "qualitative" or "arbitrary") moment in the process of design. Computer programming and magnetic tape, he explained, were set to be the operators in this technological milieu and they would reconcile all too well the current divide between design and production. "[T]he groundwork has already been laid for the object to lose its position of isolation, with respect to both production and form," Tafuri cynically commented, a situation even facilitating a new scope for mystification—a "nostalgic longing for magic" found in the compensatory allusions or semantic references which for him in fact served to reconcile a disengaged design profession with the system of consumption.[91]

Tafuri had traced architecture's turn away from a modernist ideology of the plan or "utopia of the project" to an engagement with the apparent chaos of capitalism a number of years earlier in the 1969 publication "Per una critica dell'ideologia architettonica" [Toward a Critique of Architectural Ideology] in *Contropiano*. Writing of a shift from a historical avant-garde project of pursuing "collective freedom" to one of working "within the current relations of production," Tafuri argued that avant-garde critique, in figuring a dialectical opposition, was all too easily recuperated as an "ideological tool of the current critical phase of the capitalist world."[92] When Tafuri reworked the essay to become *Architecture and Utopia* in 1973, he referred at this point in his text to the "interiors and the negative-designs worked up for" *Italy: The New Domestic Landscape* (while refuting Pierre Restany's argument that immersion in new technology harbored potentials for collective liberty). Cited alongside Fuller domes, the fourteenth Milan Triennale, and "the erotic exhibitionism" of Sottsass Jr., Ambasz's exhibition was cast as a symptom of fantasies of self-liberation that fed seamlessly back into the structures of capitalism.[93] Symptomatic of a "proliferation of an underground design of protest" that had now insidiously colonized the domestic, such practices, Tafuri believed, had been "institutionalized, propagated by international organs," such as MoMA. "The explosive contradictions of the metropolitan structures, sublimated and subjected to a cathartic irony," he wrote of the 1972 show, "enter into private life."[94]

With the foreclosure of avant-garde strategies, how then was the architect to position him- or herself within such a totalized or closed system? "It is useless to struggle for escape," Tafuri lamented, "when completely enclosed and confined without an exit."[95] Pointing to the magazine *Controspazio*, he stated, "There can be no proposals for 'antispaces': any search for an alternative within the structures determining the mystification of planning is an obvious contradiction in terms."[96] Immediately after citing Ambasz's show, Tafuri offered an example of a work which had self-consciously manifested the situation of aesthetic practice within this "constrained" situation: James Rosenquist's multipanel *F-111*. The pop artist had, in the first instance, successfully registered the artwork's fragmentation—since it could be collected (incomplete) as individual panels. In the second instance, those panels, like a "recording of the time," themselves spoke of the "deliberate formal emptiness" or muteness that architecture too had assumed in the contemporary metropolis. To demonstrate this, Rosenquist likened a single canvas to a "a vacant aluminum panel" like a "fragment of architecture from a building on Sixth Avenue and Fifty-second Street," contrasting the isolated module—the contemporary referent—to an architectural fragment of an earlier historical period—"a fancy cornice or something seemingly more human."[97] The intentionally asemantic quality of these repeatable modular units—for Tafuri akin to the reduction of the metropolitan experience to the "deadly silence of a sign"[98]—would find a correlate in contemporary practice, one ultimately tied up, however, in the same problematic as the semantic "'noise' of the neo-avant-garde."

Tafuri situated Kevin Roche's Knights of Columbus Tower in New Haven and Minoru Yamasaki's World Trade Center as unselfconscious examples of the formal emptiness at work in the logic of those vacant aluminum panels. The asemantic silence of Mies van der Rohe's Seagram Building, by contrast, implicitly acknowledged this disenchanted urban condition.[99] Tafuri argued, moreover, that the modular structure that facilitated this condition, a structure akin to the logic of postwar communication technologies (in which communication was understood as the exchange of packets of information regardless of content), was easily reconcilable to the semantic proliferation generated by architecture's engagement with artificial languages and automation. The two shared a common capitalist imperative, one that Tafuri recognized in postwar Italian design: "the necessity of an always greater integration of formal elaboration in the production cycle."[100] Moreover, as implied in the very nomination of the World Trade Center, both architecture and communication technology now functioned "to articulate with the maximum efficiency, a project of global planning of the productive universe."[101]

It was in order to comment on this condition that Tafuri added an entirely new chapter to his original essay "Architecture and Its Double: Semiology and Formalism," extending his reading of architecture's plight in the postindustrial condition. That the MoMA show was on his mind is indicated both by his citations of Peirce and Meier in this context and by his return to the Olivetti congress previously noted in his catalog essay.[102] For Tafuri, Peirce's semiotic model, the very model adopted by Ambasz, was precisely the problem, for it was Peirce who had "indicate[d] the conditions of manipulability of the pure sign devoid of any symbolic implication, of any semantic reference."[103] It was this "discovery of the possibility of inflecting signs devoid of significance, or manipulating arbitrary relationships between linguistic 'materials,'" a possibility Tafuri also traced to the historical avant-garde, that disarticulated art from politics and led to the only utopia being a technological utopia.[104]

Tafuri ended "Toward a Critique of Architectural Ideology" on architecture's instrumental, and necessarily ideological, role in the progression of a totalizing capitalism. Whether put forward as project or as "radical 'anti-project'" the impact was the same: that of reconciling, at the level of ideology, the contradictions arising in "the capitalistic reorganization of the world market." Marxist criticism had, until this point, he explained, denied or concealed the simple truth that, just as there can be no such thing as a political economics of class, but only a class critique of political economics, likewise there can never be an aesthetic, art, or architecture of class, but only a class critique of aesthetics, art, architecture, and the city.

Any "'progressive' dialogue" or projection, whether in the realm of design or its critical discourse, thus had to be rejected as simply falling into the ideological trap of "rationalizing the contradictions of capital."[105] The only role for critique was to reveal the inherent contradictions of architectural ideology. There could be no legitimate prospective function.

Ambasz seems to have agreed with Tafuri's assessment of claims to autonomy, at least as it had been set out in "Design and Technological Utopia," and he incorporated aspects of Tafuri's argument into his own summary remarks. Yet even if he was in accord with Tafuri's reading of the symptoms of architecture's malady, he would not follow him to the melancholy conclusion that the only remaining task was the critique of ideology (a notion Tafuri had drawn from the writings of the Autonomia theorist Mario Tronti).[106] Ambasz, as we have seen, retained an optimism about architecture's ongoing capacity to formulate hypotheses for change, and he believed that experimental practices might offer at least provisional strategies of institutional transformation, strategies that it was thus an imperative to push forward. Ambasz's presentation of Architettura Radicale at MoMA can thus be read retroactively as a powerful response to Tafuri's melancholy, an optimistic response that embraced lessons from the politics of the New Italian Left other than those acknowledged by Tafuri. Indeed, both behind and beyond Tafuri's legendary disenchantment might be found a more variegated model of Italian revolutionary politics from the Autonomia movement. This movement, as Michael Hardt suggests, "constituted a kind of laboratory for experimentation in new forms of political thinking that helps us conceive a revolutionary practice in our times."[107]

In his short and scathing reference to Radical Architecture in *History of Italian Architecture*, Tafuri made an oblique connection to such other Marxisms, noting that these "irresponsible" architectural practices were "deduced from a hasty reading of 'new left' reviews such as *Quaderni rossi*, *Classe operaia*, and *Contropiano*."[108] These publications mark the development of a specific, albeit heterogeneous, lineage within the extraparliamentary left in Italy. *Quaderni rossi* (Red Notebooks) was founded in 1961 by Raniero Panzieri in collaboration with Tronti, Antonio Negri, Alberto Asor Rosa, and others. Tronti, Negri, and Asor Rosa, along with Massimo Cacciari and others, subsequently split from Panzieri to found *Classe operaia* (Working Class) in 1964, and these four collaborated again to found *Contropiano* (Counterplan) in 1968, although Negri would leave shortly after its founding on account of disagreements with Tronti.[109] (Tafuri posited that Negri "had a violent crisis in 1968...as if he suffered a catharsis and went crazy."[110]) Asor Rosa later recounted that Tafuri not only participated in the early years of *Contropiano* but that his work followed the two primary lines of research that characterized the journal's intellectual project: analysis of questions concerning class struggle and the critique of ideology.[111] Tafuri was even on the editorial staff of *Contropiano* at the time of the Italian show at MoMA, but his relation to figures of the New Italian Left, from Tronti and Negri to Panzieri and Asor Rosa, was conflicted and complex.[112] His work was, for instance, notably lacking the optimism of Negri.

Connections between the architects and this intellectual milieu were noted in passing as early as Paola Navone and Bruno Orlandoni's 1974 *Casabella* publication, *Architettura "Radicale"* but have not subsequently been the focus of historical analysis of the work, let alone of the MoMA show.[113] Despite shared connections, furthermore, the work of the young radical architects was distinctly at odds with Tafuri's thinking. Yet they had perhaps made a slightly less hasty assimilation of other lessons from this reformulation of Marxism than Tafuri would acknowledge. These publications, and Negri's work in particular, were central to theorizing the transition from the mass worker (or class subject as the agent of history) to the "socialized worker" in recognition of the emergence of new social subjects as productive and dissenting forces.[114] Tronti, moreover, was central to the formulation of struggles that took place "inside and against" capitalist development, refusing traditional modes of factory work while pushing capitalism to its limits.[115] These strategies came together in what Christian Marazzi positions as "the central theme of autonomy—the struggle against work, the refusal of work."[116] As Hardt clarifies, this "did not mean a refusal of creative or productive activity but rather a refusal of work within the established capitalist relations of production."[117] Marking their connection to the New Italian Left, such refusal was, as we shall see, found in the ideals behind the young architects' conceptual projects and was coupled with forms of social and cultural experimentation characteristic of radical thought in Italy during the 1970s.

Tafuri located the emergence of the Florentine group Archizoom in a course taught by the architects Leonardo Savioli and Danilo Santi on the Space of Involvement, noting that it was "due also to the intervention of Ugo La Pietra and Ettore Sottsass." The course had set out "to use the strategies of pop art." But for Tafuri, since Archizoom had arisen in the wake of the events of 1968 as a renewed appeal to the avant-garde ("this time for its desecrating power") it had given rise to "an art that would function as a liberating psychophysical therapy devoid of codes, [one that] called upon its audience to participate in a destructive and cathartic orgy."[118] The intention, Tafuri posited, "was to haul a mythical proletariat onto the stage of psychedelic action." With reference to both Archizoom's *No-Stop City* and Superstudio's *Continuous Monument* of 1969, Tafuri argued that the work had in fact "turned the project [of engaging the proletariat] into dream material transcribed with an irony 'that made nobody laugh.'"[119] Beyond the disturbing nature of the work—Tafuri described *No-Stop City* as a "monstrous marriage between populist anarchism and liberating events influenced by those of France in May 1968"—was an "astute marketing operation" of the antidesign movement, one that he traced to the "international recognition" conferred by Ambasz's 1972 exhibition. Thus, not only was Architettura Radicale illicit for Tafuri on account of its misplaced Marxism (perhaps even founded on a misreading of Tafuri's own *Contropiano* essay), but it was enjoying an unprecedented platform of recognition, one which he had himself participated in and which was recasting the perception of Italian design. The stakes for Tafuri were thus high, and his rejection of the work far from incidental. But for Ambasz, too, as I have suggested, stakes were high.

The architects invited to produce environments for *Italy: The New Domestic Landscape* were not pursuing a single intellectual or aesthetic project, and in his final commentary Ambasz offered yet another taxonomy of discourses and practices to the viewer. (He later noted, with regard to this lack of uniformity, that Architettura Radicale "amounted to a glorious assemblage of dissimilar fragments."[120]) Bringing together the Pro-Design work with the Counter-Design practices, Ambasz proposed a strategic reconciliation of selected aspects of the Italian work, a synthesis pointing to a provisional utopian, if not entirely radical, prospect.

Ambasz wanted, on the one hand, to retain the projective ambitions of the Pro-Design approaches. Yet he read them as ultimately unable or unwilling to transform the technical and administrative structures organizing contemporary mass production and consumption. Work that engaged the semantic dimension of design continued to fall into two primary traps: either it functioned as a prophylactic through an "ambiguous layer of allusions to individual or social protest," or it simply acknowledged "the ultimate futility of their protest" by producing "deliberately unattractive objects endowed with redundant formal detail and gloomy colors."[121] Pro-Design work that harnessed technological processes evidenced two other traps: either it remained confined to individual domestic service elements—such as kitchen or bathroom ensembles—that functioned as "surrogate parts for the absent industrialized housing system" (and hence led to no actual transformation) or it reverted to recycling other industries—from freight containers to automobiles—when faced with the impasse of radically transforming the housing industry.

On the other hand, Ambasz wished to retain aspects of the Counter-Design attitude of formulating alternative, and nondeterministic, social and political agendas. Yet if such agendas harbored perhaps the last hope for a utopian prospect for architecture, their rejection of design was to him ultimately escapist, as was any utopian model predicated on advancing an image of a future entirely divorced from present social and political structures. "Since we are in battle with the present," Ambasz wrote, "it is understandable, *although not altogether acceptable* that the future be offered as the occasion for all reconciliations."[122] And here the predicament began, for how could one conceive of a better future without projecting an image of it (and hence falling into the dual pitfalls of futurology and deterministic notions)? Tafuri, too, was concerned with this question. What model of utopia, he had queried, could operate without an ideal plan, or without, in Karl Mannheim's words, "a structural vision of the totality that is and is becoming"?[123] The embrace of ambiguity and indeterminacy that the Marxist critic recognized in experimental practices was understood to eschew any model of anticipation. "Marcuse+Fourier+Dada," Tafuri scoffed, "the designer absorbs all the ingredients for a systematic reconnoitering of techniques whereby the spectator can be reconciled with the future—since the present is condemned."[124] In Tafuri's assessment, contemporary notions of utopia, such as those being presented by Ambasz, simply mimicked, or even amplified, the machinations of capitalism and the "chaos of the contemporary city."

What Ambasz recognized in aspects of the Counter-Design proposals was a diverse set of strategies for operating within the existing socioeconomic and industrial systems, that were predicated on transforming the present. The Italian radicals included in the show subscribed to neither the historical avant-garde strategies of opposition (now regarded as ineffectual on account of the totalized condition) nor to the modernist ideals of technologically driven progress (rendered ever more disturbing by the nature of a new generation of technology). Rather, their strategies acknowledged the imperative for architecture to remain engaged with, and not just submitting to, those technological and even socioeconomic forces. It is worth recounting these strategies to see how they fed back into the curator's synthetic summary.

La Pietra's Unbalancing System attempted an immanent subversion of the "productivity-oriented system" by harnessing communication networks. "Denial of utopia," he explained, "means getting involved in a head-on collision with the logics of production." Production was no longer understood as solely industrial; its participants were no longer just the factory worker but the individuated domestic subject now suspended in a cybernetic system. That postindustrial system also entailed new forms of productivity and "immaterial labor." Distancing the theses of Autonomia from the orthodox Marxism of the ICP—in which marginal workers such women, youth, part-timers, off-the-books workers were elided—Christian Marazzi notes, "These recently formed 'social subjects' are productive workers in a double sense: they produce wealth and they produce struggles."[125] If La Pietra's project was avowedly post-utopian (in the sense of refusing to project an image of an alternative future), it nevertheless harbored a techno-utopian attitude premised on interstitial moments that were not yet fully colonized by this totalized system. Deploying the domicile as a relay station, he proposed "identifying the degrees of liberty that still exist within the 'organized' social structure."[126]

Archizoom put forward an even more precisely calculated assimilation to that totalized system, one that so closely imitated the logic of capitalism as to somehow short-circuit its operations. The city was understood as a capitalist machine, one capable of resolving all contradictions: "Violent conflicts, uncontrolled disorder, and the spontaneous growth of means of communication," they argued, "are the shock tactics that the city adopts to compel the citizen to integrate himself within consumer society." In a rejection of the "image-ability" thesis of Kevin Lynch, the city was no longer to be conceived in terms of a coherent set of legible features, nor of spatial organizations or territorial divisions (which the architect might design), but as a framework for consumption within which the subject was always already immersed. And for both that urban subject and the avant-garde architect, they argued, oppositional paradigms had lost their efficacy: "Programmed electronic media has replaced direct urban procedures."[127] If up to this point Archizoom seems to be in accordance with Tafuri's disenchanted reading of the contemporary city, that was not entirely the case. For them, architecture could still perform "another function": that of harnessing the existing system to other ends. Following the logic of operating "inside and against" the capitalist system, the city became "a structure to be used"; it was redefined as "a latrine every hundred square meters" and presented as an entirely homogenous distribution of "hollow space" within which architecture offered a "neutral system available for undifferentiated use."[128] Moreover, they posited, to achieve such self-determination "one must first of all *free oneself from work*."[129]

A few years later Archizoom member Andrea Branzi expanded on that "refusal of work": "The utopia realized by radical architecture," Branzi explained, represents not so much a better model of society to propose to the world, as an instrument for accelerating reality in order to make better use of it. This utopia testifies that the end purpose of the social struggle is the liberation of man from work, and that the end purpose of the elimination of culture is intellectual production on the part of the masses.[130]

Marazzi's recent articulation of the logic of such acceleration is instructive here. Dating the thesis to Tronti's writings of 1964, he explained that ever since that time the Italian revolutionary movement has been moving toward the refusal of work as a productive force of capitalist development. Refusal of work . . . has always meant forcing capital to develop to the maximum its productive forces. Only when the worker's labor is reduced to the minimum is it possible to go beyond, in the literal sense, the capitalist mode of production.[131]

Unlike an oppositional strategy that would attempt to invert capitalist power structures (and in doing so acknowledge the hierarchy of the working class and capital), the productive refusal of work (work understood as labor power) aimed to destabilize and even dissolve capitalist power by withdrawing productive forces from that very structurals base of industrial production.

More metaphysical in character, Superstudio's project was also vectored toward eliminating this form of work. As they explained: "[W]e can visualize an image-guide: the final attempt of design to act as the 'projection' of a

society no longer based on work (and on power and violence, which are connected with this), but an unalientated human relationship."[132] Closely following Ambasz's text on Manhattan, their design, if one could still call it
that, took on the logic not only of a network but of an indeterminate mediating structure, an image-guide that operated as a virtuality that might be
actualized. As demonstrated in *Superface,* the accompanying film, their
continuous life-support grid could give rise to any number of differentiated
manifestations.

Of all the architects in *Italy: The New Domestic Landscape,* Gruppo
Strum was perhaps the most optimistic. Presenting images by architects
from Etienne-Louis Boulée to Archigram member Ron Herron, their *Utopia*
pamphlet asserted that it was "impossible not to consider a world organized
in a different way, where people would be happier and all the current shortcomings eliminated."[133] Rather than offering utopian images, they claimed
to be "concerned with rediscovering UTOPIA as an act of provocation, and
as a negation of the objectivity of the present-day system of production; in
short, we want to try to use UTOPIA as a means of intervention, directly
linked with the organization of the struggles against the programmed reorganization of capital."[134]

Ambasz did not single out specific projects in his summary remarks. His
main argument was that the counterdesign theses worked against normative or
determinate structures, thereby offering a new vocation for design. Instead
of deploying traditional signs of utopia, he explained, the architects had set
forth "negative utopias" that eradicated "formal and moral strictures."
Contradicting Tafuri's assessment that the present had been "condemned" by
such designers, Ambasz argued that theirs were utopias "not intended for the
future, but for the present." Here Ambasz was drawing upon the argument of
Menna (who was himself citing Archizoom).[135] In his catalog essay, "A Design
for New Behaviors," Menna asserted that such negative utopian projects were
not merely escapist since they had an "impact on reality." He explicated, by
way of example, how Superstudio's ironic "millenarian utopia" might produce such an impact, suggesting that the work operated by "producing models of situations that have not yet come to fruition in society." With reference
to Marshall McLuhan, he posited furthermore that they worked "by building
'Noah's arks with which to meet the coming change.'"[136] In this sense the
work was understood to produce concepts that were at once both historically

specific—in the sense of engaging the present—and at the same time indeterminate or non-normative.

Menna made a further claim for the "processes of negative thought" in these utopian projects, processes that for him could serve to "unmask the contradictions, conflicts, injustices and repression of the present and further the task of constructing a new society."[137] The projects had, he argued, a concrete, reverse plan that seeks to operate in the present: to destroy the object, architecture, and the city requires the proposal of a new philosophy of design, a kind of design that refuses, insofar as possible, to provide rigid, authoritarian structures in which the individual has no possibility for the independent exercise of his own choices.[138]

Menna was thus bringing together a negative strategy with that of an immanent transformation and in so doing engaged utopian paradigms with the present, not just the future. Such a project would have been insupportable to Tafuri, who cast Menna together with Restany as merely promulgating "aesthetic civilizations."[139] Notwithstanding the problems of assimilation and programming that remained very real traps, Menna began to suggest a function for such contestation, a sort of local negativity or dialectics that might operate without either a totalizing plan, or purely oppositional logic and yet which at the same time was not reducible to chaos.

Ambasz, as noted, found the field of counterdesign positions demonstrated by the environments in his exhibition "not entirely acceptable." Yet he also posited that one could "sense the circumstances that could lead to a change in [design's] scale, methods, and goals." As with his Italian counterparts, he entertained an ultimately utopian formulation that operated without a fixed end point or plan, and which recognized that the architect could not escape the existing system but had to work within it to transform it. But to the negative utopia of the counterdesign formulations, Ambasz coupled a dimension of social transformation mediated through physical solutions. That is, he insisted on a role for design. Both Ambasz and Menna suggested that a hegemony (their term) of political solutions confined to text restricted intellectual freedom and that a "discourse of many voices" could be forged which would recognize "the possibilities for action that aesthetic invention and imagination may reveal."[140] But how could that conceptual Noah's ark be designed not as an ironic or allegorical commentary but as an indeterminate structure?

In 1972, the answer seemed to lie in a more widespread tendency in aesthetic practice. Ambasz explained that this involved a shift from concentration on the object to "the processes that generated it, and the processes which it in turn generates."[141] In remarks addressing "The Crisis of the Object," Menna, too, had situated this "turning point in design" in relation to the wider aesthetic field. The artist, he argued, has abandoned the plastically autonomous work, an object that is an end in itself, and turned his attention to creating ambient structures (environments), to the use of the body as a means of relating and communicating (body art), and to the mental process that presides over artistic activity (conceptual art).[142]

Many such aesthetic practices were known to Ambasz from his time at MoMA. In 1968 Experiments in Art and Technology (which had advised on his audiovisual installations) had staged the *Some More Beginnings* competition in conjunction with *The Machine As Seen at the End of the Mechanical Age*. In 1970 Kynaston McShine's *Information* show had been on display at the museum, an exhibition including work by experimental architects and replete with Sacco chairs collected by Ambasz himself.[143]

For Ambasz, these conceptual strategies translated into the emergence of the environment as the task of design, an environment now understood as inextricable from larger technological and sociopolitical processes. Beyond setting out to refuse the commodified status of an object, this shift to process had other political implications. Following the theories of Alain Touraine (a speaker at Ambasz's Universitas symposium), Ambasz conceived of the environment as a space of "participation," as well as conflict, a space in which the user was recast as "the actor of the aesthetic event."[144] In *The Post Industrial Society* Touraine had distinguished two forms of participation in "the programmed society": a dependent participation, taking the form of the subject's unwitting integration into new forms of social domination and control, and a contestatory mode of participation in which the subject was engaged in economic and political decision making.[145] Ambasz concluded his summary remarks by reiterating that his concept of environment pointed toward the latter, that it "presupposes for man the role of active protagonist rather than of mere passive spectator." He explained that although the designed object or environment exerted a "power" over "the user and his behavior," this could be coupled with a political role for the participation of that subject that was specific to the object's "sociocultural context," a participatory role based on ongoing conflict within those social spaces and their technological/informatic milieu.

For Tafuri, to continue this dialogue, such a subject retained little if any capacity for action or contestation. As he explained of a related project, the body in such work had returned only as an abstract sign, a "pure sign-man," a "useless intrusion" into the all too seamless functioning of the architecture-communication machine.[146] But Tafuri need not have the last word. Ambasz's project was in many regards a final moment, or even a postmortem, for architecture's postwar engagement with general systems theory and cybernetics. Echoing Tomás Maldonado, Ambasz believed in the possibility of resemanticizing the abstract packets of information operating within the paradigm of communications theory through an insistence on giving weight to the content of the messages—not just their form or structure. In *Italy: The New Domestic Landscape*, this took the form of embracing the meaning inherent in the ritual dimensions of domestic life as well as ideals of a multiple recoding of modular kits of parts. Thus, for Ambasz, prospects remained for recuperating something like "meaning in architecture" without withdrawing from technological investigations into the pop, linguistic, or historicist paradigms prevailing in the U.S. Although his interests were increasingly moving toward the tropes of architectural postmodernism, at this time they retained a complex alliance with those earlier investigations. In this sense the project offers sites of investigation, if not necessarily contemporary lessons, for how architecture might forge a non-determinst relation to the technological advances it could not (and cannot) escape.

Following *Italy: The New Domestic Landscape*, Ambasz's curatorial work at MoMA moved toward both poles of Tafuri's dialectic (aesthetic autonomy versus engagement). On the one hand, he looked for less ironic prospects for architecture's formal and representational dimension, for instance, in exhibitions of Walter Pichler and Luis Barragán.[147] On the other, he refused the retreat to autonomy typical of the Whites and vectored certain work toward interventions into the realm of production, as manifest most provocatively in *The Taxi Project*. Within what he later referred to as the City of Information there remained for him prospects for recuperating a City of Production.[148] In 1976, while *The Taxi Project* was on view, Ambasz left the museum to engage directly in industry as a designer. It was at this time that he published "Le designer comme réalisateur," later published in English as "Designer/ Producer." Resonating with the title of Benjamin's 1934 essay "Author as

Producer," it was a working fable about a designer who, frustrated with current relations between design and industry, took it upon himself to engage directly with production.[149]

In the early 1970s, Ambasz situated his attempts to engage the technological milieu somewhere between the prevailing poles of melancholic fatalism and uncritical techno-optimism. In the *Working Papers* of the Universitas project he had explained, "It is a paradox that any system capable of allowing the greatest possible individual freedom . . . will not be some sort of unstructured Arcadia but rather a highly complex physical and socio-cultural artifact."[150] If he believed, on the one hand, that the scientific determinism of modernism foreclosed the subject's ability to "alter, by his choice of actions, the course of things," on the other hand the open-endedness and indeterminacy facilitated by postindustrial technologies were cast, at least in principle, as offering a space not just of a pernicious assimilation into the socioeconomic system but also of a mode of participation that took the form of contestatory negotiation.[151] From the model of agency implied by Ambasz's notion of an "existential operator"—a subject fully immersed in that system who nevertheless designs "structures" to mediate between man and this technological milieu—to the conception of the object as an "ensemble of interrelated processes whose interaction results in constantly changing patterns of relationships," the designer retained the task of forging new prospects for the human condition within a postindustrial society, a complex, dispersed, and inescapable network of power that Hardt and Negri have recently termed Empire.[152]

[1] These problematics are intentionally in dialogue with Fredric Jameson, in particular his work on Manfredo Tafuri. See Fredric Jameson, "Architecture and the Critique of Ideology," in *Architecture, Criticism, Ideology*, ed. Joan Ockman (New York: Princeton Architectural Press, 1985): 51–87, especially 65–68 in which Jameson demarcates the initial rejection by Marxists of the notion of "postindustrial" society, as theorized on the right by Daniel Bell, and its later recasting, by Ernest Mandel among others, as late capitalism.

[2] The literature on sixties experimental practice and its subsequent disenchantment is vast. For a reading from the period, see Manfredi G. Nicoletti, "The End of Utopia," *Perspecta* 13/14 (1971): 268–79.

[3] The term *Radical Architecture* typically refers to the practice of European architects and groups, mainly from Austria, England, and Italy, whose work was concerned less with the production of buildings than with a critical investigation of the discipline. Important early events in Italy were the *Superarchitettura* exhibition in Florence of 1966 and *Utopia e/o Rivoluzione* in Turin of 1969, and key Italian protagonists included Archizoom, Superstudio, Gruppo Strum, U.F.O., and Ugo La Pietra.

4   On this dialectic of autonomy and integration, see K. Michael Hays, "The Oppositions of Autonomy and History," in *Oppositions Reader*, ed. K. Michael Hays (New York: Princeton Architectural Press, 1998), ix–xv. In addition to the experimental work of Ant Farm, some of the more experimental work at Yale during this period can be seen to have involved utopian aspirations. See Eve Blau, "Architecture or Revolution: Charles Moore and Yale in the Late 1960s" (New Haven: Yale University School of Architecture Gallery, 2001).

5   Emilio Ambasz's relation to MoMA actually dates to earlier in 1968, when one of his posters for the Swiss Geigy Corporation had been collected and exhibited in *Word and Image: Posters and Typography from the Graphic Design Collection of the Museum of Modern Art, 1879–1967*.

6   An analysis of this intersection forms the core of my current work on Ambasz's Universitas project, including a recent paper "On the Counter-Design of Institutions" (presented at *Expertise: Connoisseurs, Consultants and Con Men*, Harvard University, Graduate School of Design, October 2002).

7   Manfredo Tafuri, *History of Italian Architecture, 1944–1985*, trans. Jessica Levine (Cambridge, Mass.: MIT Press, 1989), first published as *Storia dell'architettura italiana, 1944–1985* (Turin: Giulio Einaudi Editore, 1986), 98–99.

8   I am not suggesting that there were *no* politically motivated practices, but that we need to take seriously the failure of activist politics in architecture during this period. For an exception, see Michael Sorkin, "Radical Alternative," *Architectural Record* 152 (December 1972): 118–21. The postactivist "drop-out" formulation of hippie communities also failed to engage political processes, with the exception of important environmentalist work that remained, however, far from central to American architectural practice.

9   For a source important to Ambasz's intellectual formation, see Stanford Anderson, ed., *Planning for Diversity and Choice* (Cambridge, Mass.: MIT Press, 1968). This collected volume arose out of a symposium at MIT held in conjunction with the AIA's commissioning of Robert Geddes to study possible pedagogies for "environmental design." See also Robert L. Geddes and Bernard P. Spring, "A Study of Education for Environmental Design" (Princeton University, 1967).

10   Charles Jencks and George Baird, eds., *Meaning in Architecture* (New York: George Braziller, 1969).

11   See Kenneth Frampton, "America 1960–1970: Notes on Urban Images and Theory," *Casabella* 35, no. 359–60 (1971): 25–40.

12   See "'L'architecture dans le boudoir'" of 1974 and "The Ashes of Jefferson" of 1976, both reprinted in Manfredo Tafuri, *The Sphere and the Labyrinth: Avant-Gardes and Architecture from Piranesi to the 1970's*, trans. Pellegrino d'Acierno and Robert Connolly (Cambridge, Mass.: MIT Press, 1987), 267–90 and 291–303, respectively.

13   Jameson, "Architecture and the Critique of Ideology," 55.

14   Jameson, "Architecture and the Critique of Ideology," 58.

15   The essay appeared in the "Utopia and Anti-utopia" section of *Perspecta* 13/14; in *Casabella* 359–60, an issue prepared in collaboration with the IAUS; and in the *Working Papers* for Ambasz's *Institutions for a Post-technological Society: The Universitas Project*.

16   Emilio Ambasz, "The Formulation of a Design Discourse," *Perspecta* 12 (1969): 57–70.

17 Excerpted from a letter to Gerhard Scholem detailing the overwhelming task of his *Arcades Project*, the epigraph read, "Once I have grasped it, then an old, as it were rebellious, half apocalyptic province of my thoughts will have been subdued, colonized, set in order." Walter Benjamin, Letter to Gerhard Scholem, April 23, 1928 (Breife I, p. 470), cited in Ben Brewster, "Walter Benjamin and the Arcades Project," *Perspecta* 12 (1969): 161–62.

18 "Marx lays bare the causal connection between economy and culture," argued Benjamin. "It is not the economic origin of culture that will be presented, but the expression of the economy in its culture. At issue, in other words, is the attempt to grasp an economic process as perceptible." Walter Benjamin, "Konvolut N: On the Theory of Knowledge, Theory of Progress," in *The Arcades Project*, trans. Howard Eiland and Kevin McLaughlin (Cambridge, Mass.: Harvard University Press, 1999), 460.

19 Emilio Ambasz, "Manhattan: Capital of the Twentieth Century," *Perspecta* 13/14 (1971): 362. All citations from this text, unless otherwise noted, refer to this publication.

20 In "Design As a Mode of Thought," Ambasz notes, "The notion of an iconic structure is really a matter of methodological convenience, a way of regarding the production of man, which can be conceptual or material or, more often, a combination of both, so that they may point the way to new beginnings." Emilio Ambasz, *Working Papers* (New York: Museum of Modern Art, 1971): n.p. See also Charles Sanders Peirce, "Division of Signs," and "The Icon, Index, and Symbol," in *Collected Papers of Charles Sanders Peirce*, ed. Charles Hartshorne and Paul Weiss (Cambridge, Mass.: Harvard University Press, 1931–35), 134–55 and 156–73, respectively. Ambasz first discusses Peirce in "The Formulation of a Design Discourse," 63.

21 Ambasz's reading of Manhattan as the quintessential model of an indeterminate and experimental metropolitan structure whose immanent logic might be transferred was famously followed by Rem Koolhaas's reading of Manhattan as a system of "superimposed and unpredictable activities." See Rem Koolhaas, *Delirious New York: A Retroactive Manifesto for Manhattan* (New York: Oxford University Press, 1978), citation from page 289. That Koolhaas's parable was indebted to Ambasz's own was confirmed by Ambasz in an interview I conducted on February 24, 2001. On this aspect of Koolhaas's work, see Hubert Damisch, "Manhattan Transference," in *Skyline: The Narcissistic City* (Palo Alto, Calif.: Stanford University Press, 2001), 100–18.

22 As Ambasz explained: "The tearing of the fragment from its context, this rescuing of the irreducible word from its sentence, involves not only the usual process of bringing together where, instead of establishing fixed hierarchies, the fragments rescued from tradition are placed on the same level in ever changing continuities, in order to yield new meanings, and thereby render other modes of access to their recondite qualities." Ambasz, "Manhattan," 362. On the critical stakes of such grafting processes see Jacques Derrida, "Signature, Event, Context" (1977), trans. Samuel Weber and Jeffrey Mehlman, in *Limited Inc.*, ed. Gerald Graff (Evanston, Ill.: Northwestern University Press, 1988), 1–24.

23 Ambasz, "Manhattan," 362. For Ambasz, moreover, such a device or "structure" could act as a conceptual device to mediate between man and the man-made milieu in a non-determinate manner.

24 See Emilio Ambasz, "University of Design and Development," and "The Designs of Freedom," in *Perspecta* 13/14 (1971): 360–61 and 363–65, respectively. Two years in preparation, the MoMA symposium *Institutions for a Post-Technological Society: The Universitas Project* was held on January 8 and 9, 1972.

25   The influence of Bergson on Ambasz's thought most likely came from his primary mentor,
      Tomas Maldonado. On this paradigm, see Henri Bergson, *Creative Evolution*, trans. Arthur
      Mitchell, *The Modern Library* (New York: Random House, 1944); Gilles Deleuze,
      Bergsonism, trans. Hugh Tomlinson and Barbara Habberjam (New York: Zone Books,
      1988); and Michael Hardt, "Bergsonian Ontology: The Positive Movement of Being," in
      Gilles Deleuze: An Apprenticeship in Philosophy (Minneapolis: University of Minnesota
      Press, 1993), 1–25. On the utopian aspects of such a paradigm, see Elizabeth Grosz,
      "Embodied Utopias: The Time of Architecture," in *Architecture from the Outside: Essays on
      Virtual and Real Space* (Cambridge, Mass.: MIT Press, 2001), 131–50. In my February
      2001 interview with Ambasz he recalled having read Bergson prior to arriving in the U.S.

26   If, for Gandelsonas, Ambasz's fables were not transformative devices, he explained that such
      a role remained proper to theory. Mario Gandelsonas, introduction to Theory section,
      Oppositions 4 (October 1974): 65.

27   Gandelsonas, introduction to Theory section, 65.

28   Martin Pawley, "'We Shall Not Bulldoze Westminster Abbey': Archigram and the Retreat
      from Technology," *Oppositions* 7 (winter 1976). On this relation to experimental
      practices, see Felicity Scott, "Architecture of Techno-Utopia," *Grey Room* 03 (spring 2001):
      112–26.

29   Before the exhibit opened to the public, there was a four-day series of previews and benefit
      parties. Events began Tuesday, May 23, 1972, with an invitational black-tie preview for
      designers, sponsors, and the Italian ambassador. On Wednesday morning was the press pre-
      view, followed in the evening by a gala benefit party and preview. On Thursday was the
      museum members' preview from 11 A.M. to 11 P.M.

30   Adolfo Natalini, "Italy: The New Domestic Landscape," *Architectural Design* 42 (August
      1972): 469–73. Natalini, a member of the Superstudio group that exhibited in the show,
      also noted that a volume three times the size of the catalog could have been written on the
      "diplomatic and adventurous journeys of Emilio Ambasz in the country of beautiful design,"
      469.

31   MoMA press release, no. 26, issued May 26, 1972. The "universal" nature is noted in
      MoMA press release no. 34, no issue date noted.

32   Emilio Ambasz, cited in R. deNeve, "Supershow in Retrospect: Review of Italy: The New
      Domestic Landscape," *Print* 26 (November 1972): 63.

33   DeNeve, "Supershow in Retrospect," 67. This supplementary material was noted by many
      critics. Ada Louise Huxtable remarked, "The show's many definitions and divisions are set
      up with a fierce intellectual firmness by Mr. Ambasz. There is an indoctrinating film as one
      enters, and an audio-visual summary as one leaves." Ada Louise Huxtable, "Italian Design
      Show Appraised—Ambiguous but Beautiful," *New York Times*, May 26, 1972, p. 43.
      Robert Jensen referred to the show as "a tightly controlled polemic." Robert Jensen, "Italian
      Design show at MoMA: A Postmortem," *Artforum* 11 (October 1972): 85.

34   Emilio Ambasz, "The Museum of Modern Art and the Man-Made Environment: An Interim
      Report," *Members Newsletter* (spring 1970), n.p. He had previously held the title Associate
      Curator of Design.

35   Ambasz explained that his book series would "deal with the fact that the most crucial design
      contributions of the last decade which merit 'collecting' have in many cases not been objects
      but rather theoretical essays and design proposals." "Interim Report."

36   Along with an editorial noting that the show was "at once exhilarating and exasperating, provocative and perplexing," *Interior Design* published an angry letter to the editor that suggested such a confusion of categories was at play. The visitor noted that she was initially "disappointed and disturbed" by the show and that this "disturbing feeling intensified" over the next few days, prompting her to write. She was disturbed, in particular, by what appeared to her the suggestion that the objects could somehow think: "to attribute 'thinking' to inanimate objects not only places wrong relevance to the importance of such objects in this world but also turns the order of things around. . . . I question Mr. Ambasz's interpretation of Italian design and designers, and I feel he has presented this show as a pretentious forum and a propaganda movement for sociological and philosophical and intellectual change rather than presenting the superb and highly imaginative and creative designs." She concluded by expressing her interest in knowing "if this show represents the philosophy of all Italian designers or if it is primarily Mr. Ambasz's interpretation." Charlotte Finn, Letter to the Editor, *Interior Design* 43 (July 1972): 104.

37   In the acknowledgments detailed in the catalog, Ambasz noted the involvement of Olivetti, Giacomo Battiato, and many others in producing the sets and film that introduced the exhibition. In addition, he thanked Robert Whitman of Experiments in Art and Technology (EAT) for "advising on the setup for the film's projection system." Emilio Ambasz, ed., *Italy: The New Domestic Landscape: Achievements and Problems of Italian Design* (New York: The Museum of Modern Art, 1972), 14.

38   DeNeve, "Supershow in Retrospect," 67.

39   DeNeve presented a list of concerns: there were "far too many objects to keep track of," she complained; they were crowded and difficult to view (a situation worsened by the reflections on the Plexiglas windows); and they were difficult to identify even from the labels. "Because many of the Objects had amorphous shapes and abstract names," she argued, "matching the Object to label was often a frustrating process of elimination." DeNeve, "Supershow in Retrospect," 67.

40   Huxtable, "Italian Design Show Appraised," 43.

41   Huxtable, "Italian Design Show Appraised," 43. Ambasz recalled that this was Drexler. "Interview with Emilio Ambasz Conducted by Sharon Zane" (The Museum of Modern Art Oral History Project, 1993, 1994). See also "Some Were Excited, Some Bored," which accompanied Huxtable's opening-night review, in which it was noted that some visitors had "toured the area as if they were in a department stores."

42   DeNeve, "Supershow in Retrospect," 67. The reviewer for *Interiors* also noted that, "laid out in rows, the tall crates make delightful streets—psychologically *shopping* streets." The "big joke" on the public, she argued, was that "the final impact of the show is to lure the observer into the shopping orgy of all times. . . . One can't resist exploring. What these crates really succeed in creating is an architectural milieu giving importance to small- and medium-sized objects which would be lost in conventional open display spaces." "Italy's Supersalesmen Come to MoMA," *Interiors* 131 (July 1972): 78–83. Italics in original.

43   See Felicity Scott, "From Industrial Art to Design: The Purchase of Domesticity at MoMA, 1929–1959," *Lotus International* 97 (July 1998): 106–43.

44   Gregory Battcock, "Italy: The New Domestic Landscape," *Art and Artists* 7 (November 1972): 48–49.

45   See Walter Benjamin, "The Work of Art in the Age of Mechanical Reproduction" (1936), trans. Harry Zohn, in *Illuminations: Essays and Reflections*, ed. Hannah Arendt (New York: Schocken Books, 1968), 217–51.

46   Emilio Ambasz, *Emilio Ambasz: The Poetics of the Pragmatic* (New York: Rizzoli, 1988), 226.

47   Huxtable, "Italian Design Show Appraised," 43.

48   In addition to the intellectual and the professional levels of participation, Ambasz noted, "There is, of course, the very obvious role of the spectator who has been motivated more than anything else by wanting to see new furniture and new objects. He is an American; he has been educated to believe that by consumption will arrive redemption, and here, then are the new fetishes of the cult." Cited in deNeve, "Supershow in Retrospect," 67.

49   Superstudio, "Twelve Cautionary Tales for Christmas," *Architectural Design* 42 (December 1971): 737–42.

50   MoMA press release no. 26, issued May 26, 1972.

51   MoMA press release no. 39, not dated. These were characterized by "bold use of color, and their imaginative utilization of the possibilities offered by the new hard and soft synthetic materials and advanced molding techniques."

52   Ambasz, *Italy: The New Domestic Landscape*, 19.

53   MoMA press release no. 39.

54   One example that was added to the museum's permanent collection was the *Joe* sofa (1970), designed by De Pas, D'Urbino, and Lomazzi in the form of a gigantic baseball glove.

55   Ambasz, *Italy: The New Domestic Landscape*, 20.

56   Ambasz, *Italy: The New Domestic Landscape*, 21.

57   MoMA press release no. 127, issued December 2, 1970.

58   Ambasz, *Italy: The New Domestic Landscape*, 143.

59   Ambasz, *Italy: The New Domestic Landscape*, 12. For another Universitas speaker, Jean Baudrillard, this simply demonstrated the logic of that "system of objects" through which the object operated in consumer society. See Jean Baudrillard, *The System of Objects*, trans. James Benedict (New York: Verso, 1996 [1967]).

60   DeNeve, "Supershow in Retrospect," 68. The pamphlet "Organization of the Exhibition" referred to this as a closed-circuit presentation, with technical development by Olivetti's audiovisual department and text by Ambasz.

61   "If we could motivate the public into waiting for each letter to appear," Ambasz speculated, "maybe they would be curious enough to read it." Cited in deNeve, "Supershow in Retrospect," 68.

62   Each of the environments was to occupy an area of approximately sixteen by sixteen feet (with a height limit of twelve feet).

63   Ambasz, *Italy: The New Domestic Landscape*, 139.

64   Ambasz, *Italy: The New Domestic Landscape*, 143.

65   The majority of texts were from *Environmental Psychology: Man and His Physical Setting,* eds. Harold M. Proshansky, William H. Ittelson, and Leanne G. Rivlin (New York: Holt, Rinehart and Winston, 1970). See also Aldo Van Eyck, "Is Architecture Going to Reconcile Basic Values?" in *CIAM '59 in Otterlo*, ed. Oscar Newman (Stuttgart, 1961), 26–35; and Martin Pawley, "The Time House," initially published in *Architectural Design* (September 1968), reprinted in *Meaning in Architecture,* eds. Baird and Jencks, 121–48. Pawley was a participant in the Universitas project.

66   The two winning designs—that of Gruppo 999 and Gianantonio Mari—were shown in photopanels only in an alcove on the Fifty-fourth Street lobby.

67   Ambasz, *Italy: The New Domestic Landscape*, 137.

68   Ambasz, *Italy: The New Domestic Landscape*, 162.

69   Ambasz, *Italy: The New Domestic Landscape*, 137. To many there remained an unresolvable paradox in the suspension of "radical" projects within this institutional framework. For Ambasz, however, the museum was understood as a powerful vehicle for introducing alternative paradigms of practice to an American audience. MoMA, he argued twenty years later, "could provide institutional support, to actually become an impresario and trigger certain types of projects." He explained, for instance, that he had intended to provide "twelve Italian designers with an institutional cover of protection, so that they could actually make an environmental statement." Ambasz used the metaphor of the "hunter curator" to describe his activities, distinguishing it from the "farmer" or "agricultural curator" who was familiar with the seed and the seasons and simply waited to harvest. "Interview with Emilio Ambasz Conducted by Sharon Zane," 19–20.

70   See Archizoom, "No-Stop City," *Domus* 496 (March 1971): 49–54.

71   Superstudio, "Description of the Microevent/Microenvironment," in *Italy: The New Domestic Landscape,* 246.

72   Ugo La Pietra, "The Domicile Cell: A Microstructure within the Information and Communication System," in *Italy: The New Domestic Landscape,* 224–31. La Pietra's proposal is in response to a letter from Abraham Moles to Emilio Ambasz cited in the Design Program. See Ambasz, *Italy: The New Domestic Landscape*, 143.

73   Gruppo Strum, "For a Mediatory City," in *Italy: The New Domestic Landscape*, 254–61.

74   Mari provided a orthodox Marxist text outlining "Proposals for Behavior directed to my colleagues," and addressing issues related to communication and class struggle.

75   "Italy's Supersalesman," 82.

76   DeNeve, "Supershow in Retrospect," 68. The visual portion and its musical component were the work of Umberto Bignardi who, we learn, "prefers to be thought of as an artist who works in visual systems rather than a graphic designer." Bignardi selected images with architectural, anthropological, and political content, converted them into line drawings, then reproduced them as slides.

77   Benjamin, "Konvolut N: On the Theory of Knowledge, Theory of Progress," 456, 458. The citations are taken from [N1,3] and [N1,10], respectively.

78   MoMA press release no. 38, which documents the oral presentation.

79   MoMA press release no. 38, page 4.

80   Jensen, "Italian Design Show at MoMA: A Postmortem," 87.

81 Jensen, "Italian Design Show at MoMA: A Postmortem," 85.

82 Manfredo Tafuri, "Design and Technological Utopia," in *Italy: The New Domestic Landscape*, 392.

83 Tafuri, "Design and Technological Utopia," 393.

84 Tafuri, "Design and Technological Utopia," 388.

85 Tafuri, "Design and Technological Utopia," 392, 394. While Tafuri acknowledged affiliations with the historical avant-garde of the nineteen-twenties, he regarded those later practices as neo-avant-garde repetitions that served to cancel or even invert the political interventions of their predecessors. On this dialectic of the avant-garde, see Peter Bürger, *Theory of the Avant-Garde*, trans. Jochen Schulte-Sasse (Minneapolis: University of Minnesota Press, 1984). It is not clear from where Tafuri derived this concept, and his use of the term predates Bürger's initial German publication of 1974.

86 Tafuri later extended this critique. "Despite themselves," he argued, the "utopian-futuristic" architects had merely safeguarded architecture's autonomy. And as such they had "fail[ed] to take into account the necessity for a direct linkage between hypotheses of new modes of production and institutional reforms." Manfredo Tafuri and Francesco Dal Co, *Modern Architecture*, ed. Pier Luigi Nervi, trans. Robert Erich Wolf (New York: Harry N. Abrams, 1979), 390.

87 Jameson, "Architecture and the Critique of Ideology," 56, 75.

88 As Sylvere Lotringer explains, "Political autonomy is the desire to allow differences to deepen at the base without trying to synthesize them from above, to stress similar attitudes without imposing a 'general line,' to allow parts to co-exist side by side, in their singularity." See the editorial of Sylvere Lotringer and Christian Marazzi, "The Return of Politics," in *Semiotext(e)* 3, no. 3, special issue entitled "Italy: Autonomia, Post-Political Politics" (1980), 8. Felix Guattari argued in "The Proliferation of Margins," in the same volume of *Semiotext*(e), "For the last decade 'battle lines' widely different from those which previously characterized the traditional worker's movement have not ceased to multiply: (immigrant workers, skilled workers unhappy with the kind of work imposed on them, the unemployed, over-exploited women, ecologists, nationalists, mental patients, homosexuals, the elderly, the young, etc.). But will their objectives become just another 'demand' acceptable to the system? Or will vectors of molecular revolution begin to proliferate behind them?"

89 Tafuri, "Design and Technological Utopia," 396–97.

90 For Tafuri, such an engagement with communications would lead to nothing but despair. He recounted the effect on Benjamin himself, noting that his own biographical details bore witness to the impact: suicide. Manfredo Tafuri, "Architecture as 'Indifferent Object' and the Crisis of Critical Attention" (1976), trans. Giorgio Verrecchia, in *Theories and Histories of Architecture* (New York: Harper and Row, 1980), 88.

91 Tafuri, "Design and Technological Utopia," 399–400.

92 Tafuri, "Toward a Critique of Architectural Ideology," 30.

93 Superstudio's film *Superface* indeed included images of Fuller domes and fell into the camp of an escapist back-to-nature fantasy mediated through Fuller's Dymaxion vision.

94 Manfredo Tafuri, *Architecture and Utopia: Design and Capitalist Development*, trans. Barbara Luigia La Penta (Cambridge, Mass.: MIT Press, 1976), 142.

95   Tafuri, *Architecture and Utopia,* 181.

96   Tafuri, "Toward a Critique of Architectural Ideology," 33.

97   James Rosenquist, cited in Tafuri, *Architecture and Utopia,* 143.

98   Tafuri, *Architecture and Utopia,* 145.

99   In "Design and Technological Utopia," Tafuri also addresses this condition, noting, "The silence of the object, meant to propose an alternative to the superfluity of communications, leads to the discovery that its own 'void' is the only mute message it has to convey," 396.

100   Tafuri, *Architecture and Utopia,* 149.

101   Tafuri, *Architecture and Utopia,* 151.

102   Tafuri refers the reader to the "essays contained in the volume *Linguaggi nella società e nella tecnica,*" from an Olivetti congress in Turin, September 14–17, 1968, published in Milan in 1970.

103   Tafuri, *Architecture and Utopia,* 152.

104   Tafuri, *Architecture and Utopia,* 153.

105   Tafuri, "Toward a Critique of Architectural Ideology," 32.

106   See Luisa Passerini, "History as Project: An Interview with Manfredo Tafuri" (1992), *ANY* 25/26 (2000): 10–70. In this interview Tafuri recalled, "Tronti had coined the expression *critica dell'ideologia* [critique of ideology], which advanced the idea that it is possible to do theoretical politics, which becomes in practice the critique of ideology," 32.

107   Michael Hardt, "Introduction: Laboratory Italy," in *Radical Thought in Italy: A Potential Politics,* ed. Paulo Virno and Michael Hardt (Minneapolis: University if Minnesota Press, 1996), 1–9. "In Marx's time revolutionary thought seemed to rely on three axes: German philosophy, English economics, and French politics. In our time the axes have shifted so that, if we remain within the same Euro-American framework, revolutionary thinking might be said to draw on French philosophy, US economics, and Italian politics," 1.

108   Tafuri, *History of Italian Architecture,* 99.

109   On this, see Alberto Asor Rosa, "Critique of Ideology and Historical Practice," *Casabella* 619–20 (January–February 1995): 28–33.

110   Tafuri in Passerini, "History as Project," 54.

111   Asor Rosa, "Critique of Ideology and Historical Practice," 29.

112   In the interview with Passerini, Tafuri acknowledged his indebtedness to Panzieri's critique of Marx (in which to return to Marx meant to negate Marx himself); to Tronti's notion of *critica dell'ideologia*; and to Asor Rosa's *destruens.* He also registered his conflicts and distances with many of these figures. Other texts in this special double issue of *ANY* dedicated to Tafuri also trace out some of these connections including: Evelina Calvi, "Oublier Tafuri?" *ANY* 25/26 (2000): 21–28; and Paul Henninger, "One Portrait of Tafuri: An Interview with Georges Teyssot," *ANY* 25/26 (2000): 10–16.

113   Paola Navone and Bruno Orlandoni, eds., *Architettura "Radicale"* (Milan: Casabella, 1974).

114   See "Workerist Publications and Bios," in *Semiotext(e)* 3, no. 3 (1980): 178–81.

115   Christian Marazzi explains that *Classe Operaia* "attempted to formulate a new political strategy, which Tronti called 'inside and against': to act on the inside of capitalist development, *promoting* it through the refusal of work (thus bringing about the introduction of new

machines and new technology), but at the same time to remain *against* capitalism, *wanting everything* from it, all the wealth produced through its reformism." "Post-political Politics," 18. Italics in original.

[116] Marazzi, "Post-political Politics," 16.

[117] Hardt, "Introduction: Laboratory Italy," 2. See Mario Tronti, "The Strategy of Refusal," (1965) in *Semiotext(e)* 3, no. 3 (1980): 28–34.

[118] Tafuri, *History of Italian Architecture,* 99. This connection was recently refuted by Gianni Pettena, who argued that while these radical practices in Italy date back to the mid-sixties, and that the first projects were carried out at the School of Architecture of Florence, that "these were not the result of an institutional course." See Gianni Pettena, "Radical Architecture," in the catalog to the exhibition *Architecture radicale* (Villeurbanne: IAC, 2002), 297.

[119] Tafuri, *History of Italian Architecture,* 99.

[120] Emilio Ambasz, "Architettura Radicale," in *Emilio Ambasz Inventions: The Reality of the Ideal* (New York: Rizzoli, 1992), 81.

[121] Ambasz, "Summary," in *Italy: The New Domestic Landscape,* 420.

[122] MoMA press release no. 38, page 5. Emphasis added.

[123] Karl Mannheim, cited by Tafuri, *Architecture and Utopia,* 53.

[124] Tafuri, "Design and Technological Utopia," 398.

[125] Marazzi, in Lotringer and Marazzi, "The Return of Politics," 16. Recuperating Marx from the politics of the Red Brigade, Marazzi argues in this context that the orthodox choice of the factory worker as the agent of transformation in fact "derives more from Adam Smith than from Marx."

[126] La Pietra, "The Domicile Cell," 226–27.

[127] Archizoom, untitled submission in *Italy: The New Domestic Landscape,* 232–39. "The 'urban condition'—being a citizen—does not imply being more integrated than a noncitizen, since there are no longer any territorial regions not organized within the system," 237.

[128] Archizoom, *Italy: The New Domestic Landscape,* 238–39.

[129] Archizoom, *Italy: The New Domestic Landscape,* 235. Italics in original.

[130] Andrea Branzi, "Radical Architecture: Refusing the Disciplinary Role," *Casabella* 386 (1974): 46. This notion of the elimination of work was also central to the theses of earlier experimental practices such as that of Yona Friedman and Constant.

[131] Marazzi, "The Return of Politics," 16.

[132] Superstudio, *Italy: The New Domestic Landscape,* 242. See also page 245.

[133] Gruppo Strum, "For a Mediatory City," in *Italy: The New Domestic Landscape,* 254–55.

[134] Gruppo Strum, "For a Mediatory City," 255.

[135] See Filiberto Menna, "A Design for New Behaviors," in *Italy: The New Domestic Landscape,* 411.

[136] Menna, "A Design for New Behaviors," 411. He is citing *Gli strumenti del comincare* (Milan, 1967), the Italian edition of McLuhan's 1965 book, *Understanding Media.*

[137] Menna, "A Design for New Behaviors," 411.

138   Menna, "A Design for New Behaviors," 412.

139   Tafuri, *History of Italian Architecture*, 99.

140   Emilio Ambasz, "Summary" in *Italy: The New Domestic Landscape*, 422. See also Menna on this point.

141   Ambasz, "Summary," 422.

142   Menna, "A Design for New Behaviors," 405.

143   Curated by K. G. Pontus Hultén, *The Machine As Seen at the End of the Mechanical Age* was on view at MoMA from November 27, 1968, through February 9, 1969. *Information* was on view from July 2 through September 20, 1970, and thus premiered the exhibiting of the Sacco chair, which was included in the *Recent Acquisitions* show of 1970, curated by Ambasz and Drexler.

144   MoMA press release no. 38, page 8. See also Menna, "A Design for New Behaviors," 408–9.

145   Alain Touraine, *The Post-Industrial Society: Tomorrow's Social History: Classes, Conflicts and Culture in the Programmed Society*, trans. Leonard F. X. Mayhew (New York: Random House, 1971). On the relation of this paradigm to contemporary art practices, see Janet Kraynak, "Dependent Participation: Bruce Nauman's Environments," *Grey Room* 10 (winter 2003): 22–45.

146   Tafuri, "Design and Technological Utopia," 396. Tafuri is discussing an installation of Enzo Mari from 1967.

147   Ambasz's own work later takes on an increasingly transcendental character. In the 1985 interview with Barbaralee Diamonstein, he responded affirmatively to the question of whether his buildings were metaphors, adding, "They stand for the celestial dwelling we aspire to, we desire." Barbaralee Diamonstein, "Interview with Emilio Ambasz," in *American Architecture Now II* (New York: Rizzoli, 1985), 20.

148   Ambasz uses these terms while reflecting back on the work of *Architettura Radicale*. See Emilio Ambasz, "Architettura Radicale," in *Emilio Ambasz Inventions: The Reality of the Ideal* (New York: Rizzoli, 1992), 71–81, 79.

149   Emilio Ambasz, "Le designer comme réalisateur," *Architecture d'aujourd'hui* 193 (October 1977): 64–66. See Walter Benjamin, "The Author as Producer" (1934), trans. Edmund Jephcott, in *Walter Benjamin: Selected Writings*, ed. Michael W. Jennings (Cambridge, Mass.: Harvard University Press, 1999): 768–82. Benjamin's text was also, of course, an important one for Tafuri.

150   Ambasz, "The Designs of Freedom," 364.

151   In "The Proliferation of Margins," Guattari cautions against the likelihood of an updated dynamic of co-optation similar to that Tafuri recognized with respect to traditional oppositional strategies. But he argues, "Other forms of protest prove, on the other hand, to be much more dangerous to the extent that they threaten the essential relationships on which this system is based (the respect for work, for hierarchy, for State power, for the religion of consumption…). It is impossible to trace a clear and definite boundary between the recuperable marginals and other types of marginalities on the way to truly 'molecular revolutions.' The frontiers actually remain blurred and unstable both in time and space," 108.

152   See Michael Hardt and Antonio Negri, *Empire* (Cambridge: Harvard University Press, 2000).

THE IMMORTAL
Peter Hall

Salomon saith, *"There is no new thing upon the earth.* So that as Plato had an imagination, that all knowledge is but remembrance; so Salomon giveth his sentence, *that all novelty is but oblivion."*
— Francis Bacon, *Essays*

When I came out of the last cellar, I found him at the mouth of the cave. He was stretched out on the sand, where he was tracing clumsily then erasing a string of signs that, like the letters in our dreams, seem on the verge of being understood and then dissolve. . . .

Everything was elucidated for me that day. The Troglodytes were the Immortals; the riverlet of sandy water the River sought by the horseman. As for the city whose renown had spread as far as the Ganges, it was some nine centuries since the Immortals had razed it. With the relics of its ruins they erected, in the same place, the mad city I had traversed: a kind of parody or inversion and also temple of the irrational Gods who govern the world and of whom we know nothing, save that they do not resemble man. This establishment was the last symbol to which the Immortals condescended. It marks a stage at which, judging that all undertakings are in vain, they determined to live in thought, in pure speculation.
— Jorge Luis Borges, *The Immortal*

A great deal of industrial design and architecture might be viewed, after Borges, as the vain pursuit of immortality. Our impulse to leave palimpsestic traces and mad cities to our offspring is periodically undermined by our suspicion that all novelty is oblivion, as Bacon reminds us. If the troglodytes of *The Immortal* found refuge from this paradox in the solace of thought and "pure speculation" (as, indeed, did Borges, the writer, librarian, and voracious reader), the industrial designer faces a more troubling impasse. Historically, designers have been shackled to the idea that they must *produce* to survive. In the United States, as has been well documented, the role of the industrial designer was first defined in the 1920s as a subsidiary of advertising, to sell consumer goods through the addition of novelty, of seductive styling. "The industrial designer began as the man who persuaded industry to make those dreary household gadgets and appliances look glamorous," noted George Nelson archly in a *Fortune* magazine editorial of 1934, "thus starting a love affair with the American housewife that is not yet over."[1] The tryst is still ongoing. The annual "design" issue of the *New York Times Magazine,* despite its best intentions to prove that design is not an "affectation or afterthought," spends most of its pages actually reinforcing the point, displaying designer jeans, $20,000 phones, and *Wallpaper* magazine, which, as critic Stephen Bayley put it, presents design as "meretricious exclusivity."[2]

The industrial design work of Emilio Ambasz belongs to a critical trajectory that runs in opposition to this perceived role of design as novelty, affectation, and afterthought, a resistant strain whose notables include Nelson, R. Buckminster Fuller, and the current crop of young Dutch designers associated with Droog Design, who have turned design into defiance of built-in obsolescence. Ambasz's studio generates most of its own projects, surveying the Borgesian impasse, as it were, from the caves of pure speculation. "That thing which does not come into being does not die," as the Zen Buddhist teaching goes. According to one insider who worked in the Ambasz camp during the 1980s, for every product that saw the light of day, there were dozens that remained only as thoughts. But when speculation is taken into production, as is the inevitable obligation of every designer operating outside academia, Ambasz's objects strive to serve human needs over desires. They aim toward what Victor Papanek, scourge of the design establishment, called in 1971 "honest design (design-in-use versus design-in-sales.)"[3] Papanek famously characterized design's pioneers—Van Doren, Bel Geddes, Deskey, and Teague—as window display and stage designers who brought "visual excitement" but not nourishment to manufacturing during the Depression, much as "the swollen belly of a child suffering from malnutrition gives it the appearance of being well fed."[4] Finding more to applaud in the wartime era of design driven by performance criteria and limited materials, Papanek called for designers to make greater sacrifices, and much more innovative work that would contribute to "real human and social needs."[5]

Ambasz's Vertebra chair, designed with Giancarlo Piretti, would appear to be a prize example of what Papanek was calling for. The first automatic, articulated task chair, Vertebra sought to make the device we sit in for hours a day less unhealthy. Or, as Mario Bellini described it, Vertebra strove "to make it possible for the user to consider the chair as a dynamic and active entity, changing its configuration automatically, whenever the body desires."[6]

Aside from establishing a benchmark for ergonomic seating (a point to which we shall return), the Vertebra chair was singled out by one triumvirate of critics—Stephen Bayley, Philippe Garner, and Deyan Sudjic—as evidence of a structural change in the manner in which design is practiced.[7] In a climate of "just-in-time" inventories and computerized manufacturing systems, the consultant designer could no longer distance himself from the dreary subject of sales returns or the challenge of modifying products in response to production or market demands:

air, 1974–75.

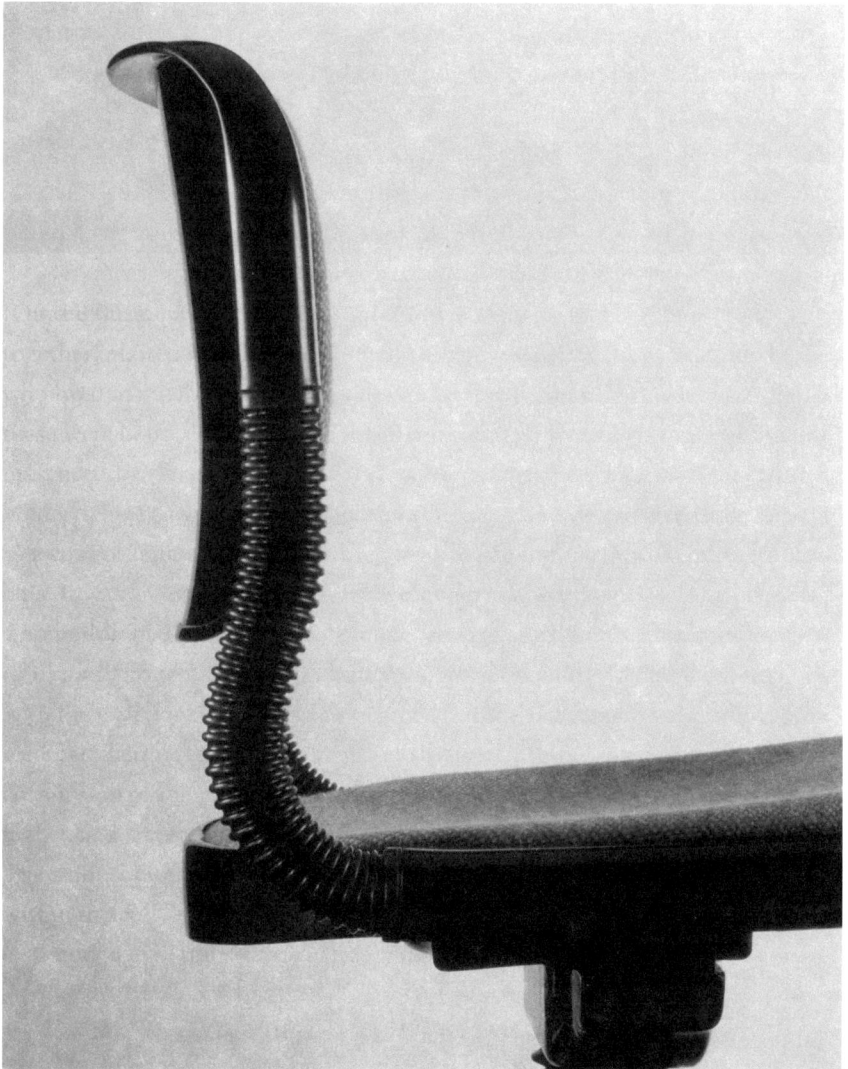

Ambasz no longer expects commissions to come to him, instead he develops his products himself. With his Vertebra chair of 1979, for instance, he sold a part of the future business to tool-makers, die-casters and upholsterers, persuading them to make tools and dies at no cost in anticipation of a share of the profits. He also carried out his own market projection, and so was able to approach the manufacturers, Castelli, with a fully costed program. The company therefore was able to undertake the manufacture of the chair, itself a design of some ingenuity, with virtually no risk because the designer had removed much of the uncertainty from the design process.[8]

In Ambasz's world, the designer becomes a figure who not only speculates on what might be, but follows through by pulling together a production team and taking on full responsibility for the costs and societal impact of that team's creations. Industrial design is thus detached from its moorings to advertising.

It would be misleading, however, to categorize the work of Ambasz as "honest design" in the Papanek mold. In addressing Ambasz's influences, and his influence on the profession, it is important to note three important fore-bears: Bucky Fuller, George Nelson, and Ettore Sottsass Jr. Fuller's utopian view of technology and tireless search for inexpensive, mobile, resource-saving structures established the foundations on which designers like Ambasz would later build. Nelson's playful experimentalism with materials and processes, his deft visual wit and ability to recognize design's impact beyond the sales curve established an equally important precedent: in 1949, Nelson argued that the profession's most important job was to reintegrate a society shattered by the pressure of new technology, infusing "emotional content" into inanimate objects.[9] The Ball Clock, launched a year later, certainly suc-ceeded in bringing cheerful modernity in through America's kitchen doors in its allusions to technological iconography—the atom and the asterisk. Nelson's position marked a departure from Fuller's version of design as a means by which technology is harnessed to man's physical and spiritual well-being. Nelson's demonstration that mass-produced perfection might be given a phenomenological twist, and that design might become the salve to—rather than the embodiment of—the march of technological progress had an important impact, in turn, on the young Ettore Sottsass Jr., who worked in Nelson's New York studio in 1956. Sottsass subsequently recalled learning from Nelson that design is not just a matter of being creative or

er for *Italy:*
Domestic Landscape.

Italy: The New Domestic Landscape
Achievements and Problems of Italian Design   The Museum of Modern Art, New York

original, but "abandoning yourself" and "understanding where society is going."[10] In Sottsass and his Italian cohorts, designed objects became capable of framing questions.

    Ambasz's pivotal contribution to the Italian-led antirationalist revolt was not as a designer but as curator of the Museum of Modern Art's landmark 1972 exhibition *Italy: The New Domestic Landscape*. The exhibition marked a significant change of perspective for MoMA, which, as Jonathan Woodham has noted, "had tended to focus on the aesthetics of the individual object or celebrated designer."[11] Featuring the work of Sottsass, Mario Bellini, Andrea

Branzi, Gaetano Pesce, Enzo Mari, and others, *Italy: The New Domestic Landscape* gave gallery space to the Italian notion of objects as part of a utopian environment in which self-sustaining technology liberated the individual from the death spiral of work and conspicuous consumption, and with symbolism—as Sottsass stressed—launched him or her on a path of self-discovery.

Ambasz took a coolly detached, curatorial tone in his introduction to the exhibition catalog, identifying three prevalent attitudes toward design in Italy at the time. The "conformist" approach referred to designers who did not question the sociocultural context in which they worked, but continued to refine already established forms and functions.[12] The "reformist" approach referred to designers who had a "profound concern" for their role in a society that encourages consumption as a means of inducing happiness, and responded with a "rhetorical mode," producing ironic revivals or seeking refuge in natural forms. The third approach, argued Ambasz, was "one of contestation"— either refusing to take part in the socio-industrial system at all or engaging in "active critical participation." In this account, Ambasz began to reveal glimpses of the ground rules that would guide his design explorations in subsequent decades:

> To the traditional preoccupation with aesthetic objects, these contemporary designers have therefore added a concern for an aesthetic of the uses made of these objects. This holistic approach is manifested in the design of objects that are flexible in function, thus permitting multiple modes of use and arrangement. To one accustomed to dealing with finite shapes that can act as points of reference, such objects can be offensive, because they refuse to adopt a fixed shape or to serve as reference to anything.[13]

The statement might be taken to apply to Sottsass's subsequent Carlton Bookcase of 1981, perhaps better described as a labyrinth of shelves in search of a bookcase. Defiantly anti-functionalist, the Carlton was a manifestation of Sottsass's argument that since there was no design solution that could not be replaced by another, one must initiate a methodology with the focus less on perfect form than on the "method of searching for form."[14] Yet the pursuit of objects that "refuse to adopt a fixed shape" applies more literally to Ambasz's Vertebra chair. Unlike the Carlton bookcase, the defiance of finite shapes inherent in the Vertebra's design has an eminently functional purpose: Ambasz claims that it emerged out of his oft-frowned-upon habit of swinging on the back two legs of a fixed chair. "I wanted it to move with me," he says.[15] As fellow task-chair designer Niels Diffrient has observed, this instinct is natural. "The more you lean back, the more you transfer weight on to the backrest instead of your spine." The Vertebra chair, noted Bellini, "does not engage the abdominal muscles, and allows the user to exercise the inter-vertebral discs, thereby actively maintaining the flowing of fluids in the dorsal spine."[16] Diffrient concludes: "It was a breakthrough product—it did what it intended to do with very few controls. The mechanisms were ingenious: It not only had a tilting back but a sliding seat co-ordinated with it."[17]

At the same time, one cannot ignore the semantic aspects of the chair's form. The now ubiquitous ribbed tubular treatment of the chair back's articulating mechanism clearly alluded to the spine, the soft flexing forms suggesting, without direct iconographic reference, that this servile seat might yet have its own soul. "Vertebra behaves like we do, as organisms in motion," noted one complementary text.[18] Subsequent Ambasz designs, as we shall see, play more explicitly with anthropomorphism, from the snail-shaped air filter to the dove-shaped water bottle. Design, as Ambasz has often stated, gives "poetic form to the pragmatic."[19]

After leaving MoMA, Ambasz found that green architecture was not enough to support him ("all my clients were other architects," he says[20]) so he turned—following the pattern of the young Italian architects he had fêted at MoMA—to industrial design. In doing so, he developed a methodology— modernist in its follow-through, but with some of Sottsass's poetic flair—that established an important concession to our desire for traces. His objects aspired toward immateriality by recalling archetypes. "It has always been my deep belief that architecture and design are both myth-making acts," begins Ambasz's fable *I Ask Myself*, perhaps titled in an echo of Borges's essay *Borges and I*. "I hold that their real tasks begin once functional and behavioral needs have been satisfied."[21]

If we were to borrow a literary mode to analyze the Ambasz oeuvre, then, we might appropriately turn to the archetypal criticism of Northrop Frye et al. Reading a text according to archetypal criticism depends on identifying themes, images, symbols, plots, and characters that correspond with recurring archetypes of myths and rituals. Its defiantly anti-Marxist premise is that these literary elements cannot be simply explained with reference to social, biological, or historical influences because they are linked to sources prior to these contexts. Such an approach, though criticized as reductivist, can in skilled hands be expansive, connecting diverse and various mythologies, enlightening the reader with the links, implications, and sometimes ambiguities embedded in a text. Borges, whose work encourages intertextual readings, offers clues to suggest that his layered topology of textual signposts might ultimately lead to a core of meta-signs, or archetypes. He once argued that there are only four basic devices of all fantastic literature: the work within a work, the voyage in time, the contamination of reality by a dream, and the double.

Ambasz declares, consciously recalling a remark from Borges, that he is a "man of few ideas many times reformulated."[22] The ergonomic chair, for example, has remained a perennial pursuit at Ambasz's studio. The chair has a status in mythology that might at first seem contradictory to contemporary perceptions of ergonomic seating. In pre-Hispanic Colombia, for example, the most common portrayal of the human form was in a seated posture. Male deities, priests, and shamans were commonly depicted in ceramics and gold, seated on benches; their demeanor was invariably impassive, suggesting inner calm and contemplation, seated at the confluence of sky and water. In Asiatic countries, the seat similarly expressed synthesis, stability, and unity. Yet contemporary understanding of human factors suggests that the body does not thrive from prolonged stasis and stability, and the best chair does not remain fixed in a "comfortable" position but moves with the body. Considered in a mobile form, as a chariot, however, the seat's symbolism gains an interesting additional meaning. J. E. Cirlot observes the following characteristics of the chariot archetype:

> The charioteer represents the *self* of Jungian psychology; the chariot the human body and also thought in its transitory aspects relative to things terrestrial; the horses are the life-force; and the reins denote intelligence and will-power.[23]

According to an archetypal reading, then, the chair in flux—the task chair—can represent both a position of power and inner calm as well as an embodiment of the human form. The division between physical seat and sitter is dissolved, the whole representing the body and mind in cohesion.

Ambasz applied the notion of the integrated sitter and seat to even the humble institutional chair, first with Dorsal (1978) and then with the basic office-worker chair Lumb-R (1981). Both incorporated a responsive backrest and contoured forms designed to maximize blood circulation and provide optimal weight distribution, but using simple flexing mechanisms. An archetypal reading might also identify in the chairs' profiles the presence of hybrid marks derived from the Greek alphabet, reminding us of the troglodyte's palimpsestic tracings and erasings in *The Immortal*. The same elemental, delineated approach is apparent in the later VoX Contract Chair (1996) and the Stacker Contract Chair (1998), both folding and stackable institutional chairs that employ the letter X as legs and the structural means of support for the back-rest, seat beam, and optional armrest and writing tablet. Again, a simple flexing backrest, made in Delrin (VoX) and ABS (Stacker), aims to provide better sup-port for sitters in public places, who may find themselves spending up to three

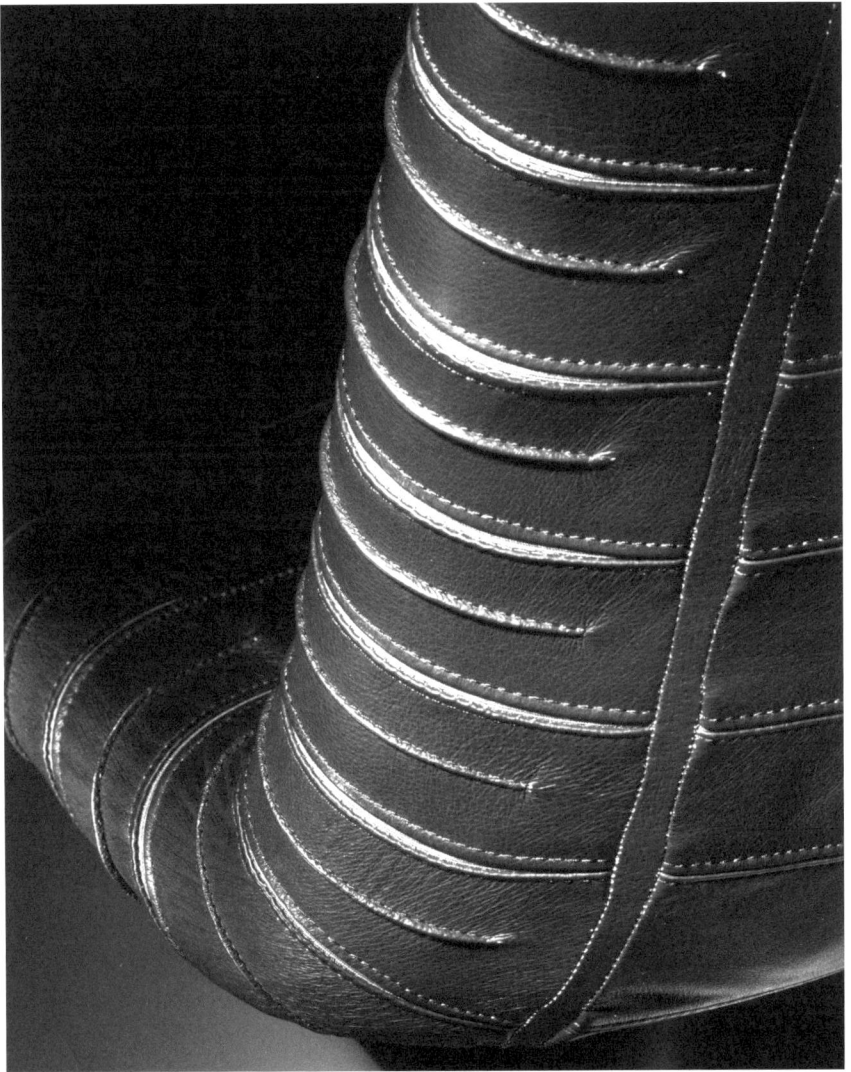

hours in such a seat in a school, waiting area, or factory. Symbolically, the X, at least according to symbols scholar Harold Bayley, denotes the union of two worlds—the superior and inferior.[24] It would seem a perfectly appropriate letter to support the union of mind, body, and man-made environment.

The 1991 Vertair chair pursues more anthropomorphic associations in an upholstery system, a series of narrow, overlapping leather bands stitched to elastic, all expanding and contracting with the sitter's motion. Unlike the recent spate of hard-edged, airily named high-tech ergonomic chairs that have emerged from the furniture giants and that boast dozens of operational levers and tension controls, Vertair's automatic adjustment does not require the office worker to read and digest a hefty instruction manual before sitting down. Levers, buttons, and knobs are banished from the form in favor of a minimalist form Ambasz calls "soft-tech," but might equally be described as crustacean. Allusions to animals as life-forces are common enough in mythology; in Ambasz's designs, the reference recurs as a playful hint.

In three subsequent designs—Brief (1995), Max Operative (1996), and Tennis (1997)—the seating system gains a more sail-like quality, becoming the wingéd chariot, perhaps. Formal origins might be traced to the earlier Qualis seating system (1989), which poses the question "what is it?" through variations on a theme: high-tech features, such as a self-adjusting tilt-forward to relieve pressure on the thighs, are underplayed in favor of a soft, folded rectangular form gently hinting, perhaps, at Magistretti's Sinbad chair (inspired by a thrown blanket). The soft geometry is then applied to various configurations, with arms, without, with wheels and without (again, recalling the inscribed letter). With Brief, Max, and Tennis, however, ergonomic issues are more thoroughly addressed. Office chairs, until recently, were designed for the 50th percentile man, a somewhat mythical figure in himself, vastly outnumbered in offices these days by men and women of various shapes and sizes. One solution to the diversity of sizes in the workplace is to manufacture chairs in three sizes—small, medium, and large. The downside is that office workers are less likely than ever to stay in the same job for more than a few years, increasing the likelihood that he or she will bequeath an ill-fitting seat to his or her replacement. Ambasz's solution: a height-adjustable backrest and armrests, to provide lumbar support for a variety of sizes. The function is visually expressed in the sail-like forms of the backrests, which convey their independent maneuverability.

If the Ambasz task chairs are an extension, to paraphrase Marshall McLuhan, of the entire human form, then his pens are an extension of the

office seating. 1995.

ax Operative
96.

is office seating.

hand. Ambasz first explored this contention, or that "everything is a prosthetic device," as he puts it, in a collection of durable, brightly colored ballpoint pens designed for schoolchildren.[25] The personal challenge was to create a pen that doesn't break in the pocket when you sit on it. Ambasz's solution was a polypropylene form which, like the human finger, transforms from flexible (for carrying) to rigid (for writing). A central ribbed midsection on the pen shaft flexes with movement, but the tubular lower and upper housings on each side can be twisted and snapped together to form a rigid shell that encloses the center. The upper housing also serves to protect the nib when the pen is in its "flexible" mode. Designer Eric Chan, who assisted Ambasz on the project, notes: "It's a very poetic idea, with a distinct before and after. Emilio always wants to simplify a mechanism, not in a mechanical way, but in an organic way. He's very good at non-traditional ways of solving problems."[26] To underline the point, Ambasz's later Magic Wand Automatic Roller Pen (1998) eliminates even the act of removing a pen cap or depressing a button to begin writing. Using a hidden automatic mechanism, the Magic Wand only proffers a writing nib when the user takes the pen out to write. As Chan puts it, "For Emilio an idea has to be groundbreaking or it's not worth doing."[27]

The literary critic James E. Irby has written of Borges that he demonstrates the "magic in obtaining the most powerful effects with a strict economy of means."[28] Sottsass has extended a similar notion to Ambasz's design, arguing in 1988 that Ambasz's body of work is "born from an obsessive search for primary principles, from a careful and wise observation of the surrounding reality, from an identification of humanistic problems."[29] Ambasz's various lighting projects are the result of a search for a primary geometrical principle that might maximize the degrees of freedom available to a cylindrical form.

The first manifestation, the Polyphemus flashlight (1983), demonstrates the answer: an elliptical cylinder is sectioned at a forty-five-degree angle, producing a highly maneuverable one-eyed head. When the top half is rotated, the light forms an L-shape that is easier to carry and more direct than the conventional cylinder flashlight. The beam can also be directed with the light in standing position or, using a magnet in the light base, attached to any metal surface. Characteristically, the one-eyed light is named after the Cyclops who was blinded by Odysseus on the island of Sicily.

Clearly, there is certain magician's delight inherent in developing this array of elemental forms that do not reveal themselves as lights or pens until used. In

Flexibol pens, 1985.

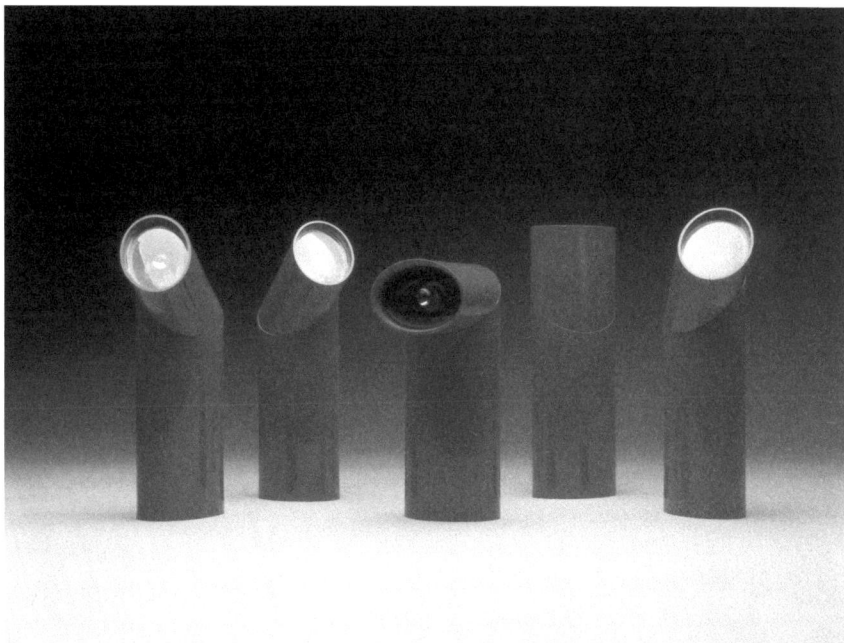

this respect, Ambasz shares something in common with a peer whose work he greatly admires, Richard Sapper. Sapper exemplified the transformational product in a series of IBM Thinkpads, which expand out of slick black cigar-box-sized volumes. Indeed, Ambasz produced a version of the IBM computer that extended the notion to a user-determined modular system. The IBM Portable Desktop (2000) proposed a one-size-fits-all smoked, tinted acrylic container, out of which would spring, as per the user's requirements, a height-adjustable screen (twelve- or sixteen-inch), a laptop-sized CPU, a DVD player, a wireless keyboard, and a handheld device/GSM phone. Again, a literary parallel for the transformative container can be found in James E. Irby's account of Borges, who "uses mystery and the surprise effect in literature to achieve that sacred astonishment at the universe."[30] When the black Pandora's box contains a customizable computer—a window to the mysteries of the World Wide Web—sacred astonishment might admittedly be more akin to the *horror* of Joseph Conrad's *Heart of Darkness*.

More slicing of geometric volumes produced Oseris, a range of low-voltage spotlights named after the Egyptian god Osiris, who was murdered by his brother and sliced into fourteen pieces that were distributed around Egypt. Extending the principle behind Polyphemus, Ambasz established that if a semispherical volume is cut twice (if not fourteen times) with a plane, the intersections generate perfect circles, which, when turned against each other, describe a movement from zero to ninety degrees. The light can also turn on its vertical axis, providing a high degree of maneuverability that can be orchestrated in museum and other exhibition settings with the help of a printed scale.

Most ambitiously, Ambasz's Soft Series designs for handheld consumer electronics foreshadowed the much-ballyhooed ubiquitous computing age into which we are rapidly being thrust. With the soft Portable Radio/Cassette, Notebook Computer, Handkerchief TV, and Phone—which encased all the mechanical and electrical components inside padded leather skins—Ambasz made our communications and entertainment devices "wearable." The Handkerchief TV, like Sapper's Thinkpads, only reveals its function when unfolded like a piece of origami; in folded form it resembles a wallet. Each leather plane is opened to expose a distinct function: screen, antenna, battery/speaker, and external ports. But where Sapper celebrates the engineered mechanisms of his unfolding designs, Ambasz pursues simpler, more organic guises. The very human, ceremonial aspect of unfolding a soft leather case to reveal a phone is ultimately more important to Ambasz as a ritual than showcasing the mechanical feats required to create it.

As was noted in the catalog of Ambasz's 1992 exhibition at the Institute of Contemporary Art at Tokyo Station, "The miniaturization of technology has led to the increasing portability of televisions, computers, cassette tape players, and other commonly used products, but the forms and materials of these products have not fundamentally altered to reflect this technological development." Indeed, many of the forms proposed for these consumer electronics goods were derived from their mechanical forebears—the anachronistic typewriter interface as a means of inputting data into computers being the prime example. The Soft Series was a response to this perceived lack of momentum in design, positing a "zoological species" in place of hard-edged products with forms derived from their former, mechanical forebears.[32] The seeds of this foray into metaphor, however, can be traced back to Mario Bellini's "zoomorphic" Divisumma 18 calculator of 1970, which sported soft, nipplelike buttons and a rubbery, seal-like surface. Today, the old mechanical tropes are increasingly vanishing. Boomboxes have since 1992 mutated into an endless array of personages, from submarines to jeeps to compacts; cellphones are "clamshells" or—increasingly—resemble hearing aids; and cassette tape players have become miniscule MP3 players resembling bars of soap or jewelry.

Perhaps more than heralding the plunge of industrial design into

metaphor, the Soft Series anticipated the eventual absorption of electronic devices into the fabric of the built environment. In this respect, the immortality/materiality paradox posed at the beginning of this essay is compounded when we consider what happens to the industrial designer when a manufacturing-based economy turns into a New Economy and then a Now Economy. The implication might seem to be that the designer is left without a job to do, without an opportunity to leave a trace for posterity. "The visual design of objects and places becomes less relevant," writes Ole Bouman in *Archis* magazine, "if those objects and places, the good old As and Bs, are displaced by the movement between them as the criterion of our existence."[33]

One of the most beguiling recent Ambasz studio projects, the Saturno Street/Highway lighting, would appear to embrace this critical shift of attention away from objects and toward flows. The Saturno light not only provides a design solution to a problem of infrastructure, the highway, or what Marc Augé would call a "non-place,"[34] it aspires toward a form of "almost transparent presence," as Ambasz puts it.[35] Like crotchets and quavers on a musical score, their delicate forms are designed to be seen in sequences of motion. Yet a closer inspection of the lights reveals that a great deal of design work is required to make these objects a "transparent presence" in the built environment: the stainless-steel fabrication reduces maintenance costs to a minimum for highway authorities, a matte-polished surface enhanced by colored bumpers maximizes visibility, and ultraviolet-resistant polycarbonate light shields are colored to help drivers visually identify different quarters of the city or upcoming exits. The lights are even designed to bend easily when struck by a car. Furthermore, they incorporate an additional layer of infrastructure in the form of signage to alert drivers of traffic conditions.

Design in the age of ubiquitous computing, then, may be less concerned with the contrived symbolism of objects and places than with their cumulative effect. The designer's role becomes less of a sole artisan, turning mass-manufactured objects into art or criticism, than that of a director, preoccupied with the interactions between objects, environments, and humans.

It might be tempting to conclude from Ambasz's prodigious writings and rich array of designs, with their various symbolic properties and metaphysical aspirations, that we are dealing with an aesthete. But as the brief history of industrial design has proven, aesthetes rarely get beyond the walls of the Academy. Ambasz, an unrepentant pragmatist, goes to some lengths to provide bare-bones accounts of his designs: "I cannot make a non-utilitarian object," he says.[36] But the figure who identifies a problem, imagines a solution, and proceeds to pull together a team of modelmakers, engineers, and fabricators to build a prototype, and finally persuades a manufacturer to take this into production is arguably not a designer at all—he is an entrepreneur, a businessman. As Eric Chan puts it, Ambasz is a "hard core negotiator," who presents his ideas as "end results" to manufacturers, refusing to compromise the design.[37] Sudjic, Bayley, and Garner note that this approach "reduces the role of the manufacturer." They conclude:

> Emilio Ambasz is a quixotic figure and it is not to be expected that every other designer would wish, or even be able, to emulate this initiative. But new technology is going to lead increasingly to this kind of approach.[38]

The idea that this quixotic figure is not a designer at all is a pleasingly Borgesian way to conclude an essay assessing the industrial design of Emilio Ambasz. In *The Immortal,* Homer the writer has ceased to write; he is a cave-dweller scratching in the sand, a bookseller with an intimate knowledge of all books. Ambasz's own semi-autobiographical fable *Designer/Producer* is the tale of a designer who, frustrated with the compartmentalization of design and with manufacturers' unwillingness to take risks, forms a co-operative with a modelmaker, mechanic, production engineer, and mold-maker. The tale ends with a wicked twist:

> The reputation of the co-operative and its products grew; young designers came from far to offer their services. But the answer they

received at the door was always the same one: "You are an industrial designer? So sorry, so sorry, we have no use for them. Now if you were a cosmologist. . ."[39]

Or, as Papanek once put it: "It is about time that industrial design, *as we have come to know it*, should cease to exist."[40]

[1] Stanley Abercrombie, *George Nelson: The Design of Modern Design* (Cambridge, Mass.: MIT Press, 2000), 49.

[2] *New York Times Magazine*, December 1, 2002.

[3] Victor Papanek, *Design for the Real World: Human Ecology and Social Change* (New York: Pantheon Books, 1972), 33.

[4] Ibid., 31.

[5] Ibid., 39.

[6] Mario Bellini, in *Emilio Ambasz: The Poetics of the Pragmatic* (New York: Rizzoli, 1988), 13.

[7] Stephen Bayley, *Twentieth-Century Style & Design* (New York: Van Nostrand Reinhold Company, 1986), 287.

[8] Ibid.

[9] Abercrombie, *George Nelson,* 52.

[10] Sottsass, quoted in *George Nelson,* x.

[11] Jonathan Woodham, *Twentieth Century Design* (New York and London: Oxford University Press, 1997), 194.

[12] Emilio Ambasz, *Italy: The New Domestic Landscape* (New York: Museum of Modern Art, 1972), 19.

[13] Ibid., 21.

[14] Volker Albus, in *Icons of Design: The 20th Century* (New York: Prestel, 2000), 121.

[15] Emilio Ambasz, interview by author, September 16, 2002.

[16] Bellini, in *Emilio Ambasz: The Poetics of the Pragmatic,* 13.

[17] Niels Diffrient, interview by author, October 3, 2002.

[18] *Emilio Ambasz: The Poetics of the Pragmatic,* 242.

[19] Charlotte and Peter Fiell, *Industrial Design A–Z* (London: Taschen, 2000), 212.

[20] Emilio Ambasz, interview by author, September 16, 2002.

[21] *Emilio Ambasz: The Poetics of the Pragmatic,* 24.

[22] Emilio Ambasz, interview by author, September 16, 2002.

[23] J. E. Cirlot, *A Dictionary of Symbols* (London: Routledge & Kegan Paul, 1984), 43.

[24] Ibid.

25 Emilio Ambasz, interview by author, September 16, 2002.

26 Eric Chan, interview by author, September 20, 2002.

27 Ibid.

28 James E. Irby, introduction to *Labyrinths,* by Jorge Luis Borges (New York: New Directions, 1988), xx.

29 *Emilio Ambasz: The Poetics of the Pragmatic,* 10.

30 James E. Irby, introduction to *Labyrinths,* xi.

31 Emilio Ambasz, *Inventions: The Reality of the Ideal* (New York: Rizzoli, 1992), 288.

32 Ibid.

33 Ole Bouman, in *Archis* (November 2002).

34 Marc Augé, *Non-places: Introduction to an Anthropology of Supermodernity* (London: Verso, 1995).

35 *Emilio Ambasz: Natural Architecture and Artificial Design* (Milan: Elemond Electa, 2002), lxv.

36 Emilio Ambasz, interview by author, September 16, 2002.

37 Eric Chan, interview by author, September 20, 2002.

38 Stephen Bayley, *Twentieth-Century Style & Design,* 287.

39 *Emilio Ambasz: The Poetics of the Pragmatic,* 48.

40 Victor Papanek, *Design for the Real World,* 38.

MYST
Jerrilynn D. Dodds

eum of History.
ona. 1989.

RUINS

Kublai Khan does not necessarily believe everything Marco Polo says when he describes the cities visited on his expeditions, but the Emperor of the Tartars does continue listening. It is the desperate moment when we discover that this empire, which had seemed to us the sum of all wonders, is an endless, formless ruin, that corruption's gangrene has spread too far to be healed by our scepter, that the triumph over enemy sovereigns has made us the heirs of their long undoing. Only in Marco Polo's accounts was Kublai Khan able to discern, through the walls and towers destined to crumble, the tracery of a pattern so subtle it could escape the termite's gnawing.
—Italo Calvino, *Invisible Cities*

The famous mythology, the mysticism, the primordial pull that are the basis for much discussion of Emilio Ambasz's work (including his own) are terms so reductive and grandiose as to erode a useful sense of specific meaning. And this is a shame, because subsequent scholarly attempts to meet those values with theoretical or art-historical arguments become similarly overblown. That the sense of wonder excited by Ambasz's proposals for, say, Houston Center Plaza or his house for Leo Castelli should cause otherwise quite sober scholars to lunge for Foucault or Jung is, I think, to obscure the earthbound nature of those projects and to suggest that they are somehow *sui generis,* or occur outside of the structure of history and historicity as it is worked through in contemporary architecture by other mortals. Ambasz's projects are in fact personal and specific, created with, as Michael Sorkin has observed, "the full certification of the subconscious."[1]

The difficulty in dealing with Ambasz lies in that very ambivalent frontier between the architect's personal vision and his representation of primordial desire: between the architect as storyteller and the architect as Olympian. What results are self-contained worlds, true to their own laws, the stories told by a particular architect and fabulist to a particular patron: each a dike against a particular set of hegemonic and cultural ruins.

Which is perhaps why ruins need to figure in what otherwise seem somewhat whimsical and innocent designs. Riley has made a connection between a number of Ambasz's schemes and Enlightenment-era Arcadian images of America, suggesting that they function today as a buffer for "the existentialist angst of the pre- and postwar periods."[2] But there is a melancholy, he maintains, a nod to the evanescence and "transience of the man-made world" evoked in Ambasz's work by images like "future ruins arranged along an ever-moving stream or bathed in an evanescent cloud of steam."[3]

This might be said in particular for the schemes that consciously evoke romantic garden designs, historical *topoi* meant to arouse just such a sensibility. The functions of the Schlumberger Research Laboratories are "arranged casually around a man-made lake," according to the architect, "in the manner of an English landscape garden."[4]

Here the earth berms familiar from much of Ambasz's work nose into the light like cartoon crocodiles, their glowing columnar teeth breaking the surface of the campus lawn. But there are also quietly overt classicizing features, temples and follies barely removed from Stourhead or Stowe. These undisguised historical quotations anchor the proposal for the Schlumberger laboratories in time and give it a humility and lucidity harder to discern in projects where the historical reference is more oblique and serves a more mythic image.

These veiled uses of history can have specific or elusive relationships to the programs they ultimately serve. Perhaps the most conscious of these temporal excavations is Ambasz's project for the Phoenix Museum of History, where geological and cultural history peek demurely from beneath the blanket of an urban meadow. Here, eroded, terraced rock gives way to an adobe wall that winds into the slope in a fetal spiral, suggesting the layered vestiges of the city's history; the past of the actual place is only partially uncovered in a generous, austere kind of understatement. The subterranean galleries include a stream, a pond, and a rupestral hypostyle hall that suggests the intersection of an underground parking garage with a rock-cut temple: a descent into the city's messy and ambivalent past, a ferreting into its actual stratigraphy.

The strategy employed at Phoenix is like a distilled, mythologized version of the one born at the Stuttgart Neue Staatsgalerie in 1984, where James Sterling used labyrinthine changes in elevation and a juxtaposition of ancient and pseudo-ancient architectural forms, confusing the created and the curated. Sterling scattered new ashlar blocks, like the vestiges of an ill-kept Mediterranean amphitheater, next to suggestive holes in the contemporary building's fabric, a lighthearted riff on the nature of monuments and on their ultimate destination as artifact.

Ambasz's own review of Sterling's work, entitled "Popular Pantheon," praises it with a kind of hysterical, enthusiastic laying-on of scent; he explains Sterling's every gesture, deconstructs for us each level of parody and self-consciousness, and baptizes it "memorable architecture" with the authority of an aging, if slightly agitated, sage. This was clearly territory Ambasz meant to occupy himself, though in a different way.

At Phoenix, Ambasz employed the archaeological conceit but avoided the kind of specificity that gave Sterling's work both its intellectual hook and its monumental, self-effacing humor. Even the historical forms—"triangular wall sections functioning like the buttresses of indigenous adobe architecture"[6] reads one description generated by Ambasz himself—are reduced to a kind of organic common denominator, so that a sense of a specific time, or even of a specific fictive history, is absent from the design. It rather conveys an experience akin to history, one so general as to nurture Ambasz's search for the ultimate history. "I long for an architecture that has been reduced to essentials, and which, at the same time, is an architecture full of potential meanings," he says in one part of "Fragments for a Credo," and in another, "My work is a search for primal things," and "Architecture is for me one aspect of our quest for cosmological models."[5]

The distillation of forms and the masking of historical reference are Ambasz's strategy for evoking the primordial, a strategy that also requires dissociation from specific models.

So in the architectural discourse that splits historicist reference into divergent camps—explicit reference, and a kind of mock archaeology—Ambasz nestles comfortably among the ruins. But his insistence on appearing *sui generis* clouds the interpretive waters. And Ambasz's refusal to relinquish the tempting grandiosity of time travel, his distinct lack of the humor that tempers Sterling's grand project, makes generation of meaning in Ambasz's work more problematic.

Even in projects where the layering of history does not nestle so perfectly within a building's voice as it does in Phoenix, the melancholy of ruins is present in Ambasz's work, though now they serve more elusive goals. And the pleasurable irony of finding them in a golf course is particularly gratifying. At the Mycal Cultural and Athletic Center at Shin-Sanda, the exterior face of an L-shaped wall is disembodied by splayed, undulating greenhouses. Its interior facade is opaque and monumental, and is made to confront an encroaching hillside that mounds up and obscures the steplike terraces inscribed on the wall. Like the seats of an amphitheater buried through time, these terraces are made to yield to nature. Looking through the exterior glass walls and the building's greenhoused structure, one finds any remaining traces of the terraces on the interior are dematerialized by the invading plants, which seem to have pushed through an ancient masonry to repossess the land inhabited by this ruin.

It is the disembodiment of the monolithic monument, its violation, which is celebrated here, and which gives the yielding-to-nature its particular drama and pleasure. Without the ruin, the power of the possession of place by nature would be lost. Like the taxidermed head of an ancient quarry, the ruin of the monument is the fetishized proof of the power of nature to reassert life in the face of despotic and overweening architectural culture.

So at the heart of the impact of many of Ambasz's designs, celebrated for their empowerment of nature, is the notion of the evanescent monument, impermanent in the face of nature. The violation of the monument is also meant to represent, in many regards, the violation of historical reference. Ambasz has spoken quite lucidly of his disdain for the traditions that license the profession to have its way with history.

> I am not striving to maintain a continuum with history, nor am I against a search for ornament. Architects returning to historical sources only to utilize elements that make sense to each other, end up talking in a hermetic language that can be understood only by those initiated into the cult.[6]

oridge Trade
ent Center.
laryland, 1989.

que,
xico.

Ambasz's resistance is not to history, but to historical reference as the basis for a discourse, and his challenge to insular, intra-professional theories can be seen as an echo of the values explored in the works just discussed, values that undermine the immutable hegemony of the monument over the land.

The tensions present for an architect like Ambasz in a program as large and demanding as the Worldbridge Trade and Investment Center, designed for a site in Baltimore, are significant. Despite the fact that the building was required to impose as little as possible on the landscape, the office complex— the largest part of the program—looms over the site like a Mayan ruin. In plan the design of the complex is quite organic: undulating terraces that simulate topographical elevations. But in profile the structure is steep and rises from the site in a composed and coherent mass that suggests building rather than land- scape, despite the fact that it is meant to drip with vinelike growth. In fact, its steps and pyramidal massing mimic Saqqara or Palenque. And so again there is the suggestion of an ancient monument digested by the land. Like the tem- ples at Angor Wat and Thom, repossessed by the Cambodian jungle, the Worldbridge Center excites a morbid thrill from the specter of a monumental past consumed by a devouring nature.

Here the historical references are oblique because the forms are suggested rather than articulated, and yet they are infinitely legible, because they belong to the architectural vocabulary of mass culture. This might be one fragment for Ambasz's contention that his work evokes the primordial or mythic. For in history "mythic" values are established by a combination of recognition and erasure. Recognition, because form has penetrated the collective conscious of a society and culture in a deep and pervasive manner; and erasure, because an evocation of primordial necessarily demands that the actual circumstances under which that form was created are erased: its specific function and meaning for those who built and used it, cannot interfere with the collective fantasy which is the creation of a "universal" drama.

At Worldbridge a pyramid—the prime image of New Age pan-spiritualism, its universality confirmed by its appearance in multiple pre-Industrial cultures— is softened and kneaded, then slowly possessed by a fecund and unstoppable vegetation. Ambasz has succeeded in bringing his discourse beyond the insular professional theories he so despises, in some part because he harnesses collective awe of apparently immutable ancient monuments, and then makes us witnesses to their consumption by a more powerful nature. Ettore Sottsass's words come to mind here: "Each element of [Ambasz's] edifices is a bit like a talismanic instrument of a wager, of a hidden ritual to fascinate some immense natural deity."[7]

Sometimes Ambasz lets us witness vestiges of the struggle, and then the images seem to emerge from a sort of benevolent *Road Warrior* script vetted by Piranesi. His design for the winter garden of Union Station in Kansas City, which does not itself demand mechanical heating or cooling, glories in the obsolescence of the towering historical station upon which it encroaches. One part of the Museum of Modern Art and the Cinemas Museum in Buenos Aires [MAMBA] is described as an "obsolete modernist concrete frame office building" which can now only be given over to a "complex facade of 'hanging gardens.'"[8]

Perhaps the most romantic cinematic image, one as humorous and pleasurable as it is portentous, must be Ambasz's proposal for a Mercedes-Benz showroom in the wilds of New Jersey's commercial and industrial sprawl. This is how it is introduced in a catalog of the firm's recent work: "A showroom for new Mercedes-Benz automobiles finds itself on a small site with typical commercial buildings to its left. In order to hide an unattractive diner from the view of people approaching the showroom via the primary road access, a tall wall of polished black stone is erected."[9]

Ambasz's rather coy, understated description of the environmental impediments to be overcome for the success of the design evoke for those more familiar with this landscape of gas stations and oil refineries the aftermath of some future nuclear or environmental disaster, an aftermath we have already created, a microcosm of what might be with which we already live. This is why the image that polished black wall brings to mind—the monolith from Kubrick's

2001: A Space Odyssey—sits so easily in that imagined place. It is the ultimate primordial archaeological artifact of this century's Arcadian generation, embodying equally its idealism, its humility before nature and history, and its philosophical hubris and grandiosity. That this most presumptuous of all images is applied to a Mercedes-Benz Showroom is of course the best part of this fabulous ruin and its disintegration of time, for it gently echoes this same generation's consumption of such privileged products, the easy way in which materialism and commercialism share a table with Arcadian values.

Of course, the shining black monolith of the Mercedes-Benz Showroom does not suggest a specific reference to the cinematic one, any more than the Worldbridge Trade and Investment Center means a specific evocation of Saqqara or Tikal. In each case a whiff of history supplies a purposeful, reductive, ahistorical link to a collective subconscious which is increasingly global.

The collapse of time in this group of works by Ambasz occurs in the representation of a future, a utopia in which nature and basic values have had their way with culture, a future time in which the evanescence and fragility of humanity's bond to nature that we feel and fear so keenly today is a forgotten anxiety. The presence of history is necessary, not only to give weight to this fictive triumph of nature, but also to place this fantasy in an illusion of time, to give it a kind of chronological scale, and, importantly I think, to make the work's values broadly accessible.

Ambasz seems acutely aware of the extent to which culture, and architecture in particular, have laid claim to spiritual territories in Euro-American secular life. And yet his claim to have created, in his own oeuvre, a kind of answer is stunning for its hubris:

The architecture I create is steeped in mysticism. On one hand, I am playing with the pragmatic elements that come from my time, such as technology. On the other hand, I am proposing a certain mode of existence that is an alternative, new one. My work is a search for primal things. They have to do with existence on an emotional, passionate and essential level.[10]

Ambasz presents himself as consequently concerned with harboring humane values, with their separation from the petty vanities and theories of the profession. Complaining that the profession uses history as an arcane insider language (they "return to historical sources only to utilize elements that make sense to each other"), he offers us instead his explanation for his own distillation of history. And when he complains that architects "end up talking hermetic language that can be understood only by those initiated into the cult,"[11] he distances himself from the use of theory as an explanation and justification for design.

Despite this discursive distancing from theory and contemporary architectural practice, a number of Ambasz's designs fit neatly into Decon's mock archaeological strategy, as it has been practiced by both Sterling and Eisenman. In some projects, such as Eisenman's University Art Museum at Long Beach, the project might be theorized in terms of metaphysics, but the working through of primordial values and the passage of time is strikingly similar. It is not clear, in fact, that Ambasz's reluctance to talk theory actually results in a new approach, or in a more purely generated style.

There is, of course, a difference between the idea of working outside theory—which many would argue impossible in any case—and simply not bearing responsibility for the synthetic values one generates. In particular, the acceptance of a reductive and mythical historical narrative—acquiescence to Emilio Ambasz's seductive primal storytelling—is a difficult intellectual exercise for a historian in a postcolonial environment. The assumption of a common primordial subconscious strikes one as puerile and provincial; dangerously colonial in its belief in a single human language of experience conceived in the land of Descartes. And yet the failure of regionalism to create something potent enough to defy the overwhelming power of the global collective, or complex enough to acknowledge the deep and at times resisted bonds— some ribbons, some chains—that bind us, makes us look twice. For that perhaps we are drawn into Ambasz's tale, and we begin to wonder about the possibility of a primal language again. Like the tortured American and the

Iraqi torturer in David O. Russel's *Three Kings*, we listen to the same music, attend the same schools, speak the same language, nurture the same children. Our mutual survival depends on recognition of a common humanity. Does it follow then that there is a valuable exercise in the creation of a common myth, one that supercedes culture, through architecture?

MYST

These words were developed for a specific task—that of creating other worlds—of writing them. Yes, Atrus, I made this world. I made the rock on which we stand and the very air we are breathing. I made the grass and the trees, the insects and the birds. I fashioned the flowers and the earth in which they grow. I made the mountains and streams. All that you see, I made.
—Rand Miller, Robin Miller, and David Wingrove, *Myst, The Book of Atrus* (backstory for *Myst*, the computer game)

I think that in opting to write fables rather than write theoretical essays I have grasped something basic: fables remain immutable long after theories have crumbled.
—Emilio Ambasz, "Fragments for a Credo"

Perhaps the attempt to create a common myth is valuable, if the story grows from Ambasz's more delicate experiential and ecological designs, but it might not be, if Emilio Ambasz is writing it. The design work, which has, at times, the capacity of a Baroque choir or a Safavid courtyard to excite real wonder, is markedly trivialized by his written fables.

Consider "Fabula Rasa," the story that ends with the words "Some people say this was how architecture started." In a "little village" in fear of the divine, an enterprising man conceives of a temple, a city perimeter, his own palace. "Fabula Rasa" is written in an unassuming, childlike style, nestled in a blanket of earthy irony that, like its title, distances the tale from experience and excludes it from any sort of historical accountability. Like the fictive tales of cities told to Kublai Khan by Marco Polo in Calvino's *Invisible Cities*, "Fabula" has the innocent conviction of a postmodern fairy tale, a charming lie aimed at deeper truths. Only the most obtuse would try to challenge primordial assumptions so magically and charmingly protected. But I'll bite.

"Fabula" is fabulously unquestioned. To give the most obvious example, all architecture in "Fabula" begins through the act of creation of a single male individual. The issue here is not to demonstrate that "Fabula" is historically incorrect—though the possibility that the earliest habitations were likely constructed by a female collective would have been, if anything, a more lively template to explore—it was not meant to be answerable to history at all. The point is that these myths, meant to position Ambasz beyond theory, serve as critiques of his own pretensions to represent the universal; their assumptions of what is primordial nail him to a specific set of social values, place and time, and to a remarkably unchallenged social and historical position.

The same childlike language is used to weave an aura of unaccountability around Ambasz's project for Barbie Knoll, the "ecological embodiment of the 'Barbie Doll,'" designed for a Mattel Corporation international traveling exhibition.[12] The design involves a sunken entrance, a "sacred entry courtyard" likened by the architect to a Greek temple, but showing equal affinity to the temples of Abu Simbel. Or, even more aptly, Hatshepsut, with its iconic representation of the now timeless Barbie, and its use of the terrain to create a transformative, awe-inspiring experience. In a subterranean space, there is an exhibition "showcasing the history of Barbie" through, among other devises, statue columns of the doll at different moments in her historical and social development. The chance to see Malibu Barbie take her well-deserved monumental place in architectural history is terrific fun, and the flat-out temple imagery makes Michael Graves's dwarves look like unctuous Disney yes-men. But then there is:

> "Barbie Knoll" silhouetted on the horizon, covered in grass and wildflowers. Children can climb upon her, tumbling and playing, making her become not only an ageless symbol of youth, but an enchanted playground. Lying protected in a green, outdoor courtyard, Barbie lies resting in the sun, an icon to the happiest times of days gone by and days to come.

I suppose it was necessary for the architect to imagine Barbie as "an ageless symbol of youth." Because if one represented her for what she is—a useful image of adolescent sexuality through which pre-adolescent girls imagine themselves into social and sexual viability—then the bikini-clad, recumbent, receptive image in the earthwork, fingers running through her hair (something that a Barbie doll cannot be made to do) and twisting her hips (Ambasz would say to accommodate the terrain) might be seen as better serving the fantasies of the Olympian storyteller of "Fabula Rasa" than the children who frolic in the courtyard of "Barbie Knoll."

"We must create alternative images of a better life to guide our actions," Ambasz has declared, "if we do not wish to perpetuate present conditions. I believe that any architectural project that does not attempt to propose new or better modes of existence is immoral. The task may stagger the imagination and paralyze hope but we cannot avoid it."[13]

If hope is not to be paralyzed, my personal hope is that my children, both male, will never be brought to frolic on the supine body of a recumbent bikini-clad Barbie, or to be asked to consider such an image primordial.

"Fabula" and Barbie Knoll must stem from that part of Ambasz's identity in which he poses as a whimsical yet wily primitive. They thus inadvertently reveal the palimpsest of desire that must layer any building, or any complex proposal for a building, and part of that is fueled, not just by a fable of humanity's connection with the earth (the theme he is concerned to make conscious), but also in a grandiose myth of individual male creation with the architect at its center. Though it does not have the effect of discrediting the depth and value of Ambasz's design work, it does free us from living in the callow tale that his fables construct.

Ambasz's designs are more layered and specific than the "mythic" and "primordial" discourse suggests; and so they plead for more discipline in the telling of the story. Against the backdrop of "Fabula Rasa," the primal concerns of Emilio Ambasz begin to recall nothing so much as the worlds created in the video game (and lively novelizations that followed) *Myst*, in which a super-race is able to write worlds into existence: to write their ecologies and cultures in magic, talismanic books that materialize these worlds, complete with nature, weather, and peoples. In more than one episode, the protagonist writes an ideal mate for himself into the world he controls. The adolescents who play *Myst* relate to the seductive image of masculine creation and control over that which is primordial in each created world.

And yet, distanced from the fables and credos, Ambasz's own designs can display an exquisitely delicate, experiential response to the specific, and the personal, which challenges the grandiose visions of agency manufactured in his written work. It is not the design, in the end, that grates; it is the grandiose claims of Olympian distance and the juvenile fantasies that grip the writing that accompanies it.

These two sides of Ambasz, unfettered from fable and credo, are present in a remarkable project, which has recently seen the light of day. "A contemporary reformulation of the traditional Andalucian house," the model for the Casa de Retiro Espiritual is, on one hand, an elegant, lyrical etching in the earth. Aquatic, wave-like forms seem to ache for the sea here in Spain's most arid, mounding landscape of wheat fields and blinding light. The cool submerged living spaces, the diffused light received through colored-glass tiles, the dazzling white heat of the open court answer climate, tradition and the kind of humility toward nature that seems at the core of Ambasz's concerns.

The facade of the house model emerges as another other side of Ambasz's architectural identity, the one that celebrates monument and maker. The issue becomes whether or not to consider it in light of the architect's own writing. He offers the following interpretation for the Casa facade:

> In Cordoba, I actually wanted to eliminate architecture. The only thing that was to stand was the facade, which would only be a mask, a surrogate for architecture. The architecture would disappear; you would only see the earth. You might say that by this device I seek, rhetorically, to eliminate architecture as a culturally conditioned process and return to the primeval notion of dwelling. I seek to develop an architecture that is both here and not here.[14]

Is the facade, which rests like an empty white book cover on the horizon, meant to seem a ruin, a piece of *spolia* from the time of architecture that somehow underscores its obliteration? There is no indication that he means us to see it quite in this way, and its wall is so unmolested—a sharp white geometric form rising from the model's featureless flat plain—that it seems more than anything else to be wall for its own sake. Then what is the part of architecture Ambasz wishes to eliminate if it is not the facade, for he continues to validate his own nurturing of spaces, textures, materials, the workings of light and shadow, the creation and erasure of ornament, in the same house?

The design, first of all, reflects substantial indebtedness to the work of John Hejduk,[15] in particular in the imposition of a stark geometric wall in opposition, even defiance, to its natural surroundings. But Hejduk would have owned up to his alienation from the environment, to his alliance with the object. Ambasz tries with words to will his wildly monumental gesture into a kind of negation of architecture as fetishized object, but this vast, blinding

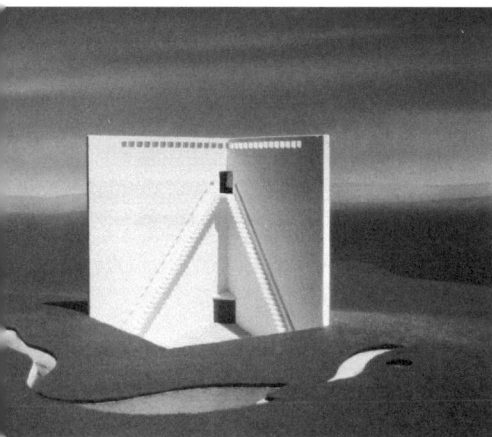

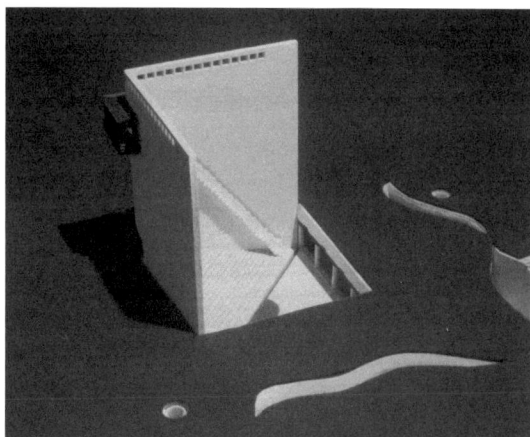

RIGHT: Casa de
itual (model).
pain, 1978.

asa de Retiro
as built).
pain, 1978.

billboard to architecture just cannot be made, visually and experientially, to mean "the obliteration of architecture" through words—especially through the words of an architect asking himself questions in a self-administered interview.

The sympathy of the Casa de Retiro Espiritual for the environment as depicted in the model has to do with a landscape as austere and featureless as the surface of the wall. It lends a timeless quality to both model and landscape, and draws one into a Bramante-esque primal discourse in which geometric form approximates the spiritual.

It is quite a shock, then, to see the Casa de Retiro Espiritual as finally built, rising like a grain elevator or a drive-in movie screen from a furry, arid olive grove. The mythic lunar landscape of the model gone, the house struggles with the ancient grove that embraces it, and material, color, and form suggest more the industrial orphan of a faulty planning code than a rustic retreat or "the obliteration of architecture." It is still striking, austere, and riveting in its exploitation of the raw light and shade of the Andalucian sun. But it is also a gratuitous personal mark on the landscape, and volumes of stories, whole worlds of words cannot make it otherwise.

Thanks to Michael Sorkin for numerous substantive comments that enormously enriched the content of this essay, and to Peter Wolf for wonderful and stimulating conversations about Ambasz and design. Thanks also to my son, Sanford Gifford, for suggesting the alliance of the writing styles of Ambasz and Calvino.

1   Sorkin, "Et in Arcadia Emilio," in *Emilio Ambasz: The Poetics of the Pragmatic* (New York: Rizzoli, 1991), 17.

2   Terence Riley, introduction to *Architettura Naturale. Emilio Ambasz: Progetti e Oggetti* (Venice: Electa, 1999), xii.

3   "Emilio Ambasz: The Architecture of the Marvelous," in *Architettura Naturale. Emilio Ambasz: Progetti e Oggetti,* introduction by Terence Riley(Venice: Electa, 1999), xiii. Translation provided by Emilio Ambasz.

4   Emilio Ambasz. *The Poetics of the Pragmatic* (New York: Rizzoli, 1991), 126.

5   Emilio Ambasz, "Fragments for a Credo," in *Emilio Ambasz: Inventions. The Reality of the Ideal* (New York: Rizzoli, 1992).

6   Ambasz, "Fragments for a Credo."

7   Ettore Sottsass, in *Emilio Ambasz: The Poetics of the Pragmatic,* 10.

8   *Architettura Naturale,* li. Author's translation.

9   *Architettura Naturale,* xxxiv. Translation provided by Emilio Ambasz.

10   Ambasz, "Fragments for a Credo."

11   Ambasz, "Fragments for a Credo."

12   *Architettura Naturale,* xlviii.

13   Ibid.

14   Emilio Ambasz, "I Ask Myself," in *Emilio Ambasz. The Poetics of the Pragmatic,* 3.

15   As does the Mercedes-Benz showroom design. For the connection to Hejduk I am indebted to Peter Wolf.

PROGRAMMATIC UTOPIAS: NOTES ON THE PREHISTORY OF AMBASZ'S PRAGMATIC POETICS

Anthony Vidler

Ambasz's "Manhattan: Capital of the Twentieth Century"[1] proposed a new site for the architecture of the information age; if Paris had established the metropolitan form for consumer culture, epitomized in the arcades, and had become, by the 1930s of Benjamin's research, the site of a prehistory of modernity, New York was already, by 1969, the consummate network city, exhibiting all the characteristics of an architecture of infrastructure. New York was, so to speak, only "delirious" in the sense that its nineteenth-century institutions—from Coney Island to the Racquet Club—acted as cultural cover for what Ambasz discerned as the far more serious, and not at all delirious, "White Collar Culture." Each of these formulations, Benjamin's Paris and Ambasz's New York, was developed out of its own intellectual prehistory. Benjamin's arcades project displays its "origins" in hundreds of citations and notes, but its principal epistemological source has to be seen as surrealism; not the pure and single-issue surrealism of a Dalí or even a Breton, but the critical, almost scientific surrealism of an Aragon. In his *Paysan de Paris*, Aragon took on the environments of Paris—the Buttes Chaumont, the Passage de l'Opéra—as an exercise in modern urban pathology. The "modern myth" he thus outlined was a myth based on an arcade about to be demolished, which through imaginary projection Aragon cast as living only in memory, and a park, constructed by Haussmann, that "resembled" nature only through the most extreme artifice. The "Paris" of Aragon's "Peasant" was, in this sense, no more than a phantom, but a phantom that lived on in the traces of its materiality in order to obscure a present hidden from all but the future. Benjamin, taking Aragon's wager to the extreme ("I am a limit, a line," Aragon wrote), worked in the Bibliothèque Nationale, itself a storehouse for the first consumer age, to identify and concretize the myth in material terms. If there is a parallel prehistory for the "Fables" of Ambasz, however, it will not be found in the New York Public Library but rather in those paradigmatic architectural visions of information and its networks drawn up by the so-called utopian visionaries of the mid-twentieth century—Archigram, Archizoom, Superstudio, and the rest: those who responded in different ways to the call, initiated by the Situationists, to find, beneath the cobblestones of Paris, the sand of a new beach, a tabula rasa for a new urban future. Urban futures, as William Gibson has recently pointed out with respect to George Orwell's *1984*, are inevitably rooted in their urban present—*1984* was, in this respect, Orwell's 1948. In the same way, the "utopias" of these 1960s groups, while ostensibly drawing their imagery from science fiction, were firmly based in a present that was, from the space program to IBM, always already there. The following remarks will sketch a few of the characteristics of this prehistory, a prehistory that was to be explored not in the library, but in the continuity of a project, not yet completed, launched by the twin events of *Italy: The New Domestic Landscape* (its material fabrication) and the Universitas Project (its intellectual speculation).

UTOPIA

We can imagine the complete mobilization, not of the population, but of space. A space taken over by the ephemeral. So that every place becomes multifunctional, polyvalent, transfunctional, with an incessant turnover of functions. . . . In this way, utopia, an illuminating virtuality already present, will absorb and metamorphose the various *topoi*.
—Henri Lefebvre, 1970[2]

Archigram, Archizoom, Superstudio: images of mobile megastructures, of magical realist landscapes, of inflatable shelters, of postapocalyptic per-spectives, of nomadic hyper-technology, of a world transformed by an unlikely combination of futuristic optimism, negative irony, and communitar-ian activism are the now commonplace signs of what Manfredo Tafuri has termed the "international utopianism" of the 1960s. Represented by pop- and op-art visual strategies—collage, comic book *détournement*, filmic story-board narration, and the like—and ideologically covering the spectrum from technophilia to technophobia, these images, despite their internal contradic-tions, shared a common foundation in radical programmatic exploration in the spatial context of utopia. If modern functionalism elevated the program to a level of authority formerly held by classical composition, then these images proposed an extended field for function that, utopian or not, marked the devel-opment of architectural invention for the next half century. These develop-ments were set in a landscape that, in opposition to the critical movements of the Marxist left in architecture, privileged space over time, and utopia over revolution. Their programmatic images still bear reexamination at a moment when the total environment and its relation to technology has come under renewed scrutiny in a globalized space that has surpassed even their radical predictions.

But the utopian programs of the 1960s, despite their apparently radical break with 1950s modernism, and despite their apparent withdrawal from the territory of the real, were founded ideologically and even spiritually in modernist aspirations. If a unifying theme in modernism could be identified from the outset, it was that it was not simply dedicated to the pragmatic "solution" of well-known problems, but to the experimental reframing and reinventing of these problems, and, further, to the exploration of possible spaces and habitats for them. But the specific conditions of post–World War II reconstruction, and the critique of an already codified CIAM modernism by the members of Team X, had already transformed modernist utopia, as represented by the glass towers of Mies and Hilberseimer, and the Ville Radieuse of Le Corbusier, into an especially flexible vehicle for the use of the new avant-garde.

For the architects of the immediate postwar generation—Alison and Peter Smithson, Charles and Ray Eames, James Stirling, and many others—urbanism served as the frame within which architecture took its place, a frame that was itself built up piece by piece with architectural elements: no architectural project without an urban idea, hovering behind it, built into its spatial and technical structure. Not an idea that, like those of the older CIAM generation, might be diagrammed as a total image, but one that in its networks, connections, implied landscapes, and technologies would adapt and change over time—a fragmentary utopia, as Karl Popper, philosophical hero to many in the 1950s, would have called it. Thus, for the Smithsons' the Economist complex represented an entire possible city *in nuce*; for Stirling, Ham Common was a way to translate Corbusian principles into British housing standards; for Van Eyk, a children's playground was a microcosm of an entire ludic world as sketched by Jan Huizinga; for Candilis and Woods, the continuous horizontal fabric of the Free University was a counterparadigm to the isolated blocks set in parkland proposed by Corbusian urbanism; for Charles and Ray Eames, there was not a chair that did not presuppose an entire environment. Construed as the results of highly differentiated and holistically conceived programs, these architectural fragments of urban projects countered the reductive simplicity of zoning and object embedded in the Athens Charter with all the force of the human sciences—questions of psychology, anthropology, ethnology, and technology were all brought to bear on the urban question in a ramified and vastly extended functional field.

And of course, utopia is always programmatic, outlining the blueprints for a society that does not exist in the here and now, operating as a systematic critique of the present, offering a complete substitute for the real, and mapping out of desire. The *topos* of utopia has always also been architectural, a space out of time and out of place that sustains an imagined social order; since the Enlightenment, this space has also gained operative qualities, a space that engenders, machines, and institutes that social order. That is, the space of modern utopia is a programmatic space with all the instrumental characteristics of a tool. From Bentham's Panopticon to B. F. Skinner's *Walden 2*, this space has been designed and detailed according to precise forms and dimensions that equal those of the most complex industrial machines. In this sense, modern utopia is the representation of functionalism at its most pure, the specifications of functionalist desire writ large.

Utopia was very much on the agenda in the late 1950s and early 1960s. From B. F. Skinner's *Walden 2,* investigating the potential effects, for better or worse, of social and psychological behaviorism, to the commune movements with their vague evocations of Fourier and the Shakers, to the Metabolist and megastructural architecturalists, utopia was seen variously as dystopia (the triumph of totalitarianism under a sunny sky [Adorno]), an enemy of the Open Society (Popper), an idea realizable in fact (Soleri), or as a critical tool (Superstudio). Systems theorists analyzed utopia as a primitive version of a cybernetic system; some historians looked critically at the late-eighteenth- and early-nineteenth-century utopias of France and the U.S.; other historians, notably the late Robin Evans, uncovered modernity and functionalism in the shape of Bentham's Panopticon (and, it must be said, much earlier and more critically than Foucault's belated use of the metaphor).

So it was easy enough to dismiss, or at the very least categorize, Archigram, Superstudio, Archizoom, as utopians, using the mechanisms of pop to integrate and market their special brand of consumer technology as architecture. Colin Rowe, whose early essay blasting utopia had been published in *Granta* in 1959 (before his discovery of Popper), went even further. He saw Archigram simply as a kind of high-tech version of townscape, English to the core, and exploiting all the tricks of Gorden Cullen and the *AR* Townscape movement: "Archigram would seem to be making *picturesque images of the future.*" He went on:

For all of the unplanned randomness, the happy jerkiness, the obviously high-pitched tonality, the aggressive syncopation, all of the famous ingredients of Englishness in action are now given a space-age gloss. Anything might happen here: the death of architecture, non-building, Andy-Warhol bug-eyed monsters, immediacy of feeling for life, instant nomadism, the wished-for end of all repression. We are presented with townscape in a space-suit; but whereas the idiosyncrasies are supposedly attributable to the pressures of context, the Archigram images are generally presented in an ideal void which, for all intents and purposes is the same void as that in which the urban model of c.1930 is located.

In returning Archigram (and he might equally well have been referring to the Italian variants) to "the urban model of c.1930" Rowe is, then, consigning their product to the dustheap of failed architectural utopias, or rather, in his terms, of failed architectural responses to the ideological pretensions of the 1930s, Marxist or otherwise. This consignment was at least opportunistic with reference to his own program of the "return to classicism" and the assumed palliative of a "mannerist" modernism.

For many (more often than not Marxist) critics, this seemed to doom the megastructures of *Living City* and the barren perspectives of *No-Stop-City* to a futile repetition of the same, as images competing in the marketplace with all the positive programs of modern megastructures and concrete plans for urban redevelopment. Manfredo Tafuri, for example, caustically dismissed the spate of utopian images produced by Archizoom and Superstudio after 1968 as a "destructive and cathartic orgy," the intention of which was "to haul a mythical proletariat onto the stage of psychedelic action," with the aid of dream material transcribed with an irony "that made nobody laugh." "In the vignettes that illustrated *No-Stop-City*," Tafuri concluded, "neoprimitives living in an absolutely barren environment use small air conditioners, expressing a monstrous marriage between populous anarchism and liberating events influenced by those of France in May 1968."[3] An image that could equally apply to the 1965 montage of a covey of naked Reyner Banhams seated within François Dallegret's inflatable "Un-house" accompanied only by a "standard-of-living package."

In this context, it may seem surprising that Archigram, followed by Constant, Archizoom, Superstudio, and the rest, construed their critique of modern architecture and its political and social shortcomings in apparently utopian terms, when utopia was demonstrably the property of hyperfunctionalism in its most totalizing form.

Certainly the recourse of 1960s communitarians to the anti-city and agrarian, preindustrial models of the utopian socialists from Fourier to Morris was an understandable return to a long tradition of machine-era critique. And the high-tech, if not science-fiction, fantasies of Archigram, as well as the post-industrial landscapes of Archizoom, were nothing but the functionalist desire extended to its furthest limits. But thirty years later, and with the excesses of postmodern historicism happily behind us, we might begin to see real advantages for these groups in being linked to the so-called utopias of the 1930s. For at least those utopias took on the environment at a bold scale—a world scale in Le Corbusier's sketches, a metropolitan scale in the projects of Hilberseimer and Mies, and both (hypothetically at least) with the utilization of the most advanced technology. And it was of course out of the period of the thirties and forties that what Warren Chalk was to call "a strange social idealism" emerged—an idealism that was "to fade" even as the technological ideal was transformed into real technological developments during the war, and later reinvented in social and psychological terms in the early 1960s.

The destabilizing power of these images and their evident relationship to a tradition, identified by Tafuri as that of "Duchamp," was clear; but so was their equal commitment to technology, new or even uninvented, and its potential for supporting a new society, or one that was, in the same way, yet to be invented. It was as if, in the ironic stance toward traditional modernism, and despite the fundamental critique of its social, psychological, and technological failings, these utopian images were simultaneously dedicated to extending modernist principles to their extreme (and thereby ideal) limits. It was at this point that the image of utopia joined the program of total design imagined by those who, like Tomas Maldonado at Ulm, believed that an entirely new version of the traditional *gesamtkunstwerke* was demanded by the complex environmental, social, and technological conditions of mass global society. Here, the "psychedelic" aspirations of the utopian Left met, however uncomfortably, the systematic cybernetics of the rational center. As Tafuri noted, they were in fact soon literally to come together in public presentation: "Their designs conquered a market that had remained closed to the products of neoliberty; their desecrations, justified by appeals to Duchamp, finally gained international recognition at an exhibition organized by Emilio Ambasz at the Museum of Modern Art in 1972: *Italy: The New Domestic Landscape*."

EXHIBITION

Marcuse+Fourier+Dada: the designer absorbs all the ingredients for a systematic reconnoitering of techniques whereby the spectator can be reconciled with the future—since the present is condemned. Utopian space, often constructed without any irony whatsoever, leads directly back to the urban environment, sublimating its chaos, its multiplicity of dimensions, the constant mutability of its structures. These new *Merzbauten* offer the promise of a nonwork continuum, guaranteed by the most advanced forms of technology and, consequently, by the world of development.

—Manfredo Tafuri, 1972[4]

Subtitled *Achievements and Problems of Italian Design*, the exhibition might have seemed at first glance to be no more nor less than a trade show, a luxury shop window for Italian imports. But a closer look revealed that these "functionalist" and technologically savvy products, arrayed under the umbrella of a "new domesticity" and worthy of installation in the museum's modernist-oriented design collection, were presented side by side with images, produced by Superstudio and Archizoom—the very same images of utopia/ dystopia that would, in any other context, have seemed antithetical or totally oppositional to any "Bauhaus"-like tradition. Further inspection would reveal that this very utopianism—ironical, and witty in the extreme—was deeply embedded in the character of these "home designs," while the apparently utopian visions of the antidesigners were filled with technologically progressive objects, themselves icons of the new domestic design. This invasion of functionalism by utopianism, and vice versa, simply confirmed the fundamental commonalty of the two—indeed the identity of both as "hyperfunctional," or better, programmatic. For what I have characterized as the extended field of program was the "Landscape" in the title, of this exhibition. This landscape embraced the smallest object of domestic use and the widest context of domestic existence; these objects were subject to the rules of function and at the same time demanded of their environment ecological and social responses beyond these rules they were then.

What the objects and environments of the exhibition implied, and the translated critical essays confirmed, was that this expansion of the programmatic field was not simply a literal extension of modernist functionalism, whether of the rationalist or realist kind, but a radical rethinking of function itself. The subsequent relapse of architectural practice into a debate over historicism versus modernism, postmodernism versus late modernism, has obscured this fact for over half a century.

For never in the history of what might be called architecture have so many propositions, themes, openings, and experimental projects, all directed toward a fundamental re-writing of what we might call architectural theory and practice, been put forward as in this exhibition of 1972. In retrospect we might hazard that while its effect has been delayed, *Italy: The New Domestic Landscape* still has the potential to transform architecture as powerfully, and far less negatively, as the *Modern Architecture* show of Philip Johnson and Henry-Russell Hitchcock forty years before.

But of course, an exhibition both innovates and confirms, and in this case the programmatic utopianism it celebrated was the confirmation of a decade of gestation and experiment, not only in Italy, but also in Britain, the United States, and France. Thus, to take one example, the loosely constituted Archigram group, between 1961 and 1971, under the cover of what seemed to be irreverent and harmless play, launched the most fundamental critique of everything architectural since the Industrial Revolution. Inflatables, infrastructure, pods, blobs, blebs, globs, gloops, and all the rest were already there, long before their time; metamorphosis, nomad culture, pleasure and fun, comfort, hard-soft, emancipation, exchange, response—all bundled with technological poetics and problematics, placing the synthetic environment (human, psychological, ecological, and technological) firmly on the agenda for decades to come. Indeed, it might be said that the sum product of Archigram's work over those ten years, and the sum of its individual contributions since, projected into society a program for the total environment. What they delivered was, as Reyner Banham recognized, a project to investigate and promote the full implications of Banham's own conclusion to *Theories and Design* (1960): "It may well be that what we have hitherto understood as architecture, and what we are beginning to understand of technology are incompatible disciplines."[5] It was the special perspicuity of Archigram and their Italian counterparts to recognize that what was needed was not so much a redefinition of architecture, not an application of Buckminster Fuller–style technology, but a construction that would subsume both into a hugely distended vision of a future world: a utopia in conventional terms, but one that would nevertheless be founded on the real advances of technology and the human sciences.

FUTURE HISTORY

What we really need is a wholesale displacement of the thematics of modernity
by the desire called Utopia. . . . Ontologies of the present demand archeologies
of the future, not forecasts of the past.
—Fredric Jameson, 2002[6]

Despite all appearances, and against the general notion of utopia as outside or
at the end of history, these movements had a critical sense of history of its
importance and its role in generating the present. All avant-garde movements by
definition have had this sense of history. From the first Saint Simonian "avant-
garde" (he coined the word) to the Futurists, from Esprit Nouveau to the Glass
Chain, history was at once the propulsive force for the development of the new
(Hegel) and the present ground for difference and distance from the past. This
was the message of the Futurist Manifesto, and its picture of a band of young
men, seated in a nineteenth-century apartment by the waters of a canal grown
green with age and obsolescence, ready to leap into their automobiles and challenge the rural landscape with their roaring engines and their speed. They were
running from history toward a future defined only by the ever new, the ever
powerful force of war and technology. Certain other modernities proposed an
end to history and proclaimed the present as the new future. All these, however,
emerged from history as a field—a space—where change was stratified and
typified into repetition, into a ratified technology, and their universalization of
history through the mechanism of abstraction, meant that history was always,
by necessary implication, lurking in the background.

Still other modernities proposed a return to history in the hopes that it
indicates an order that might be recovered, not through a return to historicist
forms, but through—once more—abstraction; a stance that, as Terry Eagleton
recently noted of T. S. Eliot, was founded on a "Janus-faced temporality, in
which one turns to the resources of the pre-modern in order to move backwards
into a future that has transcended modernity altogether." We might add Colin
Rowe and Clement Greenberg to this ascription of historical respect.

But the vision of history espoused by the "international utopians" was a
little different. While Colin Rowe eventually concluded that Archigram "represents an engagingly incidental and accidental fusion of the retrospective and the
prospective models,"[7] Archigram in fact showed itself respectful of history in a
different mode than that of the modernists. Indeed, they were ready to learn
from history, ready to assemble kits out of history, unafraid of both historicist

style (they even used style kits unabashedly to demonstrate the potential for consumer choice in architecture), and of the burden of modern architecture. For Archigram, modern architecture had itself become historical, a past to be understood but irrevocably separated from the present; the utopian dreams of the modern movement to *be* technological had been demonstrated as just that—utopian dreams—in the face of actual technological change. *Archigram* 6, for example, was dedicated not to the future but to a consideration of the recent past: the 1940s, and what's more, to the first half of the 1940s—the war years. And not in a Futurist/Vorticist spirit of eulogy of war and power unleashed, but in a simple account of technological advances forced by the war: mass-production techniques, laminated timber, geodesic frameworks for aircraft, the welded tubular construction of bridges, the air structure of barrage balloons, as well as prefabricated housing types for the temporary housing program: all innovations that awaited their appropriate introduction into architectural/environmental design.

Now, in retrospect, from the vantage point of the twenty-first century, we can see that Manhattan, like Paris, is already a site of prehistory, a memory machine for the excavation of those decisive moments of hardware development, from the mainframe to the office building. The recent restoration of Lever House, the careful remanufacturing of its already obsolete curtain-wall panels, as if the relics of some forgotten handicraft, works on our imagination like Aragon's Passage de l'Opéra. The Capital of the Twenty-First Century is, by contrast to Paris and New York, "nowhere"; it is the *effect* of the network rather than its concretization. As Tony Negri and Michael Hardt imply, it is a global city, a city of the nomadic multitude, a city not yet locatable in a world that insists on global, not local, positioning. And yet, when the prehistory of this new capital is written, it will most certainly begin where Benjamin and Ambasz left off, and, in its shadows, we will still be able to trace the outlines of their mythological architectures, constructions that were, after all, fabricated entirely of their own present as presentiments of our own future.

[1] "Manhattan: Capital of the Twentieth Century," *Perspecta 12* (New Haven, 1972), 50–71, was perhaps the first essay by an architect to take seriously the implications of Walter Benjamin's essay, introducing his "Arcades Project" for Adorno and Horkheimer, "Paris: Capital of the Nineteenth Century," also published in the U.S. for the first time in English, following Ben Brewster's translation for *New Left Review*.

[2] Henri Lefebvre, *The Urban Revolution*, translated by Robert Bobonno (Minneapolis: The University of Minnesota Press, 2003), 130–31.
Translation of *La Révolution Urbaine* (Paris: Gallimard, 1970).

[3] Manfredo Tafuri, *Italian Architecture*, 99.

[4] Manfredo Tafuri, "Design and Technological Utopia," in *Italy: The New Domestic Landscape* (New York: The Museum of Modern Art, 1972), 398.

[5] Fredric Jameson, *A Singular Modernity. Essay on the Ontology of the Present* (London: Verso, 2002), 215.

[6] *The Architecture of Good Intentions*

AN INTERVIEW WITH AMBASZ & EMILIO
Michael Sorkin

Which of you is which?

Everyone knows that two entities live within me: Emilio and Ambasz. Emilio represents the visionary architect, and Ambasz the pragmatic industrial designer.

Ambasz is an anxious man because he wants his product to be well received by men. Emilio is an anguished person because he hopes through his architecture to be welcomed by angels. Ambasz is a socially sad man; Emilio is a solitary cheerful one. I, on the other hand, am cheerfully sad and sociably solitary. I was once asked—by you, as a matter of fact—how I would like to be remembered in a hundred years' time—as a designer, a minimal artist, a farmer, a philosopher, or an architect? As a poet.

Tell me a little something about your early formation, about life in Buenos Aires, about the pampas, about Argentina.

I was born in Chaco, a subtropical province of Argentina, almost one thousand miles north of Buenos Aires. Its never failing afternoon rain could be used to adjust one's watch to 4 P.M. Clouds of vapor, evaporating half an hour later, stood as metaphors for the impermanence of all things.

When I was seven years old my parents moved to Buenos Aires. My room on the second floor of a new house opened directly onto the leafy branches of a street tree. With my bed placed against the window it was as if I lived in a tree house. I used to stay up late, in the darkness of my room, looking at the reflection of the streetlights on the tree. I never ceased to marvel at the brightness of a raindrop as it held on to a leaf. I still remember shivering as if caressed by celestial fingers when the rustling leaves made their music. I was entranced by that tree. To this day I revere its brethren.

The stars of Buenos Aires: there are so many more visible in the Southern Hemisphere. Standing on a deep balcony projected onto the sidewalk I felt they cast a dome whose perimeter was nowhere but its center was everywhere, while I was nothing. One felt so, but so lonely, in such an overbearing universe.

Buenos Aires has always been seen by the Argentines as the incarnation of everything the provinces thought ideal. We knew it was to be a disappointment but we cherished its pretense to perfection. I have sung to that flawed Buenos Aires, as one would to a beloved son who did not live up to expectations, in an essay I wrote thirty-five years ago: "Anthology for a Spatial Buenos Aires." Its words and meanings still ring true, only the plaintive sounds have vanished.

The Pampas you ask? I remember describing the Pampa as an Indian voice for space, land where man stands alone as an abstract being who would have to recommence the history of the species—or to conclude it. I see the Pampa as a terse thread, shifting from green to earthy browns knotted onto the Atlantic to the east and onto the Andes to the west. A place of the mind, a melancholy green-gray lair inhabited by a very hard to fight resignation.

Were you influenced by any architects during your early days?
When I was fifteen years old and still in high school, I came to the realization that one can only learn the craft of poetry from poets. Accordingly, I developed a plan to work for Amancio Williams. A friend who was already in Amancio's architectural office spoke to him about me. I came to interview with Mr. Williams one afternoon—by that time I was already all of sixteen years—and he invited me to join his studio. In order to better attend to this new responsibility, I switched my attendance in high school to night classes and to Amancio's studio during the day.

Many beautiful things have been said about Amancio's work by Le Corbusier, Max Bill, Mies van der Rohe, and other great artists. I have recently read those over. I am not surprised that they had always been fascinated by Amancio's work. To them, he was like Argentina: a child of Europe. Like Argentina, he was the one they envisioned enacting the European Utopian dreams. What had been dreamt in Europe was to be given strong poetic embodiment in a virgin place, where memories could only be recalled in libraries. It was the cleanest piece of paper and the largest unspoiled natural surface left. So far away; a place Europe could call its mental dwelling of last resort.

As I look at the panorama of the twentieth century's Latin American art and architecture, Amancio shines as one of its greatest artists. He strongly practiced his belief that architecture must contribute to human happiness; that for architects to revel in historical and/or simpleminded methodological references was to skirt their responsibility. He always believed in creating and inventing master examples. He constantly searched for the irreducible solution, believing that if an architectural problem could be reduced to its essentials, its answer would stun evil and proclaim God's kingdom. He searched for prototypical pilot concepts. They were to be as unselfconsciously simple as many a child's answers. After all, what could be more obvious than to put Buenos Aires' airport on the water of the River Plate, where it would not have created urban and traffic conflicts, where it could have been easily erected by barges effortlessly bringing materials to the site, where it would stand out in poetic contrast with the river's long brown horizon that Amancio's geometrical planes were to stitch to the blue sky.

It must be said in his defense that Amancio never spoke in romantic terms; he always explained his projects with a sometimes overbearing abundance of technical details. These were always right, even in their most extreme cases. I have always suspected that by analyzing the pragmatics of his projects to such an exhaustive degree, Amancio made it possible for his explanations to become an intellectual superstructure, a shell under which dwelled the poetic core. Perhaps Amancio believed that such a blanket of technical perfection would everlastingly shield *tekne's* marriage to *poesis*.

Let these heartfelt words stand as my testimonial for all the magnificent images he has created. If someone has called him "classical"—perhaps a misnomer—it is because his work is so essential, so irreducible, and so luminously strong that it transcends materials and construction methods to embody the spirit of architecture. The country was created, it would seem, yesterday, but it is only when great artists like Amancio appear that we are able to evoke a notion of dwelling in peace with ourselves. I do not know a greater accomplishment for an architect than to have created such magnificent abodes of the heart that we can find refuge and solace even when we are away from them.

You are now going to tell me, inquisitive and suspicious soul, that I have idealized this "Amancio" in my image! We have a saying in Spanish *"A quien el saco cae bien, que se lo ponga."* "He whom the coat fits, should wear it" would be an approximate translation. Let's see, I am a size fifty and this *schmatte* is a . . .

You began as a strong modernist, then?
My first architectural project—I must have been fifteen—was for neighbors across the street, a couple of schoolteachers, and I designed a house for them. I didn't know anything about Le Corbusier or anything like that, but it ended up being a very cubistic kind of house. [At Princeton] some of the projects I did were very strongly modernistic but it was almost like an explosion of the modern. To me, the modern movement had already said so many things and

the context that gave it meaning had decayed, but only a number of fragments had survived. Therefore, I was mainly interested in operating with the fragments of the modern movement—I'm talking about 1967, '66—what you would now call deconstructivism; at that time it was called something else in several projects I did. In fact, one of the projects I did in 1966 [was] working together with Peter Eisenman for the same client, which was a theological seminary. He did one building, I did another one, but mine was what we would now call a deconstructivist building.

Not exactly a functionalist pedigree.
I am very mechanically minded. I am at the same time obsessed with the search for basic generating principles from which everything else is to sprout. My functionalist concerns are those of a gardener more interested in genetics than in engineering. As a creator, I admire—and envy—the seeds for both their life-giving and their life-conserving power. But, actually, I only like to talk publicly about faucets and cost per square meter—you know, important matters.

How would you describe your architecture today?
I seek to develop an architecture that is outside the canonical tradition of architecture. My architecture is a stage set that serves as background for the dramas of human activity. It is an architecture that is both here and not here. With it, I hope to place the user into a new state of existence, a celebration of human majesty, thought, and sensation. Though apparently quite new, the designs are permeated by devices both primitive and ancient. The result is an architecture that seems to stand for eternity. I sometimes envision my work as if it were built by the last man of the present culture for the first man of a culture which has not yet arrived.

So it's a prospective project?
I am only interested in discovery, not in recovery; in invention, not in classification. In the uncharted realm of invention, taxonomy is always in the process of being yet born. In the same way as I search for essential and lasting principles in architecture. I think that in opting to write fables rather than theoretical essays I have grasped something basic: fables remain immutable long after theories have crumbled. The invention of fables is central to my working methods and it is not just a literary accessory. The subtext of a fable, after all, is a ritual and it is to the support of rituals that most of my work addresses itself.

Surely there's a more philosophical connection as well.

The fables and the architecture I create are both steeped in mysticism. On the one hand, I am playing with pragmatic elements that come from my period, such as technology. On the other hand, I am proposing a certain mode of existence which is a different one. This is a search for essential things—being born, being in love, and dying. They have to do with existence on an emotional, passionate, and sensual level.

It is my deep belief that architecture and design are mythmaking acts. I believe that their real task begins once functional and behavioral needs have been satisfied. It is not hunger, but love and fear, and sometimes wonder which make us create. The designer and the architect's milieu may have changed but the task, I believe, remains the same: to give poetic form to the pragmatic.

What rituals in particular interest you?

There is in all of us a deep need for ritual, for ceremony, procession, magical garments, and gestures. I believe it is an archetypal search in which we all partake. In my architecture I am interested in the rituals and ceremonies of the twenty-four-hour day. I am not interested in the rituals of the very long voyage—a voyage that can take forty or fifty years. And what a tragedy to discover that for the sake of those long-term dreams, we have sacrificed our daily lives. No, I am interested in daily rituals: like the ritual of sitting in a courtyard slightly protected from both the view of your neighbors and the wind—looking up at the stars. Dealing architecturally with that type of situation attracts me. Because it is not *in* the house, the house only provides a backdrop for it.

How does this bridge to your mystical concerns?

Architecture is, for me, one aspect of our quest for cosmological models. I suspect that such an all-encompassing image, if it ever arrives, will be as simple and dense as a point suspended in mid-space. Every one of my projects seeks to possess at least an attribute of the universe. The quest for that which is infinite, eternal, and ever present, I suspect, may be contained in designs of very few lines which manifest themselves with great economy of expression. In a such seemingly simple manner those lines may, I hope, acquire the fascinating power of mythical structures. Maybe it is because I seek essentials that I love Lucretius's *De Rerum Natura* so much.

How does this jibe with a more directly ameliorative approach?

We must create alternative images of a better life to guide our actions if we do not wish to perpetuate present conditions. I believe that any architectural project which does not attempt to propose new or better modes of existence is immoral. This task may stagger the imagination and paralyze hope but we cannot avoid it.

You're a crusader then?

Of course. I have a sense of justice out of which you can really make a zealot. They burn them on a stake—if they don't disgrace themselves. Now I wear three-piece suits to do the same thing. I don't let them know I'm coming with the torches.

Justice, whether social or moral, is a conceit of the mind. Justice does not exist in nature but, despite this cruel fact, I feel very strongly that it is our ethical imperative to pursue its implementation on earth. Even if we know it to be a delicate structure, held together by such ethereal material as abnegation and altruism, but destined to collapse at night, we must every morning rebuild it.

What about the idea of environmental justice and your impact on "green" architecture?

Architects have always bled for the ills of the world. In my view, they will stand far behind in the line of those sent to hell for their environmental sins. But there they will go, inevitably, if they do not honor their ethical responsibility to propose alternative models of the future.

I know it sounds presumptuous, but I lay claim to being the precursor of current architectural production concerned with environmental problems. If there is any strength to my architectural ideas, it comes from the fact that I believe that architecture has to be not only pragmatic but also move the heart.

It has taken me thirty years to prove the practical advantages of my ideas. In the meantime, I have begotten children, grandchildren, and not a few little bastards. To see Renzo Piano, Jean Nouvel, Tadao Ando, and many others utilize vegetal matter in their projects makes me feel my mission is beginning to bear fruit. To hear some of them claim these ideas' paternity makes me feel a mythological character, but I know it is just the case of a foretold Freudian destiny.

Tell me something more about your relationship to other
contemporary figures?

Many years ago, when Peter Eisenman and Michael Graves got me promoted
from freshman to senior during my first semester at Princeton, Peter told me,
standing in one of those academic corridors where eunuchs dream of power,
that now that I was a senior he would make me into his "model" student.
My mouth opened up and, from my stomach, as if I were governed by a spirit,
I heard myself saying, "I cannot be your model, Peter, because I'm going to be
the father of a nation." I was as astonished by my words as Peter, who was,
for once in his life, speechless.

I rejoice immensely when I come upon somebody else's work that touches
me, even if it is the architecture of someone like Gehry, for example, whose
work is so different from mine, and whose concerns are totally unrelated to
mine. What matters to me is that he sings his own song. His birds may not
alight often in my garden, but I'm sure they will pollinate even my flowers.

Speaking of Gehry, he often defines his work in relation to art-world
influences. How about your own, particularly the minimalists and
earth artists?

Robert Smithson and I became instantly great friends. At the end of our first
dinner together, we felt like long lost brothers. The same things interested
us, from a different viewpoint. I was fascinated by his work and I presume he
was interested in mine. Never again did I have such a feeling of conceptual
brotherhood with anyone else. I adored my conversations with him, and I was
devastated when he died.

I have also maintained a very good friendship with Sol Lewitt, whom I
have always considered the guardian angel of the minimalist group. Michael
Heizer approached me once with a request that I write the introduction and
critical essay to a book on his work. I knew his work, of course, but I had
never met him before. I presumed he was interested in the fact that we shared
many formal interests and affinities.

It will come to you as a surprise, but I was not acquainted with the work
of Richard Serra when I designed the Mexican Computer Center in 1975.
The first time I encountered his work was at the Yonkers Museum. During the
installation time, I was taken to see the exhibition by its director, Richard
Koshalek. I was dazzled. I felt that if I ever made a sculpture I would be very
happy if it looked half as good as Serra's.

What about Rem Koolhaas's work?

Short Answer:

S, MS, VS, and XS (small, medium small, very small, and extra small)

Long Answer:

Convinced that architecture should be the work of someone else's imagination, some celebrated architectural contributors to a marketplace culture repropose good old Neo-Modernism 101—tilted, twisted, and fragmented; oversqueezed and left for dead, but still juicy—as the easily disposable clothes to dress the *à la mode* chapels of the believers in "*I consume, ergo sum.*"

What have you been reading lately? In particular, what about architectural theorizing?

I have again been rereading *Morceaux Choisis*, Paul Valéry's own selection of some of his best essays. I have also just finished reading Susan Sontag's *Where the Stress Falls*. While Valéry always elates me, Sontag needs someone to let the air out of her balloon. I am sadly disappointed by most of her essays' lack of intellectual rigor. But perhaps I'm wrong. Maybe I am dense to the altruistic fact she's just trying to emulate Pavarotti; you first sing to the masses a bolero, then a mambo, and slowly you get them to *Wozzeck*. Maybe that's the way she generously plans to introduce people to literature and philosophic thought. But by stooping so much she runs the risk of remaining bent.

To think that I discovered her in 1963, during my short interlude as a freshman. I read an article she wrote for *Sight and Sound*—a British film magazine—on Robert Bresson. I thought it was extremely subtle and perceptive. I brought it to the attention of Professor Szathmary, director of Princeton's Creative Arts Program. He made funds available for me to invite her to Princeton to give a lecture. When she came off the bus, the first question she put to me was, "Why was I invited?" It was the first time, she told me, that a university had done so. I am afraid that life tends to turn opaque such youthful sincerity. If in those days she radiated wonder, nowadays doubt does not dwell in her mind.

You have asked about my recent readings of architectural theoretical thinking. I am intermittently embarrassed and irritated by the woolly-mindedness of some of the writings on architectural subjects with which I am sympathetic. No doubt, I am unlucky in my choices. There must be pearls out there. Would you consider sending me a bibliography?

CONTRIBUTORS

JERRILYNN DODDS is Distinguished Professor of Architectural History and Theory at the School of Architecture of the City College of the City University of New York. Her work has centered on theories of artistic interchange and identity, and the problems surrounding art and minorities in pluralistic societies. She has worked extensively in Spain, Bosnia, and New York City as an author, curator, and filmmaker.

PETER HALL is a contributing writer to *Metropolis* magazine and senior editor and fellow at the Design Institute, University of Minnesota, where he is developing a book on mapping and an online journal, the Knowledge Circuit. He has published essays in several books and coauthored *Pause: 59 Minutes of Motion Graphics.*

CATHERINE INGRAHAM is the author of *Architecture and the Burdens of Linearity* and has written many other essays on architecture and architectural theory. She has lectured extensively on architecture at various universities and is currently director of the Graduate Architecture and Urban Design program at Pratt, where she also teaches. She was the winner, in collaboration with Smith-Miller and Hawkinson, Architects, of the Museum of Women competition in Battery Park City in 2001.

DEAN MacCANNELL has done a number of critical studies of the built environment, including the Statue of Liberty restoration project; the Vietnam Memorial in Washington, D.C.; Disney's new town of Celebration in Florida. His 1976 book *The Tourist: A New Theory of the Leisure Class* is still in print and is widely credited with having founded the field of tourism studies. MacCannell is currently Professor of Environmental Design and Landscape Architecture at the University of California at Davis.

FELICITY D. SCOTT is Assistant Professor of Art History at the University of California, Irvine, and an editor of *Grey Room,* a journal of architecture, art, media, and politics. She has published widely in the areas of modern and postwar architecture and is currently writing a book on the dissident modernist practices of Bernard Rudofsky.

LAUREN SEDOFSKY is a writer based in Paris.

MICHAEL SORKIN is the principal of the Michael Sorkin Studio and the Director of the Graduate Program in Urban Design at CCNY. His most recent books include *The Next Jerusalem: Sharing the Divided City, Starting from Zero: Reconstructing Downtown New York,* and *Some Assembly Required.* The Sorkin Studio is currently working on plans for Queens Plaza, the campus of City College, the Cleveland waterfront, and a housing project in Vienna.

ANTHONY VIDLER is professor and dean of the Irwin W. Chanin School of Architecture at the Cooper Union, New York. His books include *Theory and Design in the Late Enlightenment;* the prize-winning *Claude-Nicolas Ledoux; The Architectural Uncanny;* and *Warped Space.* He has received numerous honors and awards, including a John Simon Guggenheim Fellowship, a Senior Fellowship of the National Endowment of the Humanities, and a Getty Scholar's Fellowship. He is a Fellow of the National Academy of Arts and Sciences.

JAMES WINES is the founder and president of SITE, the former Chair of Environmental Design at Parsons School of Design, and currently a professor of architecture at Penn State University. His recent books include *De-Architecture* and *Green Architecture.* Winner of twenty-five art and design awards, including the 1995 Chrysler Award for Design Innovation, he is also the recipient of fellowships and grants from the National Endowment for the Arts, the Kress Foundation, the American Academy in Rome, the Guggenheim Foundation, the Rockefeller Foundation, the Graham Foundation, the Ford Foundation, and the Pulitzer Prize Organization for graphics.

LEBBEUS WOODS is a professor of architecture at the Cooper Union in New York City. He is the recipient of an American Institute of Architects Honors Award and the Chrysler Award for Innovation in Design. His works are in collections around the world, including the Museum of Modern Art (New York), the Whitney Museum of American Art, the Cooper-Hewitt National Design Museum, the San Francisco Museum of Modern Art, the Carnegie Museum of Art, and the Getty Research Institute for the Arts and Humanities. Monographs on his work include *Anarchitecture: Architecture Is a Political Act, Radical Reconstruction, Earthquake!* and *The Storm and the Fall.*